MW00914121

Gold Wars

The Battle Against Sound Money
As Seen From A Swiss Perspective

By

Ferdinand Lips

FAME

The Foundation for the Advancement of
Monetary Education
New York, NY
www.fame.org

This publication is designed to provide accurate and
authoritative information in regard to the subject matter
covered. It is sold with the understanding that the publisher
is not engaged in rendering professional services. If
professional advice or other expert assistance is required, the
services of a competent professional should be sought.

Lips, Ferdinand
  Gold Wars
  ISBN 0-9710380-0-7 (paper back)

Printed in the U.S. of America
10 9 8 7 6 5 4 3 2 1

What People Are Saying About This Book

"It is the great merit of this provocative book by Ferdinand Lips to bring back a wider understanding of why gold was a solid base for economic stability in many societies. As our overextended global economy is heading for more troublesome times, the global village will need an unquestionable economic basis again that does not bear the stamp of any particular country.

Today, as Lips shows in this book, the conceivable entity for that is gold. Gold is best suited to supply confidence to a troubled economy and anchor it in reality again. Since antiquity gold has been a symbol of highest value to humans. Gold, the sun-like shining yellow metal that has the quality of being incorruptible, is an adequate metaphor for that inner kernel in humans about which we need to become conscious during our lifetime. This aspect of gold has always fascinated and inspired us.

All of a sudden, the wish to own a solid base of this yellow metal may again become the desire of individuals and nations as it has happened so many times before. Then we may find ourselves – to our surprise – on the way back to a solid gold standard."

Dr. sc. techn. T. Abt
Professor at the Federal Institute of Technology, Zurich, Switzerland

"I have known Ferdinand Lips since 1994 and those tumultuous days of the 'Randgold Revolution' which changed the face of the South African gold mining industry. The group of men that led that change were, and for most part still are, archetypes of the term 'Gold Bull.' Mr. Lips strongly believes that gold is the only currency that politicians can't print or create. This is a concept, having lived and worked in Africa my whole life, I have come to appreciate.

History has proved time and again that gold is an effective counter to excessive risk. A scholar of monetary policy and a vociferous promoter of the gold standard, in this book Mr. Lips presents a very well researched and passionate analysis of financial and monetary history. The book comes at a perfect time; never before has the future been so difficult to predict and the civilized world been so vulnerable to politics, minority pressure groups and fanatics. Understanding more of the past might well help us to successfully navigate the future.

'Gold and freedom are inseparable'— this is the thesis of *Gold Wars*, a manuscript that I recommend every modern day business person should read!"

Dr. D. Mark Bristow, PhD, Chief Executive Officer
Randgold Resources

"In *Gold Wars*, Ferdinand Lips takes on what is probably the most talked about and least understood subject of the times, money. He is to be admired as he has performed an important task to provide understanding of this vital subject, moving through history, to recent developments, to his own experiences as a Swiss banker. It is his long career in banking that lends vitality and clarity to his text. He maintains a sharp focus by his use of extensive quotations from writers and bankers, many of whom were his friends, men who tried to show the way for sound money and banking and the folly of the decisions that were being made.

In contrast, he includes the words of other financial and political leaders, those who instituted the monetary policies that have lead to the serious monetary problems the world now faces. The earnestness of his endeavor is clear as he concludes, "The Gold War is nothing else than a Third World War. It is not only a most unnecessary but the most destructive of all wars. It should be stopped now" Indeed, this is a different kind of war story, fascinating and on-going. *Gold Wars* is valuable reading."

Elizabeth Currier, President
Committee for Monetary Research and Education

"*Gold Wars* is must reading for anyone who wants to understand the genesis of the unfolding debacle in the financial markets. Herr Lips, a former Rothschild executive and private banker in Switzerland with a career spanning more than fifty years, has brought his unique perspective and insight to bear in describing the rigging of the global monetary system and the betrayal of the Swiss nation."

Robert K. Landis, Esq.
Golden Sextant Advisors, LLC

"*Gold Wars* is an absolute 'must read' for anyone who is concerned about his financial future. It is appropriate that Ferdinand Lips, a former Rothschild executive and a private banker in Switzerland who has spent 50 years dealing with money to confirm that the world's monetary system has been rigged to plunder the savings of ordinary people worldwide for the benefit of a small financial elite."

Dr. Lawrence Parks, PhD - Executive Director
The Foundation for the Advancement of Monetary Education

"For centuries governments and currencies have been underpinned by gold. Countries and individuals measured their wealth in gold. The western United States of America, South Africa and much of Australia, to name only a few examples, owed their development and much of their prosperity to the discovery and mining of gold.

Today many financiers would have us believe that gold is simply another commodity, that it no longer can be regarded as a store of wealth. Ferdinand Lips in his book, aptly named *Gold Wars*, demonstrates that this concept is not only fallacious, but also dangerous.

Countries have been, and are being, built on the back of gold mining certain international and governmental agencies seek to control gold and its price for their own ends. *Gold Wars* shows why they should not succeed and what the consequences will be if they do. This book is required reading for anyone interested in monetary stability."

Dr. Aubrey L. Paverd, Ph.D.
Geologist

"The word "extra-ordinary" should be used carefully. And that's what this book is. It will be a classic. It is past, present & future -- not only for & about gold but about society & what hope there is for stability & liberty. At last you will understand what the gold standard really was. And why politicians make war on gold. the book is properly titled. When you have read this book, you will understand gold & more about human nature. Mr. Lips makes the history of gold come alive & will enthuse you to join the war for the sake of freedom, free markets & social peace. You will want 50 copies for your best friends, press & politicians."

Chevalier Harry D. Schultz
International Harry Schultz Letter

About Ferdinand Lips

Born in Switzerland in 1931, Ferdinand Lips, is a well-established and respected authority on gold and the gold market. His roots are in banking where he started his career, and became a co-founder and a Managing Director of Rothschild Bank AG in Zurich.

In 1987 he opened his own bank, Bank Lips AG, also in Zurich. He retired in 1998 when he sold his equity interest in the bank. Not being one to sit around idly, Mr. Lips continues to be very active in the banking, gold and financial fields. He is on the Board of various companies, among them African gold mining companies. He is also a Trustee of the Foundation for the Advancement of Monetary Education (FAME) in New York.

He has written two books previously (*Das Buch der Geldanlage* in 1981 and *Geld, Gold und die Wahrheit* in 1991). *Gold Wars* is his third book and expresses his views on gold, the gold standard and the gold exchange standard as well as the various attempts to manipulate gold and eventually push it aside. As a Swiss, he dedicates an important part of the book to the events leading up to the partial, but substantial, sale of Swiss gold reserves.

In his free time, Ferdinand Lips likes to spend time with his two daughters and the study of history, architecture and philosophy. Mr. Lips, a firm believer in the gold standard, lives outside of Zurich, Switzerland.

Table of Contents

Ferdinand Lips

Acknowledgements

The following persons had the greatest influence on the origin, writing and philosophy of this book.

Dr. D. Mark Bristow, CEO and Managing Director of Randgold Resources Ltd., Jersey, CI. As a geologist, Mark Bristow was instrumental in building and developing Randgold Resources into a gold-focused mining and exploration company. He has played a significant role in encouraging the development of mining in West Africa, particularly Mali. He taught me all I know about gold mining, and he has given me a deep insight into the importance of mining for the prosperity of African countries rich in gold.

Elizabeth B. Currier, President of the Committee for Monetary Research and Education (CMRE), Charlotte, NC, USA. Ms. Currier has the greatest merit in having brought me in contact with most of the people mentioned in the acknowledgments. Her life's work is the CMRE, which has published over fifty monographs by some of the most brilliant minds in economics. The publications have brought me to a better understanding of monetary and economic issues.

Colonel E. C. Harwood, is the founder of the American Institute for Economic Research (AIER), Great Barrington, MA, USA. I met Col. Harwood at the end of the 1960s. He taught me the essentials about inflation and about the dangers of the Keynesian revolution and socialism. His various writings, and in particular an article in the *Economic Education Bulletin* ("Keynes vs. Harwood— A Contribution to Current Debate" by Jagdish Mehra, Vol. XXV, No. 11, November 1985), are an important part of my financial and economic library. On January 21, 1980, Robert M. Bleiberg wrote in an editorial in *Barron's* that the SEC accused Colonel Harwood, who had perennially urged his followers to shun paper money and to buy gold bullion and gold shares, of violating securities laws and sought a court order to liquidate his clients' holdings. Without admitting or denying the charges, Colonel Harwood signed a consent decree in August of 1976, which effectively barred him from the securities field – and investors from what today looks like inspired money management.

John Exter, former central banker at the Federal Reserve Bank of New York and banker at the First National City Bank. In his earlier years as chief of the Far Eastern section at the Federal Reserve, he served as an advisor to the Secretaries of Finance of both the Philippines and Ceylon. In 1950, he became the first governor of the newly-organized central bank of Ceylon (Sri Lanka today). He shared his first-hand experience with the economic situation of the 1930s with me, and I learned a lot about the destructive impact of debt from him. He created the economic model of the 'inverted pyramid' in which gold is *the* supreme form of liquidity.

Joseph J. Cacciotti, philosopher and stockbroker at Ingalls & Snyder LLC, New York. He has been a friend for 30 years and a source of monetary and stock market knowledge without parallel. As a great friend of Switzerland, he thinks the Swiss government and the Swiss National Bank (SNB) have no right to dispose of Swiss gold without telling the Swiss people the truth. The doings of certain big banks, the central bank and incompetent politicians will lead to degrading the Swiss franc, thereby reducing Switzerland's role as champion of freedom and independence, eventually leading to insignificance and even poverty.

Dr. sc. techn. Theodor Abt, professor at the Federal Institute of Technology, Zurich, Department of Agriculture, member of the board of the Research and Training Center in Depth Psychology (according to C. G. Jung and Marie-Louise von Franz). His teachings and discussions further convinced me of the invariability of human nature and of the noblest task humans have been facing throughout the ages: to improve themselves and, thereby, to contribute to a more humane world. We need to return to the ageless values of religion and nature.

James E. Ewart, Seattle, WA, USA, Editor-in-Chief of Zenger News Service. In his book *Money* he expresses the view that, in the absence of the classic gold standard, the present-day 'fractional reserve' banking may be nothing more than financial hocus-pocus. Banking and political insiders use it to cause inflation and, thereby, subtly lure trillions of dollars out of the pockets, purses and bank accounts of everyone else. There is no gold or silver backing for the U.S. dollar today. I share his opinion that an unbacked paper currency and today's dishonest weights and measures may be the biggest crimes in history.

Professor Antal E. Fekete, Memorial University of Newfoundland, St. John's, Canada. Award winner of the International Currency Prize of Bank Lips AG, Zurich, Switzerland, in 1996 with his paper "Whither Gold." His profound and timely studies about the present monetary arrangements, the historic background of the demonetization of silver, the bimetallic ratio, the future of irredeemable paper currency, gold and interest, and hedging in gold mining were of invaluable help in writing this book.

Reginald H. Howe, Belmont, MA, USA, lawyer and monetary expert, Award winner of the International Currency Prize of Bank Lips AG, Zurich, Switzerland, in 1992 with his paper entitled "The Golden Sextant." His website (goldensextant.com) is a high-class refresher course about the deficiencies of the present-day destructive monetary arrangements. Mr. Howe has the invaluable merit of having shed much light on the danger of gold derivatives for the world banking system. I thank him for having filed a lawsuit against the Bank for International Settlements (BIS) in Basle, Switzerland, and the elite of central banking and banking for allegedly conspiring to manipulate the price of gold, which is of particular importance for a free gold market.

R. Brett Kebble, Johannesburg, lawyer and CEO of Western Areas Ltd., Johannesburg, and director of several other South African gold mining companies. Without Mr. Kebble and Western Areas Ltd.'s commission to write a comparative study of the gold market in the 1970s and the 1990s, the present book would not exist. Brett Kebble is one of the few gold mining executives who understand gold as money. He has given precious support and encouragement to accomplish this work.

Roger A. R. Kebble, Johannesburg, Executive Chairman of Randgold Resources Ltd. and executive member of the board of Durban Roodepoort Deep Ltd., Johannesburg. Roger Kebble championed the shareholder revolt that toppled the tired hierarchy of Randgold & Exploration Ltd. in 1994 and installed a radically different company structure, which revolutionized the entire South African gold mining industry. With his boundless energy, he was successful in saving and prolonging the life of several moribund South African gold mines. He transformed them into profitable enterprises in spite of the low gold price, saving thousands of jobs in the process. He was the driving force behind turning Randgold Resources Ltd. into a world-class gold producing and exploration company. In 2000, giant AngloGold became a partner in the Morila Mine in Mali. After my retirement from banking, Roger Kebble encouraged me to keep my interest in the mining business by staying with the companies. He has given me invaluable moral support for writing this book. Like his son Brett, he understands gold as money.

Dr. Lawrence M. Parks, author of *What Does Mr. Greenspan Really Think?,* and Executive Director of the Foundation for the Advancement of Monetary Education (FAME), New York. FAME is an institution fighting for the adoption of a monetary system based on honest weights and measures and against the economic perils of what Dr. Parks calls our fraudulent monetary system. His profound knowledge and sound advice made him an excellent and critical, in the positive sense, editor.

Last, but not least, Thomas Hofmänner, contributing editor, Rapperswil, Switzerland. He has given me greatest assistance by supervising my writing, correcting my English (which is not my native tongue) and adhering to the strictest discipline with respect to sources cited in this work. With his rich cultural background and excellent sense of humor, he has shed a good light on the book. His good spirit helped me not to give up during the difficult months of finishing the book. Special thanks, also, to Messrs. Vincent LoCascio, the author of *Special Privlege: How the Monetary Elite Benefit at Your Expense*, and Richard Esposito, for checking the final manuscript.

The greatest influence on my thinking comes, however, from the German economist Wilhelm Roepke. I saw him only once, but his books have left a lasting mark on my life's philosophy. Roepke, together with Ludwig Erhard and Walter Eucken, were the fathers of the German economic miracle. They understood economics only through the history of man and his relationship with God and nature. If not halted, he felt that abandoning the gold standard and adopting inflationary policies by governments and the ruling classes would eventually lead to the loss of freedom for all but a few.

Introduction

A "gold war" is an attempt by the government upon the constitutional rights of the individual. Why do governments resort to gold wars? Sometimes they want to wage shooting wars without raising taxes; at other times they want to indulge in "social engineering" through the redistribution of income. But in every instance there is one common thread: governments have correctly identified gold as the only antidote against their effort to build the Tower of Babel of irredeemable debt.

This book is much more than a chronicle of gold wars. It is also an account of the historic failure of "Esperanto money." Over a hundred years ago a Polish physician by the name Ludovik Lazarus Zamenhof (1859 – 1917) created a synthetic language in the hope of removing the curse of Babel from mankind. According to the Bible man had become so conceited as to challenge God by proposing to build a tower that was to reach to High Heaven. God's punishment for the temerity was to confuse the tongues of nations. The tower could never be completed for failure of communication due to the confusion of different languages. Zamenhof called his new language "Esperanto" meaning "the hopeful". However, the hope was in vain as other synthetic languages such as "Ido" sprang up. The confusion of tongues, and the curse of Babel, has remained.

Calling irredeemable currency "Esperanto money" is apt. The Biblical story may be interpreted allegorically as an admonition not to challenge God by attempting to build a tower of irredeemable debt that is to reach to High Heaven. But the admonition fell upon deaf ears. Now God's wrath is upon us. Currencies of nations have been confused. The tower can never be completed for lack of compatibility of means of payment. The hope of Esperanto money to remove the curse of Babel is in vain. Other synthetic currencies spring up such as the SDR (special drawing right), the euro, and so on. The confusion of currencies, and the curse of Babel, remains.

Ownership of gold is not about lust: it is about liberty of the individual. The gold standard is not a "game": it is the embodiment of the timeless principle "pacta sunt servanda" (promises are made to be kept.) Official hatred of gold bordering on the neurotic appears less irrational if we contemplate that gold, and gold alone, is capable of exposing the ever-present bad faith behind the promises of the powers that be.

The Americans who have defaulted on their international gold obligations in 1971 put great pressure on other countries that they, too, denounce gold. This brings to mind the fable of Aesop about the wolf that lost his tail in a trap. As he felt uncomfortable being so different from the others in the pack, he tried to persuade his fellow wolves that they, too, should get rid of this cumbersome and useless relic. But a wise old wolf pointed out to him that his proposal would have had greater merit if it had been made before his fatal encounter with the trap. Switzerland was the only country to point out that the American demand to shed the 'obsolete' gold reserves would have been less disingenuous if it had been made *before* the dollar was dishonored in 1971. This tale, however, did not have a happy ending: Switzerland had to be humiliated for being so impertinent as to run a currency superior to the dollar.

Mr. Lips has written a wonderful book for the discriminating reader who may want to understand better the challenge to God's authority involved in the construction of the Tower of Babel of irredeemable debt.

Antal E. Fekete
Professor emeritus, Memorial University of Newfoundland,
St. Johns, Canada
Consulting Professor, Sapientia University, Csikszereda, Romania

Preface

Gold is a living God.[1]

P. B. Shelley

⊙ is the Egyptian symbol for the sun and for gold. It is also the symbol for the eye. Without the sun and without the eye man cannot live.

From the beginning of recorded history some 6,000 years ago, gold made a profound and lasting impression. Gold was, and still is, the ultimate symbol of wealth, power, beauty and prestige. It has been deeply rooted in the consciousness of man ever since. History shows that whenever the acceptance and the use of gold were high, there was prosperity, cultural advancement and political stability. But most importantly, gold is not only essential for prosperity and culture but also for personal and political freedom.

"Gold is the standard of all great civilizations."[2]

Thirty-five years ago, Fed Chairman Greenspan wrote in his article "Gold and Economic Freedom":

> "... gold and economic freedom are inseparable. In the absence of the gold standard, there is no way to protect savings from confiscation through inflation. Gold stands as the protector of property rights. If one grasps this, one has no

difficulty in understanding the statists antagonism toward the gold standard."[3]

"Like liberty, gold never stays where it is undervalued."[4]

J. S. Morill
Speech in the U. S. Senate, January 28, 1878

Preface

[1] B. P. Shelley, *Queen Mab* (1813) in H. L. Mencken, ed., *A New Dictionary of Quotations on Historical Principles from Ancient and Modern Sources* (New York: Alfred Knopf, 1985), 471.

[2] *The American Federationist*, 1896 (Official publication of the American Federation of Labor).

[3] Alan Greenspan, "Gold and Economic Freedom," in *Capitalism: The Unknown Ideal.* Ayn Rand, ed., (New York: New American Library, 1967), 96.

[4] J. S. Morill, U.S. Senate in H. L. Mencken, ed., *A New Dictionary of Quotations on Historical Principles from Ancient and Modern Sources* (New York: Alfred Knopf, 1985), 471.

Foreword

Hidden in the cellar of a villa in Zurich's Seefeld Quarter, there are a dozen old copperplate engravings depicting one of the most staggering financial episodes of all time: the speculative stock market frenzy caused by the Scottish adventurer and mathematician John Law. After King Louis XIV's death, Law unsuccessfully tried to save the impoverished French economy and famine-stricken population by introducing a new currency backed by real estate. These old engravings are renditions of the dance around the golden calf and of Rue Quincampoix, Paris' eighteenth century Wall Street where it all happened.

The engravings were not always in the cellar. I had discovered them in an old Dutch history book about John Law. I was so fascinated by the art that I took some out and had them restored. Newly framed, they were hung on the walls of my bank as a vivid reminder to employees and clients alike as to what may happen when certain standards are dropped and forgotten.

The Seefeld Quarter of Zurich, not far from the shore of beautiful Lake Zurich, is one of the liveliest places within the city. On one end it borders on Bellevue Square with the Opera House, the world famous Restaurant Kronenhalle, and at its other end is Tiefenbrunnen and its old mill, which has been transformed into a vibrant center with restaurants, bars, wine shops, theatres, software firms, model agencies, health centers and boutiques. It also contains shops catering to the everyday needs of a working population generally living in modest apartments. By streetcar, the Seefeld is only a few minutes away from Zurich's financial center. Restaurants of all kinds, schools, doctors' offices, car dealerships, office buildings and, of course, a few private banks, complement the picture.

The private banks, however, were not always there. There were always the obligatory branch offices of the big banks, but only lately (starting 1989) a number of private banks, some with prominent names, opened their offices in beautiful, late nineteenth century *'fin de siècle'* villas. Before, some of the villas were empty and on a slow road to decay, as they were too big for one family to manage, and domestic help is notoriously difficult to find today. One of these houses was to become the first headquarters of my private bank. Radical squatters occupied it before the owners decided to renovate and rent it out. Without being conscious of it, I had created a new financial center in Zurich by taking offices in the Seefeld. Many were to follow my lead.

My second office in the Seefeld was in another, most attractive villa with a lovely park. The story behind the house is rather sad. With the exception of one member, the family, who had once called it their home, tragically perished on the Titanic's only voyage. For a few years, an oil trading company used the house for offices. When I became interested in the property, it had already been vacated and empty for quite some time. The engravings of the John Law fiasco were on those walls.

But why are the engravings out of sight now, hidden in the cellar and gathering dust? When I retired and sold the bank, my successors thought the engravings untimely and detrimental to their marketing effort. It seems to me that the hidden or obvious lessons of history found in the old documents were cast to the winds. We are well advised to heed the warnings from across the centuries. If we do not, we are setting ourselves up for fatal crashes. With new markets popping up all over the world, these historic documents are a timely and necessary warning to us all, unless, of course, you do not want the message to be heard, or it is against your agenda.

Daniel Defoe said of John Law that he made "money flow like water in the Seine."[1] The consequences of Law's doings never went beyond France. It is said that the country never fully recovered from the financial, economic and social devastation of his scheme. The events in the financial markets of today, however, have global implications and embrace us all. The study of history, especially financial and monetary history, is a neglected and underestimated subject. We need to respect and accept past experience. If we do not, we are damned to repeat the mistakes, and then things will not only collect dust, they will turn into dust.

The idea for this book originated in the summer of 1999 when Mr. Brett Kebble, then deputy chairman of Western Areas Ltd. of South Africa, asked me to write a comparative study about the gold markets of the 1970s and the 1990s. He thought it would be useful under current market circumstances because most people were getting the gold story wrong. The first draft was delivered in October 1999, already containing some historical background beyond the 1970s. But then we decided that there was little use in writing only about two decades because the events that characterized the gold market of the seventies had their origins in much earlier days.

Most mining executives, bankers and investors are now in their forties, if not thirties, and know little of the history of the gold standard. If they have heard about it, then only that it had failed; or that there is not enough gold in the world today to support a gold standard; or they believe Keynes, who said that "the gold standard is a barbarous relic." There is probably not one university in the world teaching monetary history. So how can anybody know?

Today, political decision-makers are nominally responsible for our money. After a century of hyperinflations, we can only conclude that they have not done their job and failed miserably. Unfortunately, there is no solution in sight that will make the purchasing power of money stable. In a world where the stock market becomes the new monetary tool to manage the economy, we are not far from the era of John Law. The scheme by John Law on a worldwide basis is, however, no guarantee for the future of the world economy and the future of society as a whole.

The only thing we can expect from the ruling political class of today is patchwork. I ask the young people of this world to turn to monetary archaeology and to change the present situation of 'The End of History' into 'The Beginning of History'. As we all know, it is more difficult to master the future without a knowledge of history. The only hope remaining is, therefore, the young generation. Unfortunately, there is little chance that anybody of the older generation is going to help them get out of the present monetary morass and away from the abyss.

I ask the world's gold mining executives to do the same. Get familiar with the history of the most precious product you are digging out of the earth day after day with great pain at high cost and by taking great risks. The product has a historic use that is far more important than jewelry. It is its use as the basis of our money. Why is this dimension not perceived? Why did South Africa, the world's biggest producer of gold, not think about a forward strategy? Why did the leaders of African gold producing countries not think of gold bond financing as did those in America, the pioneer in the field? When the importance of gold is realized, there will be no more forward sales, there will be no more sales at dumping prices. The mines will stop selling and keep their undervalued gold. Perhaps, they should form the OGMEC (Organization of Gold Mining and Exporting Countries).

I demand to know from Western bankers and portfolio managers what confused logic compels them to leave no room for gold in their portfolios. They should know from history that the future of fiat money does not bode well for the survival of their clients' portfolios. I address the Western bankers because the people of the East have a better understanding of gold. Do the portfolio managers really think that stocks of companies with no earnings or bonds in troubled currencies are sensible long-term investments? Should they not be more interested in sound monetary conditions? It would make their work easier.

I ask the central bankers of this world: Are you really concerned with what should be the main purpose of your jobs: to protect the purchasing power and the integrity of your country's currency? Are you really sincere and acting to the best of your ability when you decrease your country's gold holdings only to replace it with continuously depreciating paper claims that may not be honored? Remember, no serious farmer would sell his seeds. If not, you are clearly useless and should get out of the business.

I will not ask anything of the politicians because they will never change. All they have done with their politics is to destroy the purchasing power of money. They should learn to understand people better, and to be aware that in 5,000 years human patterns have never really changed. Free people will always believe in gold, and when the economic and monetary situation offers nothing but despair, they will want to get rid of the printing presses – and the politicians! It has happened before, and it can happen again. The monetary standard matters, but so does the moral standard.

This book does not pretend to be complete. Its purpose is to inform. Much room has been reserved for Switzerland. Switzerland has played a special role in history: protecting people's money in uncertain times (which now seem to be permanent). By protecting people, it assures their financial security and personal freedom. Today, the Swiss Government, the SNB and the big banks fail to heed history. They bought their way out of responsibility not with their own money, but with money belonging to the people. Do they really believe Switzerland still has excess gold in the event of a war? The idea has always been that for Switzerland, gold and freedom are inseparable and, therefore, necessary. Why should that change?

One final word: I am not an economist. For most of my fifty professional years, I was a practicing banker. The experience gained and thirty years of studying history, particularly monetary history, led me to recognize that the present monetary system is in disarray. It is a slap in the face of law and order, civilization and civility; but, most importantly, it is a threat to our freedom. Let us hope it will not last much longer.

---

[1] Ludovic Hunter-Tilney, "Who wants to be a millionaire?" *Financial Times*, 2 September 2000. See also *Daniel Defoe, His Life and Recently Discovered Writings*, William Lee ed. (New York: B. Franklin, 1969).

Part I: Some History

"Gold is money, and nothing else"[1]

J. P. Morgan

"Not Philip, but Philip's gold, took the cities of Greece."[2]

Plutarch

Introduction

To understand today's monetary situation, it is important to understand what has been going on in the gold markets since the collapse of Bretton Woods in 1971, or, even better, what happened since the end of the gold standard of the nineteenth century. Bretton Woods, actually, was not a gold standard but a 'gold exchange' or 'dollar exchange' standard. It was, as Wilhelm Roepke called it, a denatured gold standard, and, as such, a dangerous surrogate whose implications plunged the world economy into precarious inflationary, and subsequently deflationary, crises twice during this century. The consequence of the first version of the gold exchange standard, as a result of the conference of Genoa in 1922, was even worse. It helped produce not only the Florida real estate crisis of 1925, but also the stock market boom of the twenties and the subsequent crash of 1929, which was followed by the depression of the thirties and, eventually, World War II.

The modern gold standard of the nineteenth century evolved naturally and was not the result of any conference, but rather the product of many centuries of experience and practice. It grew step by step, almost by accident, through its own force and because of the logic and experience gained with debasement of currencies in the past.

The Egyptians were the first to mine and utilize gold on a large scale. Between 4,000 and 2,000 BC, the Egyptians may have produced as much as 750 tonnes of gold. Most of this vast treasure became the property of the Pharaohs, and a great part of it was used for the elaborate decoration of royal tombs. About 4,500 years ago, Egyptian and Mesopotamian officials received their wages in gold. Right from the dawn of history man had a high regard for gold. It was the universal metal from the beginning. The metal was sought after and held by such diverse civilizations as Babylon, China, Egypt, Ethiopia, Greece and the Incas. Gold and silver are the first metals mentioned in the *Bible*. At first they were held in temples and shrines and then filtered into primitive trade. As such they were a major contributor to the ancient world's improvements over barter trade. When gold and silver began to circulate, commercial and economic progress increased greatly. Trade became more efficient, because there was a greater division of labor.

But, it was the Greeks who were the first to use gold as money in form of coins. The first coins of pure gold were, however, struck by the legendary Lydian monarch Croesus (560 to 540 BC).

The Ancient Greeks and Gold

The Greeks, and indeed all the ancient people, had a high regard for gold coins. By 400 BC, the design and the engravings of coins reached an artistic level that has yet to be surpassed. After the Macedonian conquests, Philip, with his small gold staters, put the Greeks on something resembling a gold standard. The staters were irregularly sized and shaped coins made of electrum, a naturally occurring alloy of gold and silver. They are believed to have been made as early 750 BC. Although rudely marked to show their weight and fineness, the staters were gradually replaced by more carefully made coins starting around 500 BC.[3] Philip's famous son, Alexander the Great, completed the work of making gold coins the world's primary money by spreading the gold stater as far as India.

Roy W. Jastram in *Silver – The Restless Metal* comments:

> "It must be recognized that not all the results of man's use of precious metals were benign; quite the contrary. Greed has always been with us. The great storehouses of treasures collected in palaces, temples, and sanctuaries tempted man to looting and to wars. When Alexander the Great led the Greeks into Asia Minor, he called it a war of revenge against the Persians. Revenge was important to the proud Greeks, but the added attraction was the opportunity to

plunder the vast gold and silver treasures of the Persian Empire.

> That war, brutal as it was, became the means by which an obsolete oriental theoracy, covering much of the civilized world, was destroyed. Peoples of diverse races and cultures were brought together and the immense idle reserves of the Archimedean Empire were turned to productive use. The flow of new money minted by Alexander from captured treasure was to spread prosperity (and incidentally inflation) throughout the conquered lands."[4]

At first, the heads of gods were embossed on the coins. But, there came a point when kings replaced the gods. This change signified the crossing of a major threshold in monetary history. The first man to have his head imprinted on a coin was King Solomon, to whom God had given great wisdom. Another to play an important role in monetary history was Cyrus, King of Persia. He conquered the Lydians and took all their gold to Persia. From there it was managed and circulated as far as the Mediterranean. But the man through whose hands most, if not all, of the known gold treasures of the time passed was Alexander the Great. It is a peculiar phenomenon that this man visited or conquered all the important temples and holy shrines, one after the other. However, he did not take possession of any of those consecrated sites. He sought a new relationship with the people and their respective cultures, thus creating the first Mediterranean cosmopolitan organization reaching as far as India. This was the outstanding achievement of Alexander – and he was among the first to have his face on coins.

The Ancient Romans

Again, Roy W. Jastram:

> "Centuries later, Rome sent her legions into the known world to plunder wherever hoards of precious metals had accumulated. When plunder became scarce, she was forced to organize production. The mines of her Asian, African, and European provinces

3

financed her expansion on a grand scale. Ultimately the mines ceased to provide the precious metals she needed in sufficient quantity. The slide into debased coinage began."[5]

The Roman emperor Caesar introduced the Aureus gold coin. Later, it was improved by his successor, Augustus, and became the basis of the first common market of Europe. It served for centuries as the superior world money. Roman officers also received their pay in gold. It was the special privilege of the infamous Nero to start coin clipping. That started the decline of the Empire. However, it lasted over three hundred years and, as Gibbon wrote in his work, *The Decline and the Fall of the Roman Empire*, one should not wonder why Rome went under, but rather why it lasted so long. Stability prevailed for a period of 75 years under Caesar and Augustus. Contrary to the logical Greeks, the Romans seemed unable to resist the temptation of cheating one another on weights. They were forever tinkering with the coinage–reducing, diluting, debasing it–ultimately to the point of uselessness. Perhaps that is one of the reasons why they continuously suffered from internal disorder and civil war. In a way, the Romans can be considered the first Keynesians. They proved that no economy could prosper under conditions amounting to perpetual embezzlement by those who enjoy special privileges, e.g., the monetary authorities.

It should be of interest to modern Keynesian economists, as well as to the present generation of investors, that although the emperors of Rome frantically tried to 'manage' their economies, they only succeeded in making matters worse. Price and wage controls and legal tender laws were passed, but it was like trying to hold back the tides. Rioting, corruption, lawlessness and a mindless mania for speculation and gambling engulfed the empire like a plague. With money so unreliable and debased, speculation in commodities became far more attractive than producing them.

There were many reasons for the fall of the Roman Empire, but one decisive factor was the growing lack of gold that had gradually begun to flow eastwards.

Eastern Rome

Eventually, the Romans got an emperor, the great Constantine, who had some grasp of economics as well as the military arts. For a time Constantine succeeded in arresting the disintegration of the empire. He was the founder of the new Eastern Empire, or Byzantium, and started minting the gold 'Solidus' or 'Noumisma'. In reality, he founded a whole new nation that would survive the Western Roman Empire by a thousand years. The 'Solidus' introduced by Constantine became the basic monetary unit of the world. It is a fact that as long as the Byzantine Empire strictly maintained the purity and value of the 'Solidus, or the 'Bezant' as the Greeks called it, the Empire never succumbed to a foreign invader.

There is a lot of wisdom to be drawn from this. Even non-economic historians acknowledge that the long survival of the Byzantine Empire, surrounded by hostile neighbors, was primarily due to its superior economic organization and financial structure based on gold.

The devaluations began under Emperor Michael IV (1034-1041), but it was the tragedy of Alexius I Comnenus (1081-1118) to continue to devalue the 'Bezant' in order to pay off his private debts. From then on, eight centuries of trust and confidence were irreparably damaged, and the Byzantine gold coins were no longer considered a stable currency in international trade.[6] In the meantime, the Vandals had sacked Western Rome so that hardly a trace of a viable economy was left. The same can be said of Eastern Rome. After further devaluations, the Byzantine Empire managed a precarious existence. During the next 250 years, however, it literally became a shadow of its former wealth and splendor. Constantinople fell to the Ottoman Turks in 1453.

The Arabs

Another outstanding example of the success of standard gold coins as the primary money occurred in the great Arab Empire founded by Mohammed. This empire, which coexisted, but not always peacefully, with the Byzantine state, eventually extended from Baghdad to Barcelona. At its height, it enjoyed a civilization that rivaled that of its Byzantine neighbor and even that of Augustus' Rome. The coin of the Arab Empire was the gold Dinar, which was minted at approximately the same weight as the 'Bezant.' The imperial Arabs were great admirers of classic Greek culture and philosophy and had readily adopted the Greek attitude toward sound money and honest commerce. The Dinar circulated for about 450 years without alteration and during that time the Saracen Arab civilization flourished with astounding brilliance, while Europe languished in darkness, ignorance and despair. Ultimately, Arab civilization also collapsed with almost the same rapidity as it had been formed. Its demise was largely due to religious factions and quarrels rather than economic or financial delinquency.

The Dark Ages

The final destruction of Greco-Roman civilization left Western Europe in a state of social, political, cultural and economic anarchy for the better part of six centuries. Although some modern scholars now believe these 'Dark Ages' were not quite as bleak as formerly thought, they were grim enough to reduce most of society to a primitive subsistence economy.

Gold in the Renaissance

It was the emergence of the Italian city-states that took Europe out of the Dark Ages. It began forming what is now called Western civilization by a renewed interest in culture and rapid economic progress. In 1252, the Republic of Florence began minting the first significant gold coinage in Europe since Caesar's Aureus. The Florentines made this new coin, the 'fiorino d'oro' or gold Florin, their basic monetary medium. In reality, Florence was on a gold standard. Twenty-eight years later, the Republic of Venice followed suit by minting the Ducat to the same weight and value as the Florin. By the end of the century, nearly all other cities in northern Italy, and several beyond the Alps, were issuing gold coins in Florin/Ducat denominations.

The availability of a reliable gold coinage brought a period of great commercial success and prosperity to the Italian city-states and eventually to most of Western Europe. Consequently, gold money was the economic and financial basis of the Renaissance. Culture flourishes under conditions of wealth and not of poverty. The power and reliability of gold, once again, advanced mankind to a higher civilization.

The Conquistadors

The Conquistadors landed on the American continent shortly after Columbus discovered America in 1492. They encountered the gold-rich cultures of the Aztecs, Incas and later with inhabitants of Colombia. In all these cultures, gold played an important religious role, and they had already developed a highly skilled craftsmanship to transform the precious metal into jewelry and objects of art of incomparable beauty. However, the Conquistadors were not terribly interested in the religious and metaphysical aspects of these treasures. Their main priority was to plunder as much gold as they could, and to bring it back to their kings and queens. They found it in enormous quantities. Most of the time they took it with brute force, destroying rich cultures in the process.

Modern Times

The Paper Money Experiments of France

By contrast, the first paper money experiment in France by a Scottish adventurer John Law failed miserably.[7] Under the reign of Sun King Louis XIV, the finances of France were ruined. Because Louis XV was only five at the time of the old king's death in 1715, Duke Philippe of Orléans was installed as regent. Law, who had met the Prince Regent during one of his visits to a Paris gambling casino, succeeded in persuading him to revitalize the dismal situation by issuing a paper banknote currency.

In *Extraordinary Popular Delusions and the Madness of Crowds*, Charles Mackay wrote:

"When Law presented himself at the court, he was most cordially received. He offered two memorials to the regent, in which he set forth the evils that had befallen France, owing to an insufficient currency, at different times depreciated. He asserted that a metallic currency, unaided by paper money, was wholly inadequate to the wants of a commercial country, and in particular cited the examples of Great Britain and Holland to show the advantages of paper. He used many sound arguments on the subject of credit, and proposed as a means of restoring that of France, then at so low an ebb among the nations, that he should be allowed to set up a bank, which should have the management of the royal revenues, and issue notes both on that and on landed security."[8]

Curiously, Law's theories and practices have much in common with the current fiat money experiment at the end of the twentieth century. Thus Law can easily be called the first Keynesian. In 1716, John Law was authorized by royal edict to establish a bank under the name of *Law and Company*. This bank, and the Mississippi Company he founded later, put him on the road to what can be called the first fiat money experiment of the Western World. At first, business improved, trade and commerce picked up and tax revenues increased rapidly. A certain degree of confidence was established and the whole country felt the benefits.[9]

Law was the founder of the Banque de France, and the famous Rue Quincampoix, the site of the Paris stock market. The idea that paper could eventually replace a metallic currency led to an over-issuance of paper. Stock trading dramatically increased and resembled an orgy more than an orderly market. The inevitable happened. In early 1720, some astute speculators began to realize that this bubble could not last much longer. They began to cash in their stock and bank notes for gold. It did not take long before there were more sellers than buyers and the whole paper edifice, which was based purely on thin air, crumbled. Law fled the country but was caught when trying to cross the border. Obviously having abandoned his own beliefs, the carriage in which he was traveling was found to be full of gold and silver coins!

The Assignats

Between 1790 and 1797, Law's experiment was followed by the issue of assignats, a sort of land mortgage notes, whose purchasing power decreased to their cost of production in a very short time, namely zero. In *Fiat Money Inflation in France*, Andrew Dickson White (1832-1912), an American professor and diplomat, described how one of the most intelligent nations, France, learned nothing from the failure of John Law's experiment.[10] In his foreword to this fascinating book, John Mackay offered a commentary that also applies to the fiat money experiment of the twentieth and twenty-first centuries:

> "It records the most gigantic attempt ever made in the history of the world by a government to create an inconvertible paper currency, and to maintain its circulation at various levels of value. It also records what is perhaps the greatest of all governmental efforts–with the possible exception of Diocletian's–to enact and enforce a legal limit of commodity prices. Every fetter that could hinder the will or thwart the wisdom of democracy had been shattered, and in consequence every device and expedient that untrammeled power and unrepressed optimism could conceive were brought to bear. But the attempts failed. They left behind them a legacy of moral and material desolation and woe, from which one of the most intellectual and spirited races of Europe has suffered for a century and a quarter, and will continue to suffer until the end of time."[11]

Both paper money experiments had serious political consequences that shook the world to its foundations. There can be no doubt that the resulting French Revolution changed the world forever. It prepared the ground for the man on the proverbial White Horse as well – Napoleon.

He rapidly brought back law and order by restoring the country's legal system first and then the military. When he subsequently turned his attention to the desperate financial situation, he acted brilliantly. Although he was advised to issue some new paper currency, he absolutely refused. "Never," he answered, "I will pay cash (gold and silver) or nothing." He never broke this promise, not even during the emergency of the 100 days. Napoleon restored France to a full specie basis, thereby putting the country on a *de facto* gold standard. It lasted until 1914! The most popular French gold coins are still called 'Napoléon'.

What would Andrew Dickson White say today with not just one country, but the whole world involved in the biggest, most ambitious and reckless fiat money experiment in history? He would conclude that the world would suffer until the end of time.

The Gold Standard of the Nineteenth Century

The Example of Britain

It is a disaster what happened to the pound after the gold standard was abandoned, and Great Britain serves as a classical example of how a modern gold standard functions. The early experience of Britain with gold as money started in 1664 and lasted, with some interruptions, for 250 years until the outbreak of World War I. The gold redemption promise was interrupted in the years 1797 to 1821 when Britain was at war with France. Britain's gold standard played an integral part in the rise of the British Empire. It would never have been possible without a sound currency. As Sir William Rees-Mogg wrote in his book *The Reigning Error*, "Gold was money and money was gold."[12]

On July 13, 1974 *The Economist* published a fascinating picture of the development of consumer prices during this period. This was possible because Britain is the only country to keep reliable statistics covering that time. At the beginning, the price index was set at 100. Prices remained generally stable or below the level of 1664, with the exception of the period of the Napoleonic Wars, when, in 1813, the price level shot up to 180 only to return to its long-term average later. In 1914, at the beginning of World War

I, the index stood at 91, which meant it was lower than 250 years prior. Everybody knows what happened to the pound after the gold standard was abandoned.

By 1900, approximately fifty countries were on a gold standard, including all industrialized nations. The interesting fact is that the modern gold standard was not planned at an international conference, nor was it invented by some genius. It came by itself, naturally and based on experience. The United Kingdom went on a gold standard against the intention of its government. Only much later did laws turn an operative gold standard into an officially sanctioned gold standard.

The Example of the United States.

The periods of price stability under the classical gold standard, from 1834 to 1862 and 1879 to 1913, are without parallel. U.S. consumer prices varied in a 26% range during those 62 years and were at almost exactly the same level at the beginning and the end of both periods. In 1800, the index of wholesale prices in the U.S. was 102.2. It went down to 80.7 in 1913. From 1879 to 1913 when the U.S., and most other nations, shared the gold standard, U.S. consumer prices varied only by 17% in 34 years. Again, average inflation was near zero. The average annual variation of prices, up or down, was 1.3%. This stands in sharp contrast to the average price gyrations during and after the Civil War (6.2%), the period between World War I and Bretton Woods (5.6%) and the period since Bretton Woods (6%).

It is not the purpose of this book to give a full account of American monetary history of the eighteenth and nineteenth centuries because plenty of literature is available on the subject. However, some comments about the turbulent past may help to better understand present attitudes.

Monetary chronology:

May 10, 1775

The Continental Congress authorized the printing of fiat money (the Continental), whose purchasing power quickly eroded to a tiny fraction of its face value.

May 31, 1781

The Continental currency ceased to circulate as currency. It became an article of speculation.[13]

1787

Constitutional Convention – Creation of the *Constitution*

The basic principles of the Founding Fathers, men such as Thomas Jefferson, George Washington, James Madison, John Adams and Benjamin Franklin, and their philosophy were embodied in the *Constitution*. These men were educated in philosophy and had a deep respect for creation, religion and human nature. The main tenet was that human rights had their origin in nature. The central rights were life, liberty, property (to use and dispose of one's labor), and the pursuit of happiness. A good society existed where natural rights were recognized and protected. The purpose of the best kind of government was to see to it that these rights were observed. The *Constitution* as they wrote it still exists (with a few amendments added), but the Founding Fathers would turn over in their graves if they knew how their basic concepts and philosophy were treated 200 years later.

1789

In Article I, Section 8, Clause 5, the Constitution empowers Congress with the authority to coin money. It does not state what is to be considered legal tender. Under Section 10 of the same Article it prohibits the individual States to "… to make any Thing but gold and silver Coin a Tender in Payment of Debts…" One may consider this a recursive definition of legal tender. By stipulating that the States could not make anything legal tender other than gold and silver, Congress was forced to make the two metals the currency of the United States.

April 2, 1792

Congress passed the Coinage Act of 1792, which provided for the free coinage of both gold and silver.[14]

> "The Act created the U.S. Mint, wherein our official money, coins of silver and coins of gold, were to be manufactured. Money manufactured according

to law is called *lawful* money, and the phrase 'Lawful money of the United States' means coins of silver and of gold, which have been manufactured according to United States law in a United States Mint."[15]

Money: A Precise Definition

Money

Coins or other mechanical devices manufactured in a mint—made of gold, silver or other precious or semiprecious metals—to be media of exchange.[16]

> "Britain was on the gold standard for nearly two centuries from 1717 [according to some the starting year was 1664 –auth.] to 1914, with the exception of the period of 1797-1821, when it suspended convertibility during the Napoleonic Wars. The United States was effectively on a silver standard until 1834, thereafter, it was on the gold standard until 1914, with the exception of the Greenback era (1862-1879). No other countries have been on a gold standard for so long and, not coincidentally, no others have been so relatively prosperous as these two were during their gold standard eras. Contrary to popular belief today, gold money is not inherently deflationary, and not an impediment to economic growth and prosperity. General price levels were flat or actually declining in Britain and the United States during periods of rapid growth, an outcome that many economists today consider an impossible contradiction."[17]

Britain's banking tradition goes back further and that explains the considerable differences in its respective banking history:

> "Although the basic principles of sound commercial banking were being applied with increasing success in England in the early 1800s, these principles were not so widely understood in the United States. Hundreds of banks were started in the

various states of the Union by individuals who knew nothing of banking beyond the fact that they wanted to participate in that mysteriously profitable business."[18]

For much of the time, American monetary history does not serve very well as an example for continuity and sound money. Austrian economist Felix Somary says the following in his book *Erinnerungen aus meinem Leben* (1959):

> "Contrary to Britain, today's leading power does not have a tradition of stable money. As strange as it may sound, but since the 18th century, debtors were in the overwhelming majority in the US and still are. The Union, which was almost free of debt at the beginning of the century, has built up a debt burden of gigantic proportions and is, therefore, sharing the concerns of all other debtors. In spite of all the official declarations, which are hardly worth more than trash, the situation has remained unchanged to this day."[19]

On March 14, 1900, Congress passed the Gold Standard Act. According to this act, a gold reserve of $150 million was created by the Treasury for the redemption of Greenbacks or Treasury Notes, which could only be issued in exchange for gold. The spirit of that period was as follows:

> "We renew our allegiance to the principle of the gold standard and declare our confidence in the wisdom of the legislation of the Fifty-sixth Congress, by which the parity of all our money and the stability of our currency upon a gold basis has been secured."

Republican National Platform, 1900[20]

Four years later they were still of the same conviction:

> "We believe it to be the duty of the Republican Party to uphold the gold standard and the integrity and value of our national currency."

Republican National Platform, 1904[21]

"The Republican Party established and will continue to uphold the gold standard and will oppose any measure, which will undermine the government's credit or impair the integrity of our national currency. Relief by currency inflation is unsound and dishonest in results."

Republican National Platform, 1932[22]

The Triumph of Gold

In his book *Managed Money at the Crossroads*, Professor M. Palyi wrote:

"For the first time since the glory of Rome, the civilized world succeeded in achieving a monetary unity. The commercial and financial unity was attained without a military empire or utopian dreams. The monetary unity of the gold standard was generally accepted and recognized as the only rational monetary system."[23]

The gold standard of the nineteenth century represented the highest monetary achievement of the civilized world and seems like a miracle now:[24]

French Franc	1814-1914	100 years stability
Dutch Guilder	1816-1914	98 years
Pound Sterling	1821-1914	93 years
Swiss Franc	1850-1936	86 years
Belgian Franc	1832-1914	82 years
Swedish Kronor	1873-1931	58 years
German Mark	1875-1914	39 years
Italian Lira	1883-1914	31 years

The Austrian economist Ludwig von Mises in his work *Human Action* had the following to say:

"The gold standard was the world standard of the age of capitalism, increasing welfare, liberty, and democracy, both political and economic. In the eyes of the free traders its main eminence was precisely the fact that it was an international standard as required by international trade and the transactions of the international money and capital markets. It was the medium of exchange by means of which Western industrialism and Western capital had borne Western civilization to the remotest parts of the earth's surface, everywhere destroying the fetters of old-aged prejudices and superstitions, sowing the seeds of new life and new well-being, freeing minds and souls, and creating riches unheard of before. It accompanied the triumphal unprecedented progress of Western liberalism ready to unite all nations into a community of free nations peacefully cooperating with one another. It is easy to understand why people viewed the gold standard as the symbol of this greatest and most beneficial of all historical changes."[25]

The Experience of Sound Money and Politics

Economic progress requires sound money conditions. Many, particularly politicians, did not share this opinion in spite of all the convincing good experiences with the gold standard.

Let us again quote Ludwig von Mises in *Human Action*:

"All those intent upon sabotaging the evolution toward welfare, peace, freedom and democracy, loathed the gold standard, and not only on account of its economic significance. In their eyes the gold standard was the labarum, the symbol, of all those doctrines and policies they wanted to destroy. In the struggle against the gold standard there was more at stake than commodity prices and foreign exchange rates."

The nationalists are fighting the gold standard because they want to sever their countries from the world market and to establish national autarky as far as possible. Interventionist governments and pressure groups are fighting the gold standard because they consider it the most serious obstacle to their endeavours to manipulate prices and wage rates. But the most fanatical attacks against gold are made by those intent upon credit expansion. With them credit expansion is the panacea for all economic ills. [...] The gold standard is certainly not a perfect or ideal standard. There is no such thing as perfection in human things. But nobody is in a position to tell us how something more satisfactory could be put in place of the gold standard. The purchasing power of gold is not stable. But the very notion of stability and unchangeability of purchasing power are absurd. In a living and changing world there cannot be any such thing as stability of purchasing power. [...] In fact, the adversaries of the gold standard do not want to make money's purchasing power stable. They want rather to give the governments the power to manipulate purchasing power without being hindered by an "external" factor, namely, the money relation of the gold standard.

The main objection raised against the gold standard is that it makes operative in the determination of prices, a factor, which no government can control, the vicissitudes of gold production.

The significance of the fact that the gold standard makes the increase in the supply of gold depend upon the profitability of producing gold is, of course, that it limits the government's power to resort to inflation. The gold standard makes the determination of money's purchasing power independent of the changing ambitions and doctrines of political parties and pressure groups. This is not a defect of the gold standard; it is its main excellence. Every method of manipulating purchasing power is by necessity arbitrary. All methods recommended for the discovery of an allegedly objective and "scientific" yardstick for monetary manipulation are based on the illusion that changes in purchasing power can be "measured". The gold standard removes the determination of cash-induced changes in purchasing power from the political arena. Its general acceptance requires the acknowledgement of the truth that one cannot make all people richer by printing money. The abhorrence of the gold standard is inspired by the superstition that omnipotent governments can create wealth out of little scraps of paper. [...] What the expansionists call the defects of the gold standard are indeed its very eminence and usefulness. [...] The gold standard did not fail. The governments were eager to destroy it, because they were committed to the fallacies that credit expansion is an appropriate means of lowering the rate of interest and of "improving" the balance of trade. [...] The struggle against gold, which is one of the main concerns of all contemporary governments, must not be looked upon as an isolated phenomenon. It is but one item in the gigantic process of destruction, which is the mark of our time. People fight the gold standard because they want to substitute national autarky for free trade, war for peace, totalitarian government omnipotence for liberty. [...] The international gold standard works without any action on the part of governments."[26]

Stock and Bond Markets under the Gold Standard

In the research study "Money: A Search for Common Ground" sponsored in 1984 by the Progress Foundation, Lugano, Switzerland, I analyzed the behavior of the securities markets under the gold standard of the nineteenth century. The paper titled "The Views of a Practicing Banker" was no monetary archaeological discovery, but it was representative of a conclusion from Graham and Dodd's classic work *Security Analysis*:

"Under the gold standard, the most important currencies were stable for long periods. This stability was highly beneficial to the industrialisation during that period as stock and bond issues could easily be floated. Currency stability was particularly beneficial for flotation of debt issues and interest rates were low."[27]

Before World War I, the chief characteristic of investment grade common stock was a stable, generally increasing dividend rate based on reasonable stability of earnings, a sound financial structure, and ample working capital. Because it still represented risk capital, common stock was generally offered at a higher return than bonds of corresponding investment quality. Because stocks offered a higher return, they were considered savings instruments. The 'Greater Fool Theory' of today's stock market was unknown then. 'The Greater Fool Theory' advocates that you buy common stock at a, hopefully, cheap price and sell it, after the price has gone up, to an even greater fool who then is stuck with a high-priced stock yielding little or no return at all.

It is only under the classical gold standard that financial instruments and markets can work satisfactorily for everybody, be it for the lender, the stockholder, the borrower or, most importantly, the saver. Only when honest weights and measures prevail will financial instruments and financial markets live up to their full potential. History is full of examples of markets turning into gambling casinos under a regime of irredeemable currencies. Their present-day market behavior is the best proof of that.

The experience drawn from this period was, in essence, that bonds represented a large portion of investors' portfolios. They could easily be launched, as there was no loss of purchasing power. There is no better way to achieve economic progress than by basing it on sound money. This has, and will be, proven superior to any prior or subsequent paper money system.

In his book *The Twilight of Gold*, 1914 to 1936, Dr. Melchior Palyi wrote:

> "It was a world of balanced national budgets, wherein public debts had to be amortised as a matter of course, just as private ones had to be repaid, and fiat money was an anathema. Essential public

19

expenditures (investments) were financed by the sale of long-term bonds, not by debt monetisation. Above all, it was a world of steady real growth–with rising living standards for the masses, and with 'security' provided by the protection of savings."[28]

The world economy was operating on a full-potential basis and rising standards of living for the masses meant low or no unemployment. When today's leaders search for a new financial architecture, they should remember the experience of the gold standard.

Then, protecting savings also had another meaning. Because there was no inflation in this golden 'world of security,' people could live on their savings and concentrate on cultural activities. People are most likely to save when they are confident that they can enjoy the fruits of their labor. This implies confidence in the existing monetary standard and in the ability of government to maintain order, enforce contracts and run a stable monetary system. There is no better document of what the gold standard meant to mankind than the description of the Golden Age of Security as the Austrian author Stefan Zweig recalls it in his preface to his famous book *The World of Yesterday*,[29] as well as the tragedies that befell the world after the golden anchor was foolishly lifted.

The End of the Nineteenth Century Gold Standard

In 1914, at the beginning of World War I, the gold standard was thrown overboard within a few weekends. In order to finance wars, the world resorted to deficit financing and paper money. Had the gold standard not been given up, the war would not have lasted more than a few months. Instead, it lasted more than four years and ruined most of the major economies in the world and left millions dead in its wake.

After the end of the gold standard, sound monetary policy was a thing of the past. The duration and the extent of the War forced the nations involved to neglect all monetary discipline using the war efforts as an excuse.

Based on 50 years of experience and study of the markets and the history of money, it is my conviction that the abandonment of the gold standard of the nineteenth century is the greatest tragedy of all time. It is an event that has led the world into almost 100 years of monetary no-man's land and could ultimately lead into total loss of freedom for mankind. Since then, most economists have blinders over their eyes, but whoever takes the time and work to study the decisive events in history will find that gold is the decisive fulcrum of the world economy and world destiny. The monetary standard is closely linked to the moral standard and, as such, determines the fate of humanity.

Some Monetary Chronology

On March 14, 1900 the U.S. Congress passed the Gold Standard Act, which placed the U.S. on an official gold standard.

The purchasing power of the dollar from 1800 – 1914 remained more or less unchanged. It may even have increased a bit.

On December 23, 1913, President Wilson signed into law the Federal Reserve Act that created the Federal Reserve System.[30] Since that time, the Federal Reserve Act has been amended repeatedly. The Federal Reserve System started operations in 1914.

By 1995 a 1940-Dollar was Worth Only 8 Cents

The intention to return to the gold standard after the conclusion of World War I was practically a foregone conclusion. A true return would obviously have meant the devaluation of the currencies that were undermined by the war effort. Great Britain, however, adamantly declined such a course of action with the view that it would undermine the reputation of the pound.

Although it was the firm intention to return to the pre-war gold standard, the major nations, with the exception of the U.S.A., decided in favor of introducing a dangerous surrogate. At the Genoa Conference in 1922, the Gold Exchange Standard was introduced, under which the dollar and the pound were as good as gold and could be held as reserve currencies. Unfortunately, the world did not return to the classical gold standard. What everybody should have

21

known is that these currencies had lost purchasing power and could be expected to lose even more in the future. They could, therefore, not be as good as gold.

The immediate effect of the new system was that monetary reserves were now counted twice: first in the country of issue, and then in the creditor country that held it as a reserve. Furthermore, the reserve countries were now placed in the comfortable position that they could run balance of payments deficits without being punished, as long as the other nations had 'confidence' in their currencies.

The Temporary End

The new system set a gigantic money and credit machine in motion and created the inflationary boom of the 1920s. In the beginning it seemed to function, as it depended more on paper than on gold. But in time, the new mechanism proved an engine of inflation whose product, excess purchasing media, flowed abundantly into the real estate market and the stock market. The result was a mania that led to the real estate crisis in Florida in 1925 and the stock market crash of 1929.

Jacques Rueff in *L' Age de l'Inflation* as well as in a lecture given on March 17, 1973, *"Les doctrines monétaires à l'épreuve des faits"*:

> "It is well known and had been demonstrated repeatedly that the gold exchange standard was in large part responsible for the great depression of the 1930s."[31]

In a well-written book, *The Invisible Crash,* by James Dines we can read the following:

> "So, World War I inflation temporarily derailed the gold standard, which strictly limited the money supply, and the Genoa Convention legitimised governmental tampering with the creation of paper money. No government has ever resisted abusing that right, and the direct result was a runaway inflation in the 1920s and the inevitable corrective Great Depression."[32]

Considering that the same mistakes were repeated twenty-two years later at Bretton Woods, this shows that the world does not learn from history, even if it concerns a very central aspect of life such as money.

FDR's New Deal

As it was to be expected, the events were also blamed on gold and its inadequate supply.

However, those events took place because the tried and tested gold standard was abandoned. Further, in *The Invisible Crash*:

> "Franklin Delano Roosevelt was elected in November 1932 when the economic world was prostrate. One can see how anyone with feeling for the little man would try to take direct action to help him. In that sense he cannot be blamed. Yet all the excesses derived from the inflation to pay for World War I, all the foolishness of the Federal Reserve Board had been liquidated violently, and FDR was presented with a clean slate. A really sound currency established at that time would almost certainly have prevented World War II and surely would have changed the economic history of the rest of this century.
>
> [...] FDR's "New Deal" has always been controversial. [...] I flatly predict the New Deal will go down as the greatest short-term success (four decades) and the biggest long-term failure of any economic system the world has yet seen.
>
> Here was a God-given opportunity to liquidate the Federal Reserve, reduce taxes to virtually non-existent levels and establish a really sound currency. Instead, because he was influenced by British economist Lord John Maynard Keynes, Roosevelt took the opposite tack."[33]

In a number of discussions with former central banker, noted economist and gold expert John Exter, he saw the situation as follows:

> "When the Federal Reserve first opened in 1914, they began right away to "print money" (i.e., put money or purchasing media into circulation) by buying government debt. They continued to do so through World War I, until 1920-21. Then they tried to reduce their holdings. That reduction resulted in a very sharp but brief downturn in the economy. The Fed then resumed the expansion and continued to expand through the 1920s. In 1930 the economy went into a contraction.
>
> That contraction was so powerful, so irresistible that it took Roosevelt three terms and a war to get us out of it. Roosevelt tried everything, but nothing worked. In 1933 unemployment stood at 25%. By 1937 it had fallen to 15%, but in 1937-38, the stock market took another dive, the economy went into another contraction, and unemployment climbed back up to 21%.
>
> World War II, of course, cured unemployment. Without the war there is no telling how long it would have lasted."[34]

In this context John Exter was also referring to a discussion he had had with Milton Friedman in 1974 when Friedman said that the Federal Reserve can increase the money supply by any amount, and that this steady increase in money supply would take the U.S. economy out of the depression. Exter thought Milton Friedman was wrong. John Exter always felt that from the beginning the Fed had violated the discipline of the gold standard by buying paper assets. In his opinion they should have only bought gold.

Part I: Some History First

[1] In 1913, the Pujo Committee was blaming banking instabilities on the country's leading bankers instead of the regulation that caused it. When banker J. P. Morgan testified before the committee, he was asked about the role of gold in the financial system and whether it might be the source of problems. The answer was succinct. Taken from Richard M. Salsman, *Gold and Liberty* (Great Barrington, MA: AIER, 1995), 49.

[2] Greek philosopher and biographer comparing Greek and Roman military strategists. *Parallel Lives (Aemilius Paulus)*, c. 100 BC.

[3] James E. Ewart, *Money* (Seattle: Principia Publishing, 1998), 8.

[4] Roy W. Jastram, *Silver – The Restless Metal* (New York: John Wiley & Sons, 1977), 3.

[5] Ibid., 4.

[6] P. D. Whitting, *Die Münzen von Byzanz*, (Munich: Ernst Battenberg Verlag, 1973), 173.

[7] Charles Mackay, *Extraordinary Popular Delusions and the Madness of Crowds* (London: Richard Bentley, 1841), 1 – 45.

[8] Ibid.,10.

[9] François M. A. Voltaire, *Short Studies: The French Islands*, "After the death of Louis XIV, Law, a Scot, a very extraordinary person, many of whose schemes have proved useless, and other hurtful to the nation, made the government and the people believe that Louisiana produced as much gold as Peru ..."

[10] Andrew Dickson White, *Fiat Money Inflation in France, How it Came, What it Brought and How it Ended*, (1914, reprint, Caldwell, ID: Caxton Printers Ltd., 1972).

[11] John Mackay, foreword to *Fiat Money Inflation in France, How it Came, What it Brought and How it Ended*, by Andrew Dickson White (1914, reprint, Caldwell, ID: Caxton Printers Ltd., 1972), 5/6.

[12] William Rees-Mogg. *The Reigning Error.*

[13] Pelatiah Webster, *Not Worth a Continental*, (1950), reprint Irvington on Hudson, NY: Foundation for Economic Education). *Not Worth a Continental*, i. e., not worth anything, was a descriptive phrase borne by an early American experiment in deficit financing.

[14] *A Monetary Chronology of the United States*, (Great Barrington, MA: Economic Education Bulletin AIER, 1994), 3.

[15] Ibid.

[16] James E. Ewart, *Money*, (Seattle, WA: Principia Publishing, 1998), 9, 18.

[17] Richard M. Salsman, *Gold and Liberty*, (Great Barrington, MA, Economic Education Bulletin, AIER, 1995), 9.

[18] Ernest P. Welker, *Why Gold?*, (Great Barrington, MA: Economic Education Bulletin, AIER, 1981), 9.

[19] Felix Somary, *Erinnerungen aus meinem Leben*. (Zürich: Manesse Verlag, 1956), 411.

[20] In H. L. Mencken, ed., *A New Dictionary of Quotations on Historical Principles from Ancient and Modern Sources* (New York: Alfred Knopf, 1985), 471.
[21] Ibid.
[22] Ibid.
[23] Melchior Palyi, *Währungen am Scheideweg* (Frankfurt: Fritz Knapp Verlag 1960), 14; Engl. Edition: *Managed Money on the Crossroads* (Chicago: Henry Regnery Company, 1960).
[24] The following figures are compiled from Franz Pick, *Pick's Currency Yearbook* (New York: Pick Publishing, 1975).
[25] Ludwig von Mises, *Human Action* (New Haven, CT: Yale UP, 1949), 472.
[26] Ibid., 471.
[27] Benjamin Graham and David L. Dodd, *Security Analysis* (New York: McGraw-Hill, 1951), 1–12; and Ferdinand Lips, "The Views of a Practicing Banker," In *Money: A Search for Common Ground*, (Lugano: Progress Foundation, 1984), 65–81. These are published proceedings of a conference held by the Progress Foundation in April of 1984.
[28] Melchior Palyi, *The Twilight of Gold* (Chicago: Henry Regnery Company), 7.
[29] Stefan Zweig, *The World of Yesterday* (New York: Viking Press, 1943).
[30] The Federal Reserve was empowered to issue Federal Reserve 'Notes' that were to be exchangeable for 'lawful money'. {See James E. Ewart, *Money* (Seattle: Principia Publishing, 1998), 18.} On April 2, 1792, about five years after the *U.S. Constitution* was signed, Congress passed the U.S.'s first Coinage Act (hereinafter the Act) The Act created the U.S. Mint to be the manufacturer of the U.S.'s official money, coins of silver and gold. Money manufactured according to law is called *lawful* money, and the phrase "Lawful money of the United States" means coins of silver or gold that have been manufactured according U.S. law in a U.S. Mint. Thus, the Federal Reserve Notes could not be lawful money.
[31] Jacques Rueff, lecture given on March 17, 1933 at the "Ecole des sciences politiques", Paris, France.
[32] James Dines, *The Invisible Crash* (New York: Random, 1977), 27.
[33] James Dines, *The Invisible Crash* (New York: Random, 1977), 31.
[34] Personal discussions of author with John Exter in Zurich, Switzerland (1975 – 1987); see also F. Sanders, "How Likely is Hyper Inflation? A Conversation with John Exter." *Money Changer* (December, 1992): 2.

Part II: The Gold War of the 1930s and the Abandonment of Gold

"In effect, there is nothing inherently wrong with fiat money, provided we get perfect authority and god-like intelligence for kings."

Aristotle[1]

To explain the reasons why the war against gold has intensified with every passing year, one has to go back to the crucial and historic events of the 1930s. Keynesian economics had become the world's dominant economic theory. With interruptions, that has remained so to this day.

American lawyer, lecturer and author, René A. Wormser, wrote in his book *Conservatively Speaking*:

> "No government can operate with a monetary system consisting only of fiat money without sustaining gross economic turmoil and eventually facing a tragic day of reckoning. A fiat money system prompts legislative profligacy and inevitably produces inflation.
>
> In 1933, President Roosevelt caused us to abandon the gold standard and to surrender to the government all our gold certificates in exchange for paper money. We were even prohibited from using gold as a measure of value in contracts. (Also see "Restoring Gold Clauses" in *Contracts* by René A. Wormser and Donald L. Kemmerer, published by Committee for Monetary Research and Education Inc. Greenwich CT. January 1975).[2] Since then, and until 1975, it has been unlawful to hold gold, except for licensed or commercial use. Shortly after the enactment of these prohibitions, the President, under authority granted by Congress, devalued the gold dollar.

The steps inaugurated the era of deficit financing and inept government intervention that has brought us to our present calamitous state.

It is strange indeed that President Roosevelt did not see the immorality of gold enactments, which he persuaded Congress to adopt. Or did he not care? In a conversation in Senator Carter Glass's office, on learning of the announcement that we were to repudiate our contractual promise to pay off government bonds in gold, the Senator said:

'It's dishonor, Sir. This great government, strong in gold, is breaking its promise to pay gold to widows and orphans to whom it has sold government bonds with the pledge to pay gold coin of the present standard of value. It is breaking its promise to redeem its paper money in gold coin of the present standard of value. It's dishonor, Sir.' And so it was."[3]

It is very important to look back into history because it gives a clearer picture of why we are talking about a gold war. In a publication "How Americans Lost Their Right To Own Gold And Became Criminals in the Process" by Professor Henry Mark Holzer, the author explained how Roosevelt based his Act on an obscure subsection of The Trading with Enemy Act of World War I. The speed at which a modification of this Act was rushed through Congress clearly reminds us of the way the Federal Reserve Act was passed right before Christmas in 1913. Or in more recent history, how pressure was exercised on the Swiss people in April 1999 to vote for their fateful new constitution.

In the monograph by Professor Holzer:

"A Boston University professor of the day eloquently summed up the dubious "accomplishments" of the New Deal's gold manipulations:

'March 6, 1933, began that complex sequence [...] of correlated proclamations, messages, declarations, regulations, enactments [...] through which the President and Congress are dealing with the national emergency. The first great thing to be profoundly changed was the money of the people. Gold has been nationalized, that is, the national treasury has seized as its own all the privately treasured gold coins and bullion it could lay hands on, as well as the circulating certificates of gold deposits. Gold, the king of coinage, is a prisoner, locked up between bars of bullion and carefully guarded. No gold will be paid upon presentation and demand at the Treasury. No more gold coins are to be struck. A new felony has been created, merely having gold money, now termed hoarding and considered dishonest. [...] Further inflation is indicated as quite certain to come. [...] The Statute of 1869 pledging the Nation's faith always to pay national debts in standard gold is repealed and the pledges made under it repudiated: we're off the gold standard; many think we are off the ethical standard."[4]

Holzer's comment:

"As indeed we were. The New Deal had given birth to a new class of felons; individuals with the temerity to deny that the government had a right to confiscate their gold."[5]

Wormser:

"So after the enactments of 1933, Americans were prevented from holding gold as a measure of value. Since then we have had only fiat money, money with nothing behind it. Before 1933 our Federal Reserve notes contained the promise that they could be converted into gold. Later the caption was changed to read that a bill could be exchanged for "lawful money of the United States" except more of the same. When finally, someone recognised the absurdity of this legend, it was dropped and our bills now contain merely the comforting legend: 'In God We Trust.'"[6]

On January 30, 1934 Congress passed the Gold Reserve Act of 1934. It authorized the President to declare a new gold content or equivalent of the dollar somewhere between the limits of 50 percent and 60 percent of its former content of 25.8 grains of standard gold or 23.33 grains of fine gold. Subsequently, the President devalued the dollar to 13.71 grains of pure gold, a reduction (devaluation) of 41%.

America's Anti-Gold Policy Begins

In his book *The U.S. Dollar - An Advance Obituary,* Dr. Franz Pick in 1981 wrote the following on the debasement of gold:

> "Gold's monetary function, lasting more than 6,000 years, has not always pleased governments. The linking since the 18th century of valueless paper to a fixed quantity of gold gave a hard to resist attractiveness to monetary units, as long as the governments were ready to exchange them for the yellow metal. But since rulers, and later republics, have been unable to manage their finances and thus their currency without spending more than they take in, they have had to default in various ways on their promises or contracts and have simply cheated those who have been gullible enough to believe monetary authorities. During its heyday in the 19th century, the pure gold standard formed a basis for the Western World's most successful period of industrial and financial development. It lasted until 1914. During and after World War I, the inflations, which governments were unable to understand — much less successfully to control — led to the breakdown of the Sterling in September 1931 and to the devaluation of the U.S. Dollar in January 1934, when the gold price was increased from $20.67 per ounce to $35.00 per ounce. The gold in the possession of the American people had to be surrendered to the U.S. Treasury at the pre devaluation price — a form of ethical

hypocrisy to punish the hoarders who did not want to lose through devaluation.

Since then, America has practiced an anti-gold policy—even after gold ownership was made legal at the end of 1974—to keep people from owning a metal governments cannot master."[7] [emphasis added]

A deluge of misleading anti-gold propaganda spread by the powerful paper money interests accompanied this anti-gold policy. To this day they are trying to convey the illusion that the U.S. does not need bullion behind its bank note issue.

Gold Shares in the Deflation of the 1930s

When the stock market crashed between 1929 and 1932, the Dow Jones Industrial Average lost about 90% of its value. Even tangible assets, such as real estate, were similarly hard hit. Residential and commercial buildings lost up to 80% of their value. Most commodities suffered a similar fate. The consumer price index during 1929 and 1933 dropped by 24%. Only gold did well. Its price increased by 75% from $20.67 to $35.00. Because of the leverage effect, gold mining shares were star performers.

In the crash of 1929, gold mining shares suffered with the industrial shares but to a lesser degree. The explosive run came in 1933 when the shares of Homestake Mining went up tenfold. The shares of Alaska Juneau Mines went from $1.00 to $25.00. Dome Mines fell from $5.00 to $3.00 in late 1929. In 1931 it went as high as $7.00 and finally reached the ultimate high of $34⅞ in 1938. Silver did well during this period also.

Gold and World War II

With the outbreak of World War II, gold became a strategic commodity. Worldwide trading of the metal by individuals and corporations was banned. At the same time, the gold stock of the U.S. Treasury continued to grow because of bullion transfers for foreign purchases of military hardware. The price of the metal in black markets soared, and hoarding of gold coins in North and South America as well as in Europe gained tremendously in popularity.

31

In September 1949, the U.S. Treasury—at the high point of America's gold power—owned $24.6 billion worth of bullion (at $35.00 per ounce). Since that time, progress in destroying the dollar and a seemingly unending series of budget and balance of payments deficits have demonstrated that politicians, and especially their unqualified money managers, have been unable to retain this mass of yellow metal and its substantial power — a bulwark against further debasement of an already inflated dollar.

Bretton Woods

Towards the end of the war, another fateful event took place: the Conference of Bretton Woods, New Hampshire in 1944. Although this conference was held more than 55 years ago, it is important for the purpose of this study to know what really happened. First of all, the world had learned nothing from history, particularly from the disastrous consequences of the gold exchange standard set up in Genoa in 1922. Consequently, another golden opportunity was missed.

In July of 1944, representatives of 44 nations gathered at Bretton Woods to discuss the post-war international monetary system. This system, later crushed in the storms of the gold war, became known under the geographical name of the conference's location where the new currency order for the community of nations was being prescribed. It was nothing more than an American dictate resulting in official recognition of the supremacy of the dollar, the only currency convertible into gold by foreign central banks.

The scheme had been plotted a few years before the conference took place. In *The Invisible Crash*, James Dines described the events as follows:

> "In 1942 Harry Dexter White for the United States and Lord John Maynard Keynes of the British Treasury developed proposals for a new international monetary system. This fountainhead of financial troubles was convened at Bretton Woods, New Hampshire, in 1944 with the launching of the International Monetary Fund and the World Bank.

Since the United States was the strongest country in the world, the opportunity was seized to change the old gold exchange standard to a dollar exchange standard. Thus, the New Deal's direction was internationally legitimized, and firmly locked the world's economies on their tragic rendezvous with destiny.

The IMF required countries to define the parities of their currencies in gold or U.S. dollars and to keep exchange rates firmly locked within one percent of "parity". To give countries time to adjust imbalances in their international payments, the Fund's resources extended credit. This credit emasculated the power of gold to force countries to sell internationally in roughly equal amounts against what they were buying. This fatal flaw threw the international balance wheel out of whack. The gold lever had been tampered with and was being strapped down out of position. [This was a major blow against gold's disciplinary function and a major victory for the enemies of gold without the world noticing the disastrous impact it would have later on. – auth.] If a country could not restore its balance-of-payments without deflating its economy or imposing restrictions on current trade and payments, the country could then change the parity of its currency, thereby eliminating all deflations and creating a perpetual "high". So, all the world's currencies were expressed in terms of, and closely tied to the U.S. dollar, but in turn the dollar was still fixed to gold. The dollar was the yardstick. Only the United States could change the price of gold, and all other nations were forced to upvalue or devalue in terms of dollars. This incredible power given to the United States would eventually be devastatingly abused, but Lord Keynes and other engineers at Bretton Woods were too busy constructing their monetary monster to worry about such mundane matters.

Bretton Woods also ruled that a nation's reserves could be composed either of gold or any currency convertible into gold. This last one was the killer because it included the dollar and later the pound when it was strong and freely convertible into gold, and in no way anticipated the way the dollar would be run into the ground. This subverted virtually every currency in the world and launched an international inflation the likes of which had never been seen before."[8]

The advantages to the U.S. were obvious. It enabled painless financing of wars, economic conquests all over the world and paid for nearly limitless, expensive imports simply because the banking system could create the necessary dollars.

According to Ludwig von Mises' *Human Action,* the Bretton Woods Conference was held under very particular circumstances:

"Most of the participating nations were at that time entirely dependent on the benevolence of the United States. They would have been doomed if the United States had stopped fighting for their freedom and aiding them materially by lend-lease. The government of the United States, on the other hand, looked upon the monetary agreement as a scheme for a disguised continuation of lend-lease after the cessation of hostilities.

The United States was ready to give and the other participants — especially the European countries, most of them still occupied by the German armies, and the Asiatic countries — were ready to take what was offered them. The problems involved will become apparent once the delusive attitude of the United States toward financial matters and trade was replaced by a more realistic mentality.

The International Monetary Fund did not achieve what its sponsors had expected. At the annual meetings of the Fund there is a good deal of discussion, and occasionally pertinent observations, and criticism concerning the monetary and credit policies of governments and central banks are brought forward. [...] Monetary affairs in the world are going on as if no Bretton Woods Agreement and no International Monetary Fund existed."[9]

Under Bretton Woods, the U.S. had a commitment to maintain the value of the dollar by buying and selling unlimited quantities of gold at $35 per ounce. Ironically, it also had the commitment to pay gold to foreign central banks, but not to U.S. citizens, for whom ownership of gold remained a felony. Often that commitment went unmet, or the U.S. would have lost all its gold. Occasionally diplomatic pressure was applied to prevent gold withdrawals from the U.S. James Dines recalls an incident when President Johnson discouraged Germany, for example, from converting its U.S. dollars into gold by reminding it that U.S. troops stood between it and Russia.[10]

Devaluations and controls on the flow of capital and gold persisted. Britain devalued twice under Bretton Woods. Other countries devalued more often. Some major currencies were not even linked to the dollar until 1958. Thus in a number of critical features, the strict discipline of a classical gold coin standard was absent.

A Prominent Witness

Friend and former central banker, John Exter, recalled:

"My point is that from the very beginning the Fed violated the discipline of the gold standard by buying paper assets. They should have only bought gold, but it's almost irresistible to buy paper assets, which increases the total reserves of the banks and in turn enables them to make more loans. People, by and large, don't like discipline. The Fed is no exception.

World War II brought us out of the Depression, and once again the Fed launched a major credit expansion by buying paper assets to finance the war.

Nonetheless, our gold reserves that had poured in during the 1930s kept the Fed's balance sheet in reasonably good shape, even during the subsequent Korean War expenditures."[11]

A major reason of why it was difficult to maintain monetary and fiscal discipline, was the increased role of a government influenced by Keynesian philosophy. It eased the passage of an act that would have fatal consequences on the purchasing power of money and, consequently, financial markets.

The Employment Act of 1946

In the 1950s and the 1960s a weekly column in *Barron's* called "The Trader" was written by a certain Mr. Nelson. Week after week, he untiringly drew readers' attention to the consequences the Employment Act had on the purchasing power of the currency and, therefore, the stock market.

With the passage of this act, the U.S. government officially declared war on unemployment and promised to maintain full employment regardless of cost. Thus, it hoped to eliminate the business cycle and to prevent the country from ever sinking to the economic depths of the 1930s.

Maximum employment, production and purchasing power were the goals. Those goals were responsible for a growing conviction among banks, investors and the public at large that business risk normally associated with the business cycle was a thing of the past. It is not surprising that this led to a new business philosophy and credit ethic. It appeared that it was no longer necessary to hold much liquidity, i.e., cash. To the contrary, the notion that government would manage the country out of every crisis led to the growing belief that the accumulation of more and more debt was the right business philosophy to adopt.

Increased government spending and the resulting deficits financed by the Fed, however, were beginning to take their toll on the purchasing power of the dollar, and to put strains on the arrangements of Bretton Woods.[12]

The Fed in the Fifties

Again, John Exter recalled:

> "During the Eisenhower years the Fed behaved itself except for one bad year. I was in charge of gold and international operations at the New York Fed during those years. Bill Martin was chairman of the Fed [William McChesney Martin, Jr., Chairman 1951-1970 – auth.]. Ike kept his hands off the Fed, which stopped creating credit. It's the only period of Fed history that I'm happy about. The world monetary system was working its way to a good equilibrium.
>
> The Fed, however, had one bad year during the mini-recession of 1958 when the Fed created 2\frac{1}{4}$ billions of credit. To my astonishment, I had to sell 2\frac{1}{4}$ billions of gold to foreign central banks to maintain the equilibrium of the system; it's still the biggest Fed gold loss in one year."

(John Exter told me privately that his heart was bleeding seeing all this gold leaving the Fed.)

He added:

> "As fast as the Fed created dollars, they flowed to foreign central banks who demanded gold. Fortunately, in 1959 and 1960, the Fed came to its senses and stopped creating credit, and the gold losses ceased."[13]

In *How to Invest in Gold Stocks,* Donald J. Hoppe wrote:

> "Although it seems incredible now, in 1971 [And how much more in 1999! –auth.] after having endured a dozen years of virtually continuous monetary crisis, the events of 1958 created a near panic. Emergency Cabinet meetings were held and the lights burned late in the Treasury Department. Secretary of the Treasury Robert B. Anderson was called to testify before a special meeting of the House

Finance Committee. According to reporters Robert S. Allen and Paul J. Scott, who were present, the conversation went something like this:

Secretary Anderson: Liquid dollar balances of foreign countries are now $17,632 million, as against $12,000 million in 1952. In addition, these foreign interests now have $1,500 million U.S. securities. Meanwhile, the gold reserves of the United States have dropped to $20,582 million compared to $23 billion in 1952.

Rep. Frank Karsten (D., MO.): Just how serious is this $2.5 billion loss of gold? We hear conflicting reports about this.

Anderson: It could give us a great deal of trouble, if foreign countries and investors lose confidence in the dollar and demand their holdings in gold.

Karsten: You mean there could be a big run on our gold?

Anderson: Exactly, that is a very real danger.

Rep. Lee Metcalf (D., MT.): You mean right now?

Anderson: Right now! In fact, the situation is steadily getting worse the longer it takes Congress to act on this problem. It's a very sensitive one and does not brook trifling with. When you are dealing with the confidence of a nation's currency, you are already dealing with highly explosive dynamite."[14]

Hoppe:

"The preceding took place in 1958! Compare that particular reaction to the attitude of the Nixon administration, which viewed with "complete calm" and "amazing coolness" the disastrous $10.7 billion balance-of-payments deficit of 1970, the $5 billion first-quarter deficit of 1971 and the European dollar

38

crisis of the same year. It reminds the author, at any rate, of the bovine complacency that inevitably precedes major sociological and military disasters. Such a mood of eerie optimism prevailed in the summer of 1929 and in the fall of 1941. Familiarity, it is said, breeds contempt. We have lived with the dollar crisis for so long that we have begun to doubt its reality; that is the most dangerous sign of all."[15]

Gold Mining Shares Start to Move

In 1957, when I was a financial analyst at Dominion Securities in Toronto, the President of the company, James Strathy, who was also President of the Toronto Stock Exchange at the time, called me into his office and asked me to make an analysis of Dome Mines. This was the first company analysis of my life, and I came to the conclusion that Dome Mines was a good company, but that its stock would not perform particularly well in the intermediate future. A year later, in 1958, the stock of Dome Mines and the TSE Gold & Silver Index started their bull markets that lasted over 35 years and presumably have more to go in the future.

Many countries with which the U.S. ran deficits — Britain, Belgium, Switzerland, Italy — were demanding gold in lieu of dollars.

Private investors also showed a growing interest in gold and gold mining shares. James Grant, founder of *Grant's Interest Rate Observer* and author of several books, remarked:

"By the end of 1958, the United States' gold reserve was at a new post-war low of $20.7 billion. That was not the only sign of a growing lack of world confidence in the dollar. A new gold mutual fund, the American South-African Investment Trust, better known as ASA, had been successfully started by Charles Engelhard and Dillon, Read & Co. Charley Engelhard and the founders came to the conclusion that inflation lies ahead and investors needed an investment vehicle to protect against it.

Offered at $28 a share, the stock fell to $18 afterwards. However, it did extremely well in the gold bull markets of the 1960s and 1970s before languishing again in the disinflationary 1990s. From its offering in September, 1958 to early September, 1994, it generated a compound annual rate of return of 8.2% (before dividends), rising 17-fold in price."[16]

For many years John Exter was a director of ASA, and James Dines was noted for his slogan "All the way with ASA."

The great bull market in gold mining stocks had started.

The Experience of the 1960s

According to John Exter, the monetary crisis started with John F. Kennedy and his so-called effort to 'get the country moving again.' The Fed succumbed to political pressures from JFK and once again began expanding. (This is what James Strathy with his great experience sensed years ago, because during the last Eisenhower years, newspapers and magazines were already full of pro-Kennedy propaganda.) That was the beginning of the end of the gold dollar standard and the Bretton Woods international monetary system. The reason, of course, was Kennedy's pressure on the Fed to pursue inflationary credit expansion policies that eroded the purchasing power of the dollar.

Exter:

"All this became obvious to me as early as 1962 when I made a speech to the Detroit Economic Club, saying that the US could not maintain a gold price of $35.00 per ounce. That's when I started to buy gold. I bought British sovereigns, which contain about a quarter of an ounce of gold, for $9.00 a piece.

The rest of the story is history. Various "thumb-in-the-dike" attempts were made to retain the $35.00 gold price, but the market eventually prevailed over government stop-gap schemes, and the fixed rate system collapsed when Nixon reneged on our promise to redeem dollars in gold at $35 an ounce. That was on August 15, 1971, a watershed day in U.S. — and world — monetary history. Nixon's action ushered in the chaos we now know as the floating exchange rate non-system.

But more importantly, the abandoning of the link between gold and the dollar eliminated any restraints on the Fed's ability to create money through the purchase of paper assets. The result has been an unprecedented explosion of debt that, at some point, is going to implode in a credit contraction that will produce a deflationary collapse and a depression unparalleled in history.

The cost of monetary expansion policies to American citizens came to $13 billion of gold or 13,000 tons."[17]

There is no doubt that today the official U.S. position regarding gold would differ from the present policies had it not lost all this gold.

Richard M. Salsman in *Gold and Liberty*:

"The weaknesses of this 'dollar-exchange-system' compared to the classical gold standard are apparent. The United States had the ability to inflate the supply of dollars and then watched them pile up as reserves in the vaults of other central banks. It was possible to allow perpetual balance of payments deficits. Bretton Woods centralised the monetary system even more than the financial policies of World War I, for now the money of only one country (the United States) was the hub of all other monetary systems. The core of the international monetary system was not the credibility of gold money, but the credibility of the U.S. Government. In 1961, U.S. President John F. Kennedy described what was required of the United States to maintain this system:

'The growth in foreign dollar holdings has placed upon the United States a special responsibility

— that of maintaining the dollar as the principal reserve currency of the free world. This required that the dollar be considered by many countries to be as good as gold. It is our responsibility to sustain this confidence.'

Lofty rhetoric aside, the United States did not keep the dollar "as good as gold". It could not hope to do so, given its own explicitly chosen Keynesian policies of deficit spending and inflating. Within a decade of Kennedy's speech, the United Stated defaulted on the dollar exchange standard. The Kennedy and Johnson administrations set the United States on a course of sustained deficit spending and inflating unprecedented in the Nation's history. End of statement."[18]

In their analysis, Exter and Dines rightly put the blame on the Fed's policies. Oddly, they almost never mention the money creation by the banks, that were the principal villains in this plot.

Deficits Without Tears

Looking back and weeding out the blinding overgrowth of today's very shaky prosperity, it is unbelievable how major mistakes could be repeated by central bankers, the banking industry and apparently mindless economists. They had no sense and understanding of history and let it end in tragedy for the entire world. At the international monetary conference held in Genoa in 1922, 'economy in the use of gold by maintaining reserves in the form of balances in other countries' was recommended. To promote the wider use of this innovation, the League of Nations' Financial Committee suggested to its member countries that currencies payable in gold should also be used as a reserve for national paper money issues along with gold and credits payable in national currency. The best analyses of the Genoa and Bretton Woods decisions are to be found in Jacques Rueff's book *Le Péché Monétaire de l'Occident* and in its American edition *The Monetary Sin of the West*.

As early as 1965, in an interview in *The Economist* on "The Role and the Rule of Gold", Jacques Rueff was "convinced that the gold exchange standard attains to such a degree of absurdity that no human being having the power to reason can defend it."[19]

Jacques Rueff:

"I wrote in 1961 that the West was risking a credit collapse and that the gold-exchange standard was a great danger for the Western civilization. If I did so, it is because I am convinced – and I am very emphatic on this point - that the gold exchange standard attains to such a degree of absurdity that no human brain having the power to reason can defend it. What is the essence of the system, and what is the difference from the gold standard? It is that when a country with a key currency runs a balance-of-payments deficit – that is to say, the United States, for example – it pays the creditor country dollars, which end up with the latter's central bank. But the very same day, they are reloaned to the New York money market, so that they return to the place of origin. Thus the debtor country does not lose what the creditor country has gained. So the key-currency country never feels the effect of a deficit in its balance-of-payments. And the main consequence is that there is no reason whatever for the deficit to disappear, because it does not appear.

Let me be more positive: If I had an agreement with my tailor that whatever money I pay him he returns to me the very same day as a loan, I would have no objection at all to ordering more suits from him and my own balance of payments would then be in deficit.

Because of this situation, the United States could pay off its balance of payments deficits in paper dollars. [...] As the central banks received dollars, they used them immediately to buy U.S. Treasury Bills or certificates of deposit in New York banks, thus returning the dollars to their country of origin which thus recovered all the assets it had just paid out."[20]

This excess purchasing media, of course, was highly inflationary because the dollars that went abroad could now be counted twice, first in the country of origin and secondly in the country where they were spent. In a series of articles in leading world newspapers, Rueff warned that, if this system continued for long, it would inevitably have three consequences:

"a) A permanent deficit would develop in the United States' balance of payments whose overseas settlements would no longer automatically reduce the amount of credit available at home. [...] Thus the United States was in the privileged position of being able to buy, invest, loan or donate money in other countries without limit since its money markets would not feel any effects from this capital outflow. Having learned the secret of having a "deficit without tears", it was only human for the United States to use that knowledge, thereby putting its balance of payments in a permanent state of deficit.

b) Inflation would develop in the surplus countries as they increased their own currencies on the basis of the increased dollar reserves held by their central banks.

c) The convertibility of the reserve currency, the dollar, would eventually be abolished owing to the gradual but unlimited accumulation of sight loans redeemable in United States gold."[21]

Subsequent events perfectly bore out and confirmed his fundamental analysis. But he felt that this was not due to a failure on the part of the Bretton Woods system. The system was all too effective leading to its collapse. The breakdown must be attributed to the fact that an alien practice had been grafted onto the Bretton Woods system, namely the gold exchange standard, which alone was responsible for giving the U.S. dollar the status of a reserve currency. This was the cancer eating away at Bretton Woods until the whole organism collapsed.

Rueff was a firm believer in the discipline and the automatism of the gold standard. He strongly advocated a return to the gold standard. Regarding monetary and fiscal authorities, he had the following to say:

> "There is nothing inherently inadequate about the available monetary and fiscal instruments, but their weakness comes from a lack of decision to use them firmly and promptly. [...] It was a case of too little and too late. [...] We were struck by the fact that for many countries there remain major gaps and serious delays in the information that the authorities should have as a guide to prompt and adequate policy decisions."[22]

Rueff wrote:

> "I do not believe, as a matter of fact, that the monetary authorities, however courageous and well-informed they may be, can deliberately bring about those contractions in the money supply that the mere mechanism of the gold standard would have generated automatically."[23]

Part II: The Gold War of the 1930s - the Abandonment of Gold

[1] Aristotle, *The Nichomachean Ethics V*, 340 BC; see also Aristotle, *Politeia*.

[2] Actually, *TheTrading with the Enemy Act* did not empower Roosevelt to close the banks or suspend specie. He closed the banks and suspended gold payments on March 5, 1933. The following Friday, *The Trading with the Enemy Act* was amended retroactively to provide legal cover for Roosevelt.

[3] René Wormser, *Conservatively Speaking* (Mendham, NJ: Wayne E. Dorland Company, 1979), 79.

[4] Henry Mark Holzer, "How the Americans Lost Their Right to Own Gold and Became Criminals in the Process" (Greenwich, CT: Committee for Monetary Research and Education, Inc., 1981).

[5] Ibid.

[6] René Wormser, *Conservatively Speaking* (Mendham, NJ: Wayne E. Dorland Company, 1979), 79.

[7] Franz Pick, *The U.S. Dollar – An Advance Obituary* (New York: Pick Publishing Corporation, 1981), 69/70.

[8] James Dines, *The Invisible Crash*, 37/38.

[9] Ludwig von Mises, *Human Action* (New Haven, CT: Yale UP, 1949), 478.

[10] James Dines, *The Invisible Crash* (New York: Random House, 1977), 47.

[11] John Exter, conversations with author, in Zurich, Switzerland (1975 – 1987).

[12] The Employment Act of 1946, Sec. 2 says: "The Congress hereby declares that it is the continuing policy and responsibility of the Federal Government to use all practical means consistent with its needs and obligations and other considerations of national policy […] to coordinate and utilize all its plans, functions and resources […] to promote maximum employment, production, and purchasing power."

[13] John Exter, conversations with author, in Zurich, Switzerland (1975 – 1987).

[14] Donald J. Hoppe, *How to Invest in Gold Stocks* (New York: Arlington House, 1972), 47.

[15] Ibid.

[16] James Grant, *The Trouble with Prosperity* (NY: Random House, 1996), 49.

[17] John Exter, conversation with author, in Zurich, Switzerland (1975 – 1987); see also James Blakely, Blakely's *Gold Investment Review*, vol. I, no. I (1989): 4; and a speech by John Exter, "Problems and Possibilities of Returning to the Gold Standard," (Greenwich, CT: The Committee for Monetary Research and Education, Inc.).

[18] Richard M. Salsman, *Gold and Liberty*, (Great Barrington, Massachusetts: AIER, 1975), 74.

[19] "Return to Gold – Argument with Jacques Rueff," *The Economist*, 13 February (1965), in Jacques Rueff, *The Monetary Sin of the West* (New York: Mac Millan, 1972), 75–98.

[20] Jacques Rueff, *Le Péché Monétaire de l'Occident*, (Paris: Plow, 1971), 27; English edition: *The Monetary Sin of the West* (New York: Mac Millan, 1972) 75.

[21] Jacques Rueff, *The Monetary Sin of the West* (New York: Mac Millan, 1972), 20: see also *Le Monde* (Paris) 27 – 29 June 1961 and *Fortune Magazine*, July 1961.

[22] Jacques Rueff, *The Monetary Sin of the West* (NY: Mac Millan, 1972), 42.

[23] Ibid., 41.

Part III: The Great Gold War: 1960 - 1971

"Gold can make its way through the midst of guards,
and break through the strongest barriers more easily
than the lightning's bolt."
Horace[1]
When gold speaks, all tongues are silent.[2]

The Gold Trap of Bretton Woods

That is the title of the first chapter of a book by Charles A.
Coombs[3], former Senior Vice President of the Federal Reserve
Bank of New York, responsible for U.S. Treasury and Federal
Reserve operations in the gold and foreign exchange markets. After
33 years with the Federal Reserve Bank of New York, he retired in
1975. His book, *The Arena of International Finance* records his
recollections of the startling and controversial events that happened
in the time between the agreements at Bretton Woods, the collapse
of the dollar and the financial crises of today. Just the description of
his education and his entry into the services of the Federal Reserve
Bank of New York draws a telling picture of the period's spirit.

"As a student in the late thirties, most of my
instruction in international finance had focused on the
causes rather than the consequences of the collapse of
the world financial system earlier in the decade. I had
become thoroughly versed in the iniquities of the old
gold standard, which had allegedly punished
inefficient countries with deflation and
unemployment while simultaneously inflicting
inflation on their more prosperous trading partners.
Britain's abandonment of the gold standard [more
precisely, gold exchange standard—auth.] in 1931
had seemingly marked the end of an era. Every
examination paper quoted Keynes' contemptuous
reference to gold as 'a barbarous relic.' To most
students, there seemed now no effective alternative
but floating exchange rates.

At the Bank I soon realized among other facts of life that gold was still very much in the picture.

As a young student 'steeped in Keynes', I still thought the whole business pretty barbarous. But I also found, as my summer apprenticeship at the Bank progressed, that the breakdown of the gold standard in 1931 and the subsequent emergence of floating rates had produced a new and even more dangerous form of economic barbarism. Multilateral trade had progressively given way to discriminatory, bilateral trading arrangements, reinforced by exchanges controls, amid a welter of charges and countercharges of competitive devaluations through floating exchange rates.

On returning from military service to the New York Federal in 1946, I found that American and British Treasury officials had negotiated during the war years a sweeping reform of the world financial system at the Bretton Woods conference of 1944. Gold had again been enshrined as the central value and *numéraire* of a fixed-parity system whose operation would be supervised by the International Monetary Fund with headquarters in Washington.

I also found that during the war years President Allan Sproul and Dr. John H. Williams of the New York Federal had vigorously opposed the creation of the International Monetary Fund, even to the extent of refusing to participate in the Bretton Woods conference.

In effect, convertibility of the dollar into gold at $35 per ounce became the lynch-pin of a worldwide fixed exchange rate system. The choice of gold as the *numéraire* and ultimate reserve asset of the system conformed, of course, to historical tradition and the instinctive orthodoxy at the time of every financial community here and abroad.

From the very beginning, gold was the vulnerable point of the Bretton Woods system. Yet the open-ended gold commitment assumed by the United States government under the Bretton Woods legislation is readily understandable in view of the extraordinary circumstances of the time. At the end of the war, our gold stock amounted to $20 billion, roughly 60 percent of the total of official gold reserves. As late as 1957, United States gold reserves exceeded by a ratio of three to one the total dollar reserves of all the foreign central banks. The dollar bestrode the exchange markets like a colossus."[4]

He later explained how the vulnerability of the Bretton Woods system became increasingly visible. By the end of 1960, the American gold stock had fallen from its peak of nearly $25 billion to somewhat less than $18 billion.

There were several reasons for the continuing erosion of the U.S. gold stock. Firstly, the price of gold was still at the price fixed in 1934, $35 dollars an ounce, and did not take into account the loss of purchasing power the dollar had suffered before, during and after the war. Secondly, as European countries started to climb out of the ruins of the war, they began to build up their gold reserves. Coombs wrote that, ironically, Washington developed an inclination to classify foreign central banks buying gold from the U.S. as ingrates or worse. Those abstaining from gold by accumulating dollars were seen as the true friends of the U.S.

The main cause for the continuous drain on the U.S. gold reserves were the U.S.'s balance of payments deficits emerging in the late fifties. Various military and foreign aid programs were causing deep policy cleavages within the administration. The Treasury tried to defend the dollar on the one side, and on the other, the Pentagon and the State Department did not want to yield vital American interests abroad for lack of financing.

However, there was another important reason – not only was there a market between central banks, but there existed a private market also. At that time, Americans and Englishmen, citizens of the two nations who were the architects of Bretton Woods, were not allowed to buy gold. This private market turned into a buyer of gold as it sensed the increased difficulties the U.S. had maintaining convertibility of the dollar into gold. In other words, the U.S. was trapped by its gold commitments under Bretton Woods.

On October 20, 1960, a spectacular rise of the London gold price to the $40/oz.-level ignited an explosion of speculation against the dollar in the foreign exchange markets. European investors, the Swiss in particular, expected Senator John F. Kennedy to be elected President. They thought the new administration would bring about more inflation and, as a result, the balance of payments would suffer even more. On Monday, October 17, 1960, Swiss banks not only began advising customers to buy gold, but also started buying for their own accounts. In a very short time, the London price went above the $40/oz.-level.

The sudden crisis of confidence was later resolved by the Treasury issuing a press statement formally endorsing the Bank of England's sales of gold to stabilize the London price at the ultimate expense of the American gold stock. London was then the center of international gold trading. The daily fixing of the gold price, which takes place at Rothschild's, was the only daily international gold price fixing of its kind in the world.

But it was not only the U.S.'s problem with its balance of payments that caused increased speculative interest in gold. There were political events as well. The U-2 spy-plane incident and USSR General Secretary Khrushchev's subsequent canceling a summit meeting with President Eisenhower did not boost confidence, and the Russian decision on August 13, 1960, to build the Berlin Wall rekindled fear of a new war.

On February 6, 1961, President Kennedy, in a dramatic announcement, pledged to maintain the country's official price of gold. This personal commitment immediately returned foreign confidence in the dollar, and the free market price of gold in London sank back toward the official $35 level.

At the end of 1949, the U.S. stock of gold (about 700 million ounces, equivalent to $24.6 billion at $35 per ounce) comprised nearly 70% of the total gold holdings of all free-world governments and central banks. In the 1950s, the cumulative balance of payments deficits totaled $17.5 billion. During this period foreigners were largely content to increase their holdings of U.S. claims. Nevertheless, the U.S. had to pay out 145 million ounces of gold. In 1960, the balance of payments deficit did not diminish, and demand on the London gold market increased markedly. By the end of 1960, the U.S. gold stock had decreased to about 500 million ounces, or $17.5 billion.

Several measures were introduced to bolster the dollar. On January 14, 1961 President Eisenhower, as one of his last acts as President, prohibited U.S. residents from owning gold anywhere in the world.[5] Federal gold regulations prohibited private purchase of gold in the U.S. at the time. Curiously enough, it permitted U.S. residents to buy and hold as much gold abroad as they pleased.

Curbs such as the "Interest Equalization Tax" in July of 1963, the "Voluntary Foreign Credit Restraint Program" and "Foreign Direct Investment Controls" in February of 1965 were implemented. The U.S. balance of payments deficit, however, persisted, and, until the end of 1965, another 106 million ounces of gold were paid out by the U.S.[6]

The Creation of the Gold Pool

Rather than recognize and deal with the cause of the dollar tragedy, the Treasury's money doctors chose the typically totalitarian remedy of suppressing the free-market price of gold instead of devaluing the dollar. Early 1961, the U.S. and seven major European nations formed the 'Gold Pool' whose mission it was to stabilize the price of gold on the London market. The Gold Pool was successful in preventing a recurrence of price increases (such as those of October 1960) through sales of bullion in the London market whenever demand pushed up the price of gold. After a brief period of such sales, upward pressure on the price of gold eased, and the total official monetary stock increased. The $35 price was effectively contained until the gold crisis of March 1968, when the famous 'two-tier' price system was established, allowing a fixed monetary price and a floating commercial price simultaneously (Hoppe).[7]

What actually happened was the following. The arrival of the jet age enabled the helpless central bankers to meet for consultations in person. The so-called Basel meetings at the Bank for International Settlements (BIS) were one of these gatherings. Instead of seriously studying the fundamental cause of the recurring crisis, the central bankers cooked up the plan of the Gold Pool. It was launched at the meeting of the Governors on November 1961. The main features of their 'brilliant' plan were the following: [8]

1. All central banks had a mutual interest in keeping speculation on the London gold market to a minimum. This was to be done by means of official intervention. To minimize the effect of sudden and sharp changes in the market, the burden of intervention was to be shared by all.

2. The central banks of the following countries were asked to commit $270 million of gold to the Pool:

Germany	$30 million
United Kingdom	25 million
Italy	25 million
France	25 million
Switzerland	10 million
Netherlands	10 million
Belgium	10 million
United States	135 million
Total	$270 million

3. The Bank of England was to manage intervention on the London gold market by selling its own gold. At the end of the month the various participants, in accordance with their relative shares in the Pool, would reimburse the Bank of England.

4. The immediate object was to keep the London price from exceeding $35.20, which was roughly equivalent to the cost of delivering *loco* London gold purchased in New York. If possible, the price was to be pushed below $35.20 if it could be done without undue heavy intervention.

5. At all times the dollar proceeds of such Pool sales were to remain fully convertible into gold in New York by the recipient central bank. If a central bank's total dollar holdings remained

within normal limits, the Americans hoped that the bank would retain the dollar proceeds of such London gold sales. If, on the other hand, the dollar proceeds clearly exceeded the central bank's need for dollar reserves, they would be converted into gold in New York. Because one purpose of the pool was to soften the immediate impact of the U.S.'s intervention on the Treasury's gold stock, it was hoped that such conversions would not be made immediately after receipt of the dollar proceeds. But, it would remain the central bank's option to convert in one week, one month, several months, or not at all.

6. The participating central banks and the United States were to agree not to buy any gold in the London market or from any other source, such as Russia or South Africa. Furthermore, the U.S. was to persuade other central banks, when opportunity arose, to adopt similar policies.

Charles A. Coombs wrote in his book that it was decided to keep the Gold Pool agreement secret for the time being. Keeping with the traditional spirit of the BIS meetings, not a scrap of paper was initialed or even exchanged; the word of each governor was as binding as any written contract.

In the first month of operations of the Pool in November 1961, the Bank of England was relatively successful in limiting sales to $17.4 million.

On returning to New York from the Basel meeting, Coombs worked out a proposal to convert the Gold Pool into a gold buying as well as a selling syndicate:

> "During the spring of 1962 Russian selling appeared in such a volume that the Pool was able to recoup the $17 million of gold sold in November 1961, and by the end of May had built up a surplus of $80 million. In May 1962, however, a sharp break in the American stock market (largely in response to the confrontation between President Kennedy and U.S. Steel), together with a severe attack on the Canadian dollar, revived speculative buying in the London gold market. By mid-July 1962 the Gold Pool surplus had

been exhausted. . […] But in October 1962 a challenge of the first magnitude appeared. During the Cuban crisis, speculative demand erupted; the Bank of England forcefully intervened for a total of nearly $60 million over the three-day period, October 22-24. Curiously enough, a sizeable share of Pool intervention during these three days of crisis was financed by further sales of gold by the USSR. […] By October 24, 1962, the cumulative deficit increased to more than $80 million. […] As the Cuban crisis subsided and Russian sales continued, the Pool quickly recovered $70 million, leaving a net deficit of no more than $12 million by the end of November 1962. […] In 1963 private demand for gold fell off appreciably from the very high 1962 levels, while South African deliveries rose and the Pool steadily acquired gold in moderate volume. […] Then in the autumn of 1963 the harvest failure in Russia suddenly transformed the whole market picture. Heavy imports of wheat from Canada and other suppliers were quickly arranged by the Soviets. In order to finance the purchases, the USSR, which put great value on its impeccable credit rating, instead of resorting to international capital markets, decided to finance its entire cereals import requirements by sales of gold. […] Suddenly, the Pool was flooded with gold. During the final quarter of 1963, Russian sales of $470 million swelled Pool acquisitions to $639 million, all of which was distributed to the members of the Pool. Further heavy Russian sales totaling $438 million were made during the first half of 1964 South African deliveries also rose more than 25 percent, and by the end of September the Pool had accumulated and distributed a further $656 million. In 21 months the Pool had thus augmented the gold reserves of the BIS group of central banks by $1.3 billion, of which the U.S. Treasury's share was nearly $650 million."[9]

His conclusion about this first phase of operations was that the Pool had succeeded beyond the wildest dreams of any who had participated in its creation. What the gentleman, however, still did not understand (see Jacques Rueff's analysis in this book) was that there was no way the Bretton Woods arrangements could survive for very long, particularly when countries, and this primarily applies to the U.S., were not adhering to the strictest fiscal and monetary discipline. Given the military engagement of the U.S. in Vietnam, it was only a matter of time until the U.S. balance of payments would go from bad to worse.

Not everybody, therefore, had the same rosy view of the central bankers' accomplishment. While Charles A. Coombs clearly expressed his opinion that one could not rely on the continuation of such good fortune, he forgot that the markets are the masters. Subsequent tragic events have shown to this day that it would have been worthwhile to think hard about installing a gold standard when there still was time. The alternative was, and is, loosing time and money with a gold dollar standard that has the potential of throwing the financial market into a crisis from which it may never recover.

In *The Invisible Crash*, James Dines wrote clearly[10]:

> "Economic imperialism was a natural consequence of the type of mentality dominating Washington in the 1930s. The fascism that spawned Hitler apparently had more subtle manifestations in other countries, not all of which have been extirpated to this very day [1975]. The amount of goods that American tourists in Europe brought back to the U.S. was reduced, and new tourist taxes sprang up everywhere. This chipping away at the freedoms of Americans was met without complaints. Pressure was placed on U.S. corporations to repatriate U.S. funds under the lure of capitalism. Actually this was a fascist act of expropriating the assets of U.S. stockholders so that government could spend that money instead. This is not capitalism. Such chicanery by people in high office is not the kind of free government that can support capitalism. [...] So great

was their fear of the metal that the people in Washington stopped at nothing to demonstrate that gold was an unsatisfactory investment. Their anti-gold hysteria became self-fulfilling prophecy from 1933 to 1968. But as great as the power of these politicians was, even greater was the power of gold.

That anti-gold policy would virtually drive the entire United States gold mining industry out of business, Canada had to subsidize its gold mines and South Africa was forced to pay pennies to their workers, because it was all they could afford. All of this was blithely ignored by the powers in Washington. I wonder if the people responsible for these outrages will ever be brought to justice.

The government, completely misreading the gold crisis, immediately blamed it on the "gnomes of Zurich" and "currency speculators". Thus the guilty parties, that is the creators of inflation, immediately sought a scapegoat. Their reaction would prolong the crisis because it concealed the true culprits.[11]

The Gold Pool was designed to dump gold on the gold market whenever it began to rise. This suppression of free market price is not free enterprise. [...] The United States provided 50% of the total net gold sales of the Pool, which gives an indication of the geographical location of the true culprit. In June 1967, France wisely withdrew from the Pool amidst heavy criticism and pressure."[12]

In addition to a gold crisis or rather dollar crisis, there was also ... a Silver Crisis.

The Other Monetary Metal – Silver

There can be no discussion of gold without also discussing some historic facts about silver, the first metallic monetary standard in ancient times. While gold was also known, it was mostly concentrated in royal or religious temples and treasuries and rarely entered trade. The value attributed to silver in relation to gold was not measured according to a worldly but to a cosmic yardstick. The ancients had an explanation for this. As the moon travels 13.3 times faster through the zodiac than the sun, it was thought that gold was 13.3 times more precious than silver.[13] Man was made aware that in money there also ruled a divine order. The gold treasures of Egypt were known for their relationship with the sun. The silver amulets and temple pictures of Ephesus were thought to be related to certain influences of the moon.

Some men believed that gold and silver were ordained, not by elected governments, but by millennia of human experience under divine guidance, and that they are the true monetary metals that have been handed down to us from Biblical times. In Egypt, the symbol for gold and the sun were the same, and gold was considered to be the metal of the gods. In antiquity, gold and silver were stored in shrines and temples, but as they entered circulation, they facilitated trade forever, and the barter economy was a thing of the past.

The Gold/Silver Ratio

One of the most fascinating questions of monetary history, and also one of the most mysterious, is the economic interpretation of the gold/silver ratio and its changes. This ratio was as low as 10 in antiquity. By the beginning of the Modern Age, it crept up to 14. Governments tried to stabilize it at 15 in the eighteenth century, but without success. In the nineteenth century the ratio was completely destabilized as it raced towards 60, only to come down to 16 by the end of World War I. In the post-war years it rose again and hit 100 during the Great Depression in the early 1930s, when silver was selling for 25 cents an ounce. From this all-time high, the ratio started its long descent *pari passu* with the deliberate debasement of world currencies to reach a low of 16 in 1980. From there it began climbing again. At the time of this writing the Au/Ag ratio is at 61.

For thousands of years, the ratio fluctuated between 10 and 15. There was only one exception. During early Egyptian history the ratio was as low as 2.5, but there was good reason for that: There was a shortage of silver, which came mainly from Greece.[14, 15]

57

From Bimetallism to Monometallism

The end of silver as a monetary metal came in the middle of the nineteenth century, first as a consequence of the Legal Tender Act in the U.S. in February of 1862, and the National Banking Act of February 25, 1863. The champion of silver demonetization was, however, Imperial Germany, which, as a consequence of its victory over France in 1871, had accumulated a large hoard of gold. The treasuries declared bimetallism a failure and selling silver became a genuine source of revenue to them.

The most probable reason for the sale is that in the middle of the nineteenth century large-scale government interventions in monetary affairs had begun. Otherwise the Au/Ag ratio would have continued its almost imperceptible secular rise. However, large-scale credit manipulation was possible only if the government and the banking system assumed control over one of the monetary metals. The first step in this direction was the decision to scrap bimetallism and introduce monometallism.

Because silver was more widely distributed among the population, the control over silver as a means of credit manipulation appeared, therefore, less promising. Consequently, gold became the only monetary metal. That was probably the most likely reason for the demonetization because, even during my lifetime, I remember very well how silver coins circulated peacefully with paper bank notes in Switzerland until 1968.

In that year the silver price exploded. Because of rising inflation, hoarding began and silver coins disappeared from circulation. Currency debasement was another reason why silver lost its monetary role and not the 'failure of bimetallism'. In the final analysis, it was a result of governments meddling with money and credit.

Antal Fekete conveys a view not found in books on economics:

> "The Coinage Act of 1792 initiated a new statutory system fixing the bimetallic ratio (gold/silver price) at 15. This was an attempt of valorization. It was clearly based on the belief that the

government can create or destroy value by fiat. Enemies of freedom later took full advantage of this mistake. After one hundred years of monetary experimentation, which had seen the de facto monetary standard shift back-and-forth between silver and gold, as well as changes in the official bimetallic ratio in 1834 and again in 1837, not to mention of the reckless experiment with the irredeemable greenback during the Civil War and its aftermath, the government started the demonetization racket. It first demonetized silver by abrogating the constitutionally guaranteed right of the people to the free coinage of the standard silver dollar, an act the firebrand political orator William Jennings Bryan dubbed *The Crime of 1873*. One hundred years later the government demonetized gold, an act that can aptly be dubbed *The Crime of 1971*. These acts were further efforts at valorization, as were the numerous pieces of legal tender legislation that followed. At the turn of the century and millennium the U.S. government is still indulging in valorization. It is trying to cap the gold price by hook or crook, in order to conceal the true extent of dollar-debasement that has taken place in the 20th century.

There are a number of lessons to be learned from these experiments. First, while the government may succeed temporarily in valorizing one monetary metal or the other, it is notoriously impotent when it tries to valorize both. The second lesson is that, while valorizing one monetary metal may temporarily prevent a runaway increase in the price-level itself, it could *not* prevent a runaway increase in the *volatility* of the price level."[16]

Then, Fekete asks the question:

"What is the bimetallic ratio trying to say?

Since time immemorial the bimetallic ratio displayed a most remarkable stability, one unmatched by any other economic indicator. Although never constant, the bimetallic ratio has been stable while displaying a slight upward bias. This stability was no accident. It indicated the wisdom of a long succession of generations who understood well that the only danger threatening their monetary system was the danger of a corner. Should pirates or piratical governments try to corner one of the monetary metals thereby destabilizing the bimetallic ratio, people would restore the ratio through arbitrage. They would sell the dearer monetary metal and buy the cheaper one. This state of affairs came to an abrupt end just after the American Civil War and the Franco-Prussian war of 1870/71. A victorious north and, independently, a victorious Prussia started a course of empire building. They flexed their monetary muscles by settling the demonetization-racket into motion. They spent their booties – by far the largest in all history up to that point – on destroying the natural monetary order. They defrocked silver. Not only was the bimetallic ratio destabilized but, as if in the wake of a "Big Bang", a cataclysmic increase in its volatility was set off that has continued to this day. While varying between a lower bound of 15 und an upper end of 100, both the amplitude and the frequency of changes in the bimetallic ratio have been on the rise.

There has been precious little interest on the part of mainstream economists in questions related to the bimetallic ratio and its variation. This is a clear indication that their paymaster, the governments, are anxious to keep the issue out of public debate. Yet the question cannot be ignored. It is natural to ask for an explanation of this singular historic phenomenon. How could the bimetallic ratio, involving the first two metals ever mentioned in the *Bible*, after having shown a remarkable stability for several thousands of years, all of a sudden be destabilized and become ever more volatile?

It is the thesis of this Manifesto that the bimetallic ratio has faithfully recorded the history of the violent and evil interference of governments inspired by *The Communist Manifesto*, in the spontaneous monetary order. Governments were hell-bent on politicizing the monetary system and centralizing credit in their own hands, in fulfillment of the prophecy of Marx and Engels, even if it meant a systematic destruction of the constitutional monetary order and the overthrow of representative government. The destabilization of the bimetallic ratio by the deliberate policy of driving monetary gold into the coffers of governments and their central banks. It reflects the recognition that, if they could not valorize both monetary metals then the governments ought to act in concert to valorize one of them. The governments' choice was gold. They thought that they could bring gold under control more easily than they could silver."[17]

Fekete's analysis and conclusion show, that before the "Gold Wars" there were "Silver Wars". The following and later chapters demonstrate they continue to this day.

Silver is Sacrificed

Don Hoppe, in his excellent book on investing in gold mines, revealed how the silver issue was mishandled:

"For residents of the United States, silver dollars and subsidiary silver coins were the only intrinsic-value money still available, and Gresham's Law inevitably drove them into hiding. At first, the Treasury Department, with inexcusable ineptness, sought to blame the growing scarcity of silver coins on the activities of numismatic coin collectors. However, to assume that the disappearance of the Federal Reserve's entire stock of silver dollars (some

$350 million worth) plus nearly the entire circulating supply of half-dollars, was the work of the nation's 'coin collectors' requires a rather broad definition of what constitutes a coin collector. Certainly the hoarding of common coins has nothing to do with traditional numismatics.

During the following transition period from intrinsic value to non-intrinsic value coinage, the Treasury Department vowed to maintain the $1.29 ceiling on silver by continuing to supply the market from government stocks. The Treasury boasted that it could hold the line on the price of silver until 1980 if necessary. But, speculators and investors alike rushed to exchange their depreciating Federal Reserve notes for silver bullion in such quantities at the bargain price of $1.29 that direct Treasury sales had to be suspended by the summer of 1967. The price of silver immediately soared above $2 per ounce.

In August 1967, the Government tried once more to get the price of silver under control. It was feared that an uninhibited rise in the price of silver would cast further doubt on the integrity of the credit dollar and encourage additional withdrawals of gold by foreign holders. As it turned out, it was a needless worry. The gold stock kept right on declining according to its own apparently inflexible schedule.

At any rate, a weekly auction was established by Washington, in which its remaining stock of silver bullion, including .900 fine silver then being removed from melted coins, could be sold by sealed bids to industrial users through the General Services Administration, rather than the Treasury. This program remained in effect until November 1970, when the Government announced triumphantly that it had no more silver to sell. The latest, and hopefully the last, great cycle of government intervention in the silver market, which had begun in 1933, was finally ended."[18]

Silver, The Restless Metal

This is also the title of a book by Professor Roy Jastram on the history of silver:

> "Although silver has become predominantly an industrial good, it has not left behind it the characteristics of a precious metals market. It is still bought by individuals and institutions as an investment, as a protection against inflation, and as a speculative object.
>
> During the decade of 1970-1980, families in the Middle East and the Hunt brothers in the United States accumulated large amounts of silver. Other large operators made accumulations of their own but escaped Hunt's publicity. [...] Thus, a large base was being built for a vigorous price move. In 1979 and early 1980, speculative buying reached a crescendo. New silver price records being set daily stimulated the speculative motive further. Then, dramatically, from a high of $48.00 the price collapsed to $10.80 within seven weeks. The restless metal showed how explosive it could be."[19]

Some believe that the silver/gold ratio will ultimately again fall to 16:1, but it should not be forgotten that silver is no longer a monetary metal. However, in future inflationary periods, it may again resume its monetary role as the gold of the 'little man', and there may be renewed silver speculation and crises as long as money creation remains under the purview of a small specially privileged cabal.

The Breakdown of the Gold Pool

The Pool continued to suffer losses. There was the chronic illness of sterling. The Labour victory in the elections of October 1964 not only brought heavy selling pressure on the pound but simultaneously ignited a burst of speculative demand for gold. According to Charles A. Coombs, buying pressure in the London gold market continued to mount in early 1965 as President de Gaulle launched a strong attack on the U.S. dollar and called for a return to the gold standard. Here again, it shows how a senior official of the Federal Reserve, in this case Mr. Coombs, did not seem to understand what the real reasons for the crisis were. However, General de Gaulle understood, and his advisor, Jacques Rueff, understood even better. But Coombs makes de Gaulle responsible for the demise of the ill-fated, ill-constructed Bretton Woods agreements:

> "But de Gaulle's arrogant pronouncements served only to polarize the issue in a new and confusing dimension. And his advisors who urged him to put a gun to the American head by cashing in dollars for gold succeeded only in hastening the downfall of Bretton Woods and ensuring that gold would never again play the same role as before. Between 1962 and 1966, the French government bought nearly $3 billion of gold from the U.S. Treasury, shipped the bulk of its gold custody holdings at the New York Federal Reserve to Paris, and generally challenged the functioning of the Bretton Woods system."[20]

He continues:

> "In March 1965 even the Chinese government started to buy gold in the London market. By August 1965 the Pool had spent more than $200 million on interventions. [...] Then late in 1965 there were new heavy offers of Russian gold and the Pool was back to a surplus of $1.3 billion by the end of the year. [...] This was followed by increased inflow of gold from South Africa to help finance their balance of payments deficit. [...] Demand for gold in 1965 had also been swollen by such a factor as the war in Vietnam. [...] Industrial demand also started to climb. [...] In June 1967 the deficit was now totaling $365

million. [...] Speculation arising out of the September 1967 meeting of the IMF in Rio de Janeiro coupled with sagging confidence in sterling, pushed the Pool deficit to $434 million by the end of October. [...] In July 1967 the first break occurred, as the Banque de France regretfully indicated that it could no longer continue. [...] In November events overtook. The sterling crisis, building steadily to a climax since the Middle East war of June 1967 culminated with the devaluation of the pound from $2.80 to $2.40 led to a tidal wave of speculation now sweeping through the London market and over the following week beginning November 20 the Pool sustained a crescendo of losses, $1,006 millions from January to November 20-24, 1967."[21]

From now on, Charles A. Coombs repeatedly refers to the London gold market as the London gold bazaar. The crisis culminated when Senator Jacob Javits called for a cessation of Gold Pool operations in March of 1968 as well as for other basic changes in U.S. gold policy. Pool losses were snowballing.

By March 1968, the U.S. gold stock had plummeted to around $10.5 billion or about 300 million ounces, due to the Treasury's unwise insistence on suppressing gold at $35. In an emergency weekend meeting in Washington DC on March 17, 1968, it was decided to close the Gold Pool and to establish a two-tiered gold price. According to Mr. James Dines it was:

> "[...] an obvious last-ditch attempt by the currency manipulators of the Washington Economic Establishment to suppress the gold price. In April 1968 the gold price reached a high of $44. The end result was an indisputable victory of gold over the monetary authorities, central bankers, economists and politicians."[22]

In the words of Dines:

"This left gold as the unquestioned financial master of the world, and the world's ultimate money to those who would see."[23]

On March 18, 1969 Congress removed the 25% gold reserve requirement for Federal Reserve Notes. This action severed the last mandated restriction between the Nation's money supply and its stock of gold.

On December 30, 1969, in a reversal of the policy announced when the 'two-tier' market was established, the IMF announced an agreement to purchase newly-mined South African gold (thereby establishing a method for increasing the world's official stock of monetary gold) at $35 per ounce if the market price fell to $35 or less. The agreement also provided that the South African central bank could sell gold on the free market from its official reserves to meet foreign exchange requirements, regardless of the free market price.

The 'Gold Shortage' Myth and the Creation of the Special Drawing Rights (SDRs)

Whenever monetary experts did not know what caused the recurring monetary crises, they usually blamed it on gold by creating the myth about the shortage of physical gold. This, as we know from the history of the gold standard, was a clear misinterpretation of the situation and far from the truth. The real problem always was that too much fiat money was being created, and so it should be with the invention of the SDRs. This so-called 'Paper Gold', created by the Treasury under its Secretary Fowler and Undersecretary Paul A. Volcker, was designed to complement gold. This was done because it was believed that there was not enough gold and foreign exchange, i.e., dollars, in the market. However, in reality, the world had plenty. In 1969 the SDRs were integrated into the international monetary system.

Jacques Rueff commented:

"Meanwhile monetary experts devised an ingenious scheme for concealing the United States' insolvency by allocating every country a quota of special international reserves to be held only by central banks. But to avoid added inflationary effects, the amount of SDRs had to be limited. Thus, even with the help of SDRs, the United States could not have redeemed more than a fraction of its dollar debt."[24]

The Wall Street Journal greeted this achievement in modern financial alchemy enthusiastically. Hoppe summed it up:

> "'U.S. SCORES PAPER GOLD TRIUMPH' and Undersecretary of the Treasury Paul A. Volcker told newsmen with a broad smile: 'Well, we got this thing launched.' *The Journal* welcomed it as a 'major success for the American school of economic thought, since it dealt a blow to old-style backers of gold as the sole yardstick for monetary value and economic cure-all.' *The Journal's* comment overlooked the fact that the SDRs had to be denominated or defined in a certain amount of gold. So gold was still the undisputed 'yardstick' of monetary value. Furthermore, it was specifically noted that the SDR could never be 'devalued.'"[25]

D. Hoppe was convinced that the SDR plan was one of the greatest financial swindles ever perpetrated, and that:

> "[…] it would, one day, be ranked by historians along with such other gems of human opacity as John Law's Mississippi Scheme, the assignat madness and the South Sea Bubble. Somehow defining the SDR unit as being 'equal' to gold and then just as solemnly declaring that it is not redeemable in gold, strikes one as a patent absurdity. A paper currency or unit of credit can be regarded as 'equal' to gold only if it is in fact convertible into gold at a fixed price or rate, without restriction."[26]

Richard M. Salsman thought that the SDRs were the farthest thing from gold one can imagine.[27] That central banks thought that they could create such fictions and call them gold was a sign of how removed they were from the practical workings of the markets. Dubbed 'paper gold' at the time, SDRs were a brazen attempt to practice modern alchemy. The creation of SDRs neither created gold nor did anything to solve the real problem of excessive fiat money creation and its result: worldwide price inflation. If anything, SDRs contributed to it by creating more fiat claims instead of more wealth. The U.S. went on losing gold after SDRs were created.

Nevertheless, the view was widely accepted at the time that the creation of SDRs or money-out-of-thin-air spelled the end of gold as a monetary metal.

How did the price of gold and the gold mining shares react? The price of gold on the London market briefly plunged below \$35; and in London, New York and Johannesburg, speculators fell over each other trying to get out of their gold stocks.

The late economist Dr. Melchior Palyi had some harsh words for the idea of paper gold:

> "The new SDR reserve currency will serve only to encourage a more reckless financial expansion and inflation on a world-wide basis. The adoption of the SDRs will be the triumph of the inflationists. It will remove the last obstacle on the road to a fully managed 'world currency,' one that presumably will never be allowed to become short in supply. It is literally the old 'greenback' policy on a global basis."[28]

Dr. Palyi did not indicate just who would do the managing. Presumably it would be the IMF directorate.

Apparently American representatives pressured other IMF delegations to accept the SDR scheme. They gave them to understand that if the plan was not accepted, the world could face a financial catastrophe, and it was hinted that they might run the risk of foreign-held dollars no longer being redeemable in gold.

When I asked former central banker John Exter about his opinion, he answered:

"Under the gold standard, paper currency notes promised to pay to the bearer on demand a fixed amount of gold in exchange for the note. Today, our paper money is nothing more than an 'I-O-U nothing.' The IMF's attempts to substitute so-called paper gold for the real thing is one of the most absurd concepts I've ever heard in my life. I call the IMF's Special Drawing Right a 'who-owes-you-nothing-when' — there is no obligor, no promise to pay, no maturity date. It is the most preposterous credit instrument ever conceived by the mind of man."[29]

The U.S. Stock Market in the 1960s

After WWII, the U.S. stock market started a long bull move leading to an overvaluation of many stocks in the early 1960s. This could not last and was, subsequently, corrected. The first thunderstorms occurred in spring of 1962. The dark clouds could already be seen in the fall of 1961 when some stocks reached absurd valuations. In spring 1962, a serious bear market got under way and on May 20, 1962, a real washout took place and many stocks were cut in half from their December 1961 levels. That Tuesday was called 'Black Tuesday', and even very serious bankers believed that this was 1929 all over again. Far from it, the overall situation was still sound and the most extreme overvaluations corrected. From then on, the market recovered strongly, and the Dow Jones Index reached a new all-time high in 1966 of 1000, only to fall back to 744 in October of the same year.

Interest rates had been continuously rising since 1945 and reflected not only higher demand for capital but rising inflation. From a level of a little over 1.5% in 1945, 10-year Treasury bond yields increased to around 8% in 1970, and short-term paper yielded around 10% or more. The market got sicker and sicker, but few realized that the world was in the midst of a serious monetary crisis. Even fewer understood that it was because gold was mistreated.

Speculation, especially in conglomerate stocks, was rampant. A wild take-over game was underway. Conglomerate companies were not paying any dividends but using their stock primarily to take over other companies, often much bigger ones, only in order to grow. The word "synergy" was most frequently misused, because in many cases the activities of the acquiring companies and the acquired ones did not have anything in common.

Then the situation really got out of hand. When I was in New York in the fall of 1968, stock market analyst and operator Bob Wilson thought that the markets looked like 1929. Soon afterwards, in 1969, the market started a decline. The Dow in the spring of 1970 fell to 631 only to recover to 1000 again. After 1972 a new serious bear market started and, in December of 1974, the Dow went as low as 577. Considering the rising rate of inflation, the situation was even worse. Nobody thought that things that were happening could possibly have anything to do with the gold crisis. In many established Keynesian-trained circles, anti-gold propaganda was fashionable, and gold was a four-letter word.

Part III: The Great Gold War: 1960 - 1971

[1] Horace, Carmina III, c. 20 BC.

[2] Italian proverb.

[3] Charles A. Coombs, *The Arena of International Finance*, (New York: John Wiley & Sons, 1976).

[4] Ibid, 3.

[5] *The Pocket Money Book*, (Great Barrington, MA: AIER, 1994).

[6] Ibid.

[7] Donald J. Hoppe, *How to Invest in Gold Stocks*, (New York: Arlington House, 1972), 169.

[8] Charles A. Coombs, 62/63.

[9] Charles A. Coombs, *The Arena of ...*, 62-68.

[10] Anyone interested in the day-to-day events of this period should read James Dines' *The Invisible Crash*. Particularly Chapter 9, "An Odyssey Through the Gold comments in the Dines Letters, 1961 – 1974," reads like a personal diary as Dines recalls the explosive currency and gold situation of the period and the general ignorance about the importance of gold.

[11] The culprits, of course, were politicians, central banks and their respective banking systems, which achieved the special privilege of being able to create demand deposits (money) out of thin air. [auth.]

[12] James Dines, *The Invisible Crash* (New York: Random House, 1977), 48/49.

[13] Gérard Klockenbring, *Geld - Gold – Gewissen*, (Stuttgart, Verlag Urachhaus, 1974), 18.

[14] C. H. V. Sutherland, *Gold, Its Beauty, Power and Allure*, (Vienna and Munich: Verlag Anton Schell, 1970), 46.

[15] James U. Blanchard, *Silver Bonanza*, (New York: Simon & Schuster, 1993), 82.

[16] Antal Fekete. "The Bimetallist Manifesto," private correspondence with the author, September 2, 2000.

[17] Ibid.

[18] Donald J. Hoppe, *How to Invest in Gold Stocks* (New York: Arlington House, 1972), 174.

[19] Roy W. Jastram, *SILVER: The Restless Metal* (New York: John Wiley & Sons, 1977), 157.

[20] Charles A. Coombs, *The Arena of ...*, 152-173.

[21] Ibid.

[22] James Dines, *The Invisible Crash* (New York: Random House, 1977), 51.

[23] Ibid.

[24] Jacques Rueff, *The Inflationary Impact the Gold Exchange Standard Superimposes on the Bretton Woods System* (Greenwich, CT: Committee for Monetary Research and Education, 1975), 19.

[25] Donald J. Hoppe, *How to Invest in Gold Stocks* (New York: Arlington House, 1972), 181.

[26] Ibid.

[27] Richard M. Salsman, *Gold and Liberty* (Great Barrington, MA: American Institute for Economic Research, 1995), 75.

[28] Melchior Palyi, "A Point of View," *Commercial and Financial Chronicle* (24 July, 1969): . Also Hoppe *"How to ... "*, 180.

[29] "Classic Exter Opinions," *Blakely's Gold Investment Review* (1989): 10.

Part IV: Gold Rush and Gold War

"Gold and silver have been ordained not by corrupt governments and their handpicked henchmen but by millennia of human experience under divine guidance. They are the true monetary metals that have been handed down to us from Biblical times."
Antal E. Fekete[1]

"Gold is the sovereign of all sovereigns."
Democritus[2]

The Aftermath and Consequences of the Collapse of the Gold Pool

The gold market was closed on March 17, 1968 at the request of the U.S. The London market remained closed for two weeks. When it reopened, the gold business had a fundamentally new structure. First, at a meeting in Washington, central banks and the IMF had created the 'two-tier' market. On one level, central banks and monetary institutions continued to deal with each other at the official price of $35 an ounce, i.e., no devaluation of the dollar, while, on the free market, the price would find its own level. As part of the Washington Agreement, central banks were forbidden to have anything to do with the 'free' market; they could neither buy nor sell in it. The two-tier system divorced monetary from non-monetary gold for the next seven years.

Then something very dramatic happened. After the Gold Pool was closed, the London bullion houses also shut their doors for two weeks. During this period the 'Big Three' Swiss banks took over and formed their own gold pool. The Swiss banks always had an excellent relationship with South Africa, and when nobody was willing to finance the South African government or South African enterprises, the Swiss, and also the Germans, helped. South African bond issues could easily be launched on the Swiss capital markets. Furthermore, contrary to the London houses, the Swiss banks had enormous placement power. They were operating as principals and, therefore, were in a situation to finance huge gold positions. The English had no placement power at all.

Not only did the Swiss banks put 10% of their international clients' portfolios into gold, but they were also suppliers to the booming Italian jewelry industry, the biggest in the world, and to other trading centers, such as the Middle and Far East, which for a long time did their banking through Switzerland. So it was easy to persuade the South Africans to channel their physical gold through Switzerland.

However, the Swiss were also handling most of the Russians' physical gold supplies. The Russians liked Swiss secrecy and discreteness. Contrary to London, no statistics were published on how much Russian gold was sold through Switzerland. As a consequence, the secretive Russians transferred much of their gold trade from London to Zurich. They even set up their own Wozchod Handelsbank in Zurich. Subsequently, it became a very important gold trading bank.

According to Timothy Green in his *The New World of Gold*, originally published in 1981, the Russians channeled just over 2,000 tonnes of gold into Switzerland between 1972 and 1980.[3] By 1968 the Swiss had captured an estimated 80% of the world's physical gold market. Not only could they offer the most modern banking facilities, but each of the big banks also had their own precious metal refinery.

Since gold could no longer be taken up by central banks under the Washington Agreement, and speculators were holding about $2 billion[4] worth of gold, suddenly there was a huge overhang of physical metal. In this situation, the Swiss banks played a crucial role for South Africa, and they were rewarded for their valuable services. From then on, Zurich was the biggest gold trading center in the world. London only began to regain some of its prominence with the launching of the Gold Futures Markets. In Switzerland, trading of 'call options' and 'put options' to potential buyers and sellers of gold in units of 100 ounces of gold had begun.

The Closing of the 'Gold Window' by President Nixon

As U.S. short-term dollar liabilities to foreigners were continuing to rise, French economist Jacques Rueff recommended doubling the gold price in order to restore confidence in the dollar. When he suggested this to President Kennedy during his visit to Paris, Kennedy answered that he could not do this to the American people. But, by August of 1971, the situation had reached a critical stage. Neither the two-tier system nor the appeasements by politicians and economists of all sorts helped. In August, U.S. short-term dollar liabilities to foreigners were estimated at about $60 billion, of which about two-thirds were owed to foreign official institutions. At $35 per ounce, U.S. gold holdings had shrunk to $9.7 billion.

On August 9, 1971, the price of gold had reached a new high of $43.94. After a sharp correction, interest in gold mining shares was on the rise again. Germany's Mark had gained 7% since being floated on May 10, 1971. This meant that the U.S. dollar effectively had been devalued by 10%. Swiss banks also temporarily suspended trading dollars in an attempt to stem the growing monetary panic.

The end of this monetary tragedy was reached when the Bank of England and the SNB asked for gold in exchange for their dollars. Salsman in *Gold and Liberty* writes:

> "By 1971, more than half of the gold supply that was forcibly taken from U.S. citizens in the 1930s, ended up in the vaults of foreign central banks. This was the biggest bank heist in world history. It happened in slow motion and may not have been the intent of every official who participated in it."[5]

President Nixon responded and, on August 15, 1971, closed the Gold Window by refusing to allow the Treasury to redeem any foreign-held dollars in gold. "Closing the Gold Window was," according to Salsman, "a polite expression for defaulting on gold payments and repudiating an international monetary agreement. This default was not substantially different from the 'third world' debt defaults that would later take place in the 1980s. The U.S. gold default was the act of a banana republic. The U.S. dollar has been unhinged from gold ever since."[6]

Also Salsman:

> "When gold was 'demonetized' in 1971, many critics of gold predicted that its price would fall below $35 per ounce. They assumed that the paper dollar gave value to gold, not the other way round. [Unlike J. P. Morgan, they did not know that gold was money. –auth.] Federal Reserve Board Governor Henry Wallich referred to the activity in the gold market as a 'side show'.
>
> *Such was the result, and many officials and economists actually applauded* the *abandonment of gold money at every step.*"[7] [Emphasis added by auth.]

It is most revealing to read the *Extract from the Executive Statement* of August 15, 1971.[8] President Nixon suspended convertibility of the dollar and blamed international money speculators for monetary crisis no less than five times. Blaming imaginary scapegoats was certainly not worthy of a U.S. President. Also his Secretary of Treasury, John Connolly, was not particularly known for his monetary expertise.

It is tragic that the public, be it American or European, did not understand what was going on. The Asian people (not their central banks) always had a far better understanding of the virtues of gold holdings. A watershed occurred that would change the world forever. It is even more tragic because no current leaders in politics and finance appear to remember those events today.

John Exter told me the following story, which is absolutely authentic, as he was physically present:

> "On August 10, 1971, a group of bankers, economists and monetary experts held an informal meeting at Mantoloking on the Jersey shore to discuss the monetary crisis. Around 3 o'clock in the afternoon, a big car rolled up with Paul Volcker in it.

He was then Under-secretary of the Treasury for Monetary Affairs.

We discussed various possible solutions. As you would expect, I was for tight money – raising interest rates – but that was overwhelmingly rejected. The others thought the Fed would not slow credit expansion for fear it would trigger a recession [...] or worse. As for raising the gold price, as I suggested, Volcker said it made sense, but he didn't think he could get it through Congress. Governments, especially world leaders like the U.S., don't like to admit to their citizens that they have been debasing the currency no matter how true. It's too embarrassing, and the crisis we were facing at the time was all but unknown to the public at large. It wasn't a national emergency like 1933 when Roosevelt was able to do anything he wanted.

At one point Volcker turned to me and asked what I would do. I told him that since he wouldn't raise interest rates and wouldn't raise the price of gold, he only had one option open. I told him he'd have to close the Gold Window because it made no sense to go on selling off our gold stock at $35 an ounce. Five days later Nixon closed the Gold Window.

The final link between the dollar and gold was broken. The dollar became nothing more than a fiat currency, and the Fed [and especially the banks] were then free to continue its monetary expansion at will. The result, as you know, was a massive explosion of debt. I estimate the dollar debt in the world today is in excess of $16 trillion.

The problem with this mountain of debt is that it simply cannot be repaid. Debt is a funny thing: it always must be repaid, if not by the debtor, then by the lender, or worse still, the taxpayers."[9]

In the U.S. total debt at the beginning of 2001 was about $27 trillion. Worldwide debt is estimated to be over $70 trillion. It is expected that a large part of this debt cannot be serviced, nor will it ever be repaid.

The World Bank and the International Monetary Fund

The World Bank and the IMF were originally established to help countries 'manage' their balance of payments in order to stay on the dollar exchange standard – in other words, to keep the Bretton Woods system operational. According to Salsman in *Gold and Liberty*:

> "When the link between the dollar and gold was broken in 1971, there technically was no longer a need for these agencies. But as with all government bureaucracies, they fought to stay in place. They contributed to the 'third world' lending crisis of the following decade by guaranteeing loans to uncreditworthy governments for state projects. These agencies, funded as they are by the taxpayers of industrialized countries, continue to transfer wealth from producers to non-producers."[10]

Since 1971 their activities have expanded. The International Monetary Fund (IMF) has become a mechanism to transfer wealth from poor people to rich people. In recent years, it has, however, come under growing criticism. Not only has its gold policy been a disaster, but also countries in trouble were too often prescribed the wrong medicine: austerity and devaluation. As will be discussed in Chapter VII, the widespread opinion is, even in U.S. high places, that the organization would not be missed if it were to be dissolved. Most of its useful functions could be performed by the Bank for International Settlements (BIS) in Basel .[11]

The 'Smithsonian Agreement'

Meanwhile nothing was solved. Flight from the bankrupt dollar continued. During this period, the Deutsche Bundesbank and the SNB bought billions of dollars in order to support the U.S.

currency. Four months after the closing of the Gold Window, the finance ministers of the G-10 countries, at a meeting at the Smithsonian Institute in Washington, DC, agreed to set new parities, but the basic idea of Bretton Woods, fixed exchange rates, was maintained against all reason. For the first time since 1935, the dollar was devalued from $35 to $38 per ounce of gold. This did not make much sense because the market was already at $45 per ounce. The next official devaluation of the dollar was from $39 to $42.22 per ounce, and came on February 13, 1972, when the market had priced gold at $75 per ounce.

As could be expected, the understanding called the Smithsonian Agreement solved nothing. Hoppe tells us that President Nixon, with his usual penchant for overstatement, hailed the new arrangement as the most significant monetary agreement in the history of the world.[12] He would continue to promise that it would create more jobs, restore stability to world finance, benefit farmers, stimulate exports, end U.S. balance-of-payments drain and generally bring prosperity to all.[13]

Nixon did not understand, or did not want to understand, that the U.S., with its exploding balance of payments deficit and facing a rapidly expanding European market, had lost the ability to redeem dollars for gold at a fixed rate. It was not because of gold that the dollar and its exchange could no longer be controlled; it was because the banking system was creating too many dollars. As the value of a currency is determined by its scarcity, the dollar could only lose value. There was increasing manipulation in the foreign exchange market, because a growing group of currency speculators took advantage of the depreciating dollar. At the same time this drove the price of gold up.

Meanwhile, towards the end of 1972, the Dow Jones reached 1000 again, but inflation was dangerously on the rise, representing not only a threat to the stock market, but to the whole economy. In January 1973, France, once more, sought to restore gold as the basis of the world currency system, but the Americans had no intention to follow the recommendation from Paris. In March 1973, the system of fixed exchange rates (Bretton Woods) collapsed completely. By

March 26, the gold price in London reached a record high of $90 per ounce.

From then on, the world currency system became a 'non-system'. All currencies 'floated' against each other. This opened the door for more currency debasement; hardly a satisfactory situation. Money is one good whose quantity and quality cannot be left to the profit motives of specially privileged private bankers.

Floating became a mechanism that transferred the ills from one country to the next, and aggravated the world's economic situation. It was the consequence of not wanting to understand that, historically, gold was the money chosen by the collective wisdom of mankind since the dawn of civilization. The ongoing war against gold was essentially a war against the choice of the market and was, therefore, doomed.

Birth of an Atomic Time Bomb

It did not take long to find out how disastrous the monetary situation had become. As long as the world was on fixed exchange rates, there was no need for currency hedging. This changed forever when exchange rates started to float. This created a grave problem for producers of goods that took a longer time to manufacture, such as airplanes, locomotives and turbines.

With volatility of foreign exchange markets as high as 50%, serious problems affecting survival loomed for every exporter and importer. Due to currency fluctuations, they were in danger of losing what they intended to earn through production. Therefore, a tremendous need for currency hedging evolved. The cost of this hedging were revenues to the financial sector.

At first, the volume and the number of instruments were small, but over the years the number of derivative contracts, swaps, options or futures grew at a frenetic pace creating an industry of its own. The basic idea was that derivatives should enable companies and investors to manage their risks better. But a number of financial disasters were proof that the ever-inventive human mind had also created a new Las Vegas. In the case of Long Term Capital Management (LTCM—a hedge fund that hired a handful of hot-shot economists from academe, including a few Nobel Prize winners) not even the most sophisticated computer models would have tamed the genie of risk as long as the Russian government was defaulting on its debt.

As far as the gold market is concerned, it is estimated that the 'paper gold' market in 1999 is many times larger than the actual physical market. Estimates range from a minimum of 90 to an excess of 100 paper-ounce contracts being written for every ounce of physical gold that changes hands. This is not only mind-boggling, or a Frankenstein monster as James Dines calls it, but a king-size horror trip.

At Berkshire Hathaway's annual meeting in late April 1993, famous investor Warren Buffett opined that derivatives might one day trigger a catastrophic chain reaction in world financial markets. Buffett conceded in a subsequent interview that it is difficult to predict what chain of events might trigger such a meltdown. In a speech delivered in early 1992 to the New York State Bankers Association, E. Gerald Corrigan, then President of the New York Federal Reserve Bank, warned that derivatives tend to add "elements of risk and distortion" to the balance sheets and income statements of financial and non-financial institutions alike, and that managers do not always understand what their traders and "rocket scientists" are up to.[14]

In a report to members of FAME, Executive Director Dr. Lawrence Parks wrote on December 25, 1996 that Alan Greenspan has been talking about systemic risk in nearly all of his speeches in recent years. In two speeches, neither of which seem to have been covered by the popular media, Greenspan brought up the possible collapse of the banking system with taxpayers picking up the tab.[15]

The ultimate consequence of abandoning gold was the birth of a market madness which the world had never seen before. It may end one day in a financial collapse that is unparalleled in history. As Keynes said: "In the long run we are all dead." His cynical remark might turn into a prophecy. But, there is also hope because the world may see gold resurrected to its rightful place.

Paper Money Systems Always Fail

The Smithsonian System failed. The European Monetary System was abandoned only to be followed by the Maastricht System in 1999. No paper system will ever work for long. Gold is the only commodity plentiful enough when compared to yearly new production that can serve as money. Furthermore, as long as governments keep interfering, follow protectionist policies and keep spending more than they have, there is no base for an honest monetary system. In his epochal *Grundsätze der Volkswirtschaft* (1871!) and his article "The Origin of Money", Carl Menger, Austrian economic theorist and founder of the Austrian school of marginal analysis, introduced the concept of liquidity of commodities and proceeded to explain the genesis of money.[16]

> "The commodities, which under given local and time relations are most liquid, have become money. [...] The reason why precious metals have become the generally current medium of exchange among all peoples of advanced economic civilization, is because their liquidity is far and away superior to that of all other commodities, and at the same time because they are found to be especially qualified for the concomitant and subsidiary functions of money."[17]

Professor Antal E. Fekete, Memorial University, St. Johns, Canada, wrote in his introduction to the republication of Carl Menger's *The Origin of Money* 92 years after the original had been penned:

> "Governments played no essential role in the historical evolutionary process of promoting gold to the station of money. In fact, that process did not come about by design: it was the unintended social result of collective wisdom, precipitated by individual teleological forces. Gold coins, on the other hand, had one great competitor: the promise of government to pay gold coin on demand. Governments issued the promises only to dishonor them later. Menger's *Origin of Money* compels one to ponder the wisdom of our government's usurping the prerogative of the

market and trying through coercion, to promote *its debt* as the most liquid asset on earth."[18]

Sir Rees-Mogg said it beautifully in *The Times* of December 12, 1979:

> "Gold is a possession and not a promise. A government that owns an ounce of gold does not have to ask the United States or anyone for permission to cash it. The gold supply is finite; that is its monetary significance."

The dollar crisis, the collapse of the Gold Pool, the demise of Bretton Woods, and the war against gold did not happen because gold failed. It happened because those who created money out of nothing, as evidenced by promissory notes to redeem for gold on demand, could not keep their promise. Late German economist and social philosopher, Wilhelm Roepke, professor at the Graduate Institute of International Studies in Geneva until 1966, felt that Britain's and the U.S.'s decision to default on the gold standard in September 1931, and March 1933 respectively, was going to prove extremely fateful in the future.

After Roepke's untimely death in 1966, Ludwig von Mises wrote the following in the *National Review*:

> "In the 1930s Roepke had the courage to promulgate his own ideas, although he knew very well what consequences he would have to face. He was one of the first professors the Nazis fired. He went into exile, first to Istanbul and later to Switzerland. [...] In a series of brilliantly written books, all of them available in American editions, Roepke expounded his economic and political theories. These publications developed the principles that guided Ludwig Erhard and his collaborators in their endeavors to build a new German economy out of the wreckage left by the Nazis. For most of what is reasonable and beneficial in present-day Germany's monetary and commercial policy credit is to be attributed to Roepke's influence. He – and late Walter

Eucken – are rightly thought of as the intellectual authors of Germany's economic resurrection."[19]

Roepke's thinking therefore should not be taken lightly, as it is so up-to-date that the present-day generation of economists and politicians would do well to read or to reread his works. In his book *Die Lehre von der Wirtschaft* he wrote:

"Since Britain (1931) and the U.S. (1933) made the fateful move to sever their currencies from gold and to leave the international gold currency system in a shortsighted nationalistic egoism to fate, and since all currencies have begun to sway and fall under the shadow of mistrust, there no longer exists an international currency system worthy of its name. Now we know with painful certainty how the world economy looks without a gold currency. The whole mechanism all of a sudden does not function any longer because one of its most important preconditions ceased, and what is left is a questionable muddle of manipulated currencies. The nonchalance with which the leading countries have thrown the discipline of gold overboard – and this applies particularly to the U.S., where it was absolutely inexcusable, is only a detail of the general process of disintegration of legal and moral/ethical standards, that up to now were the substitute of a world legal system. Everything is melting and undermined, everything gets out of balance: The world is getting used to take existing conventions of international decency lightly, to experiment with currencies, to freeze foreign assets, to do dumping, to direct import and export depending on almost daily changing moods here and there. The danger of the process of disintegration is, that it growing stronger by its own force."[20]

The Views and Influence of Academia

The impact of the Keynesian school of economics on governments and economists is neither over nor helpful in solving today's monetary problems, because its policies are strongly inflationary. A great deal of Keynesian economic thinking was influenced by the experience of the Great Depression.

Whenever private borrowing, especially borrowing from banks, subsided, it was replaced with deficit spending by the government. This was the government's way to supply the economy with the funds that the private sector was not willing to borrow from the banks. The problem of debt, however, was never really addressed. As the government went into debt, that debt was said not to matter as it was owed to the government itself. Keynes called the gold standard a "barbarous relic".

Milton Friedman and his monetarist followers came later. They pretended to be free-market oriented, but in the most important aspect of economic life – money – they were interventionists. Central banks are a statist innovation and are not compatible with a free market. Monetarists favored floating exchange rates instead of fixed exchange rates, and advocated the need for increasing the money supply at some regular rate. According to them, that would solve most problems.

As John Exter said:

> "In such a system, no country would ever have to pay another with good store-of-value money. They see no need for the discipline of convertibility. [...] We are supposed to be able to pay for our oil with paper dollars regardless of how many we print. [...] They ignore the desire of the people for a good store-of value money like gold. In fact they refuse to call gold money and arbitrarily assert that it is an ordinary commodity like lead or zinc with no role in the monetary system. They have even proposed that the Treasury has no business holding it and should over time sell it off in the market place. Having thus disposed of gold they then arbitrarily define paper,

currency notes and demand deposits, as money and exhort the authorities to increase this money aggregate as an arbitrarily fixed magic rate. Although the rate varies in their minds from time to time, they have even advocated fixing it by law. They do not tell us how this ever-growing volume of paper IOU's should retain the store-of-value function of money. And they seem totally unaware that increasing them steadily at their magic rate will some day create a debt problem."[21]

Exter does not beat around the bush by summing up:

"Keynesianism and Friedmanism are simply 20th century versions of John Law. Their appeal is that by ignoring the discipline of convertibility into gold, and deliberately printing paper money at some economist or politician-minded rate we can somehow cheat nature and get something for nothing, eliminate the business cycle, and ensure perpetual full employment prosperity – without ever taking our lumps. It means, of course, that some economist – or council of economists – serving a politically-oriented government and not risking his own money and judgement in the marketplace, knows so much about the workings of the economy that he, in his John Law wisdom, can decide what monetary, fiscal, tax, trade, price, income, or what-have-you policy is best for all the rest of us, and can thus fine-tune our great economy."[22]

No wonder they did not like gold, not to speak of a gold standard. It is not that men like Keynes or Friedman did not understand – quite the contrary – but they bowed to the political winds of the time. The trouble is that for more than half a century their followers in academia have been corrupting the minds of generations of students with their erroneous teaching.

The economic policy makers who were the products of these new philosophies left a disastrous mark on the destiny of twentieth century life with all its panics, crashes, currency crises and, last but not least, wars. There were few men who tried to swim against the stream of conformity. Unfortunately, they had no chance, and their names are forgotten. There are a very few exceptions for whom the *res publica* always had top priority. One of these persons was Switzerland's Dr. Fritz Leutwiler. At a private luncheon with Dr. Leutwiler in the early 1970s, he openly told me that the gold standard was the best monetary system the world ever had.

Because most economists today are trained by disciples of Keynes or such men as the Nobel Prize winning author of the famous textbook *Economics,* Paul E. Samuelson, the outlook is dim. His book, published by McGraw Hill, is full of mathematical formulas and colored charts. But when one starts to read his views on gold, which are bare of any historical background, one begins to wonder why such superficiality should deserve the Swedish Nobel Prize in Economics. Samuelson is a good example of how twentieth century academia completely slept through monetary research, or missed it for compelling reasons.

The Monetary Wisdom of Paul E. Samuelson

In *The Invisible Crash,* James Dines explains:

> "Economic illiterates who were weaned on Samuelson and trained to worship Keynes have led the world to the brink of a major disaster. The full effects are at present incalculable, although it is clear that a major turning point in the history of the world began yesterday [This was after the collapse of the Gold Pool. – ed.]. The man in the street does not know it yet, although he is uneasy as would be inhabitants of a valley where the distant rumble of thunder precedes an earthquake."[23]

Samuelson in his famous volume on 'the free-market tier' as he calls the two-tier market:

"Outside the IMF Club, gold has finally been completely demonetized. [Question: How can one demonetize money? – ed.] Its price is freely set by supply and demand, just like the price of copper, wheat, silver or salt. Thus in 1973 the few American gold mines left sell their output at near the price set by auction in London or Zurich.

Newly mined gold from South Africa provides an exception. South Africa wanted to be able to sell part of her output in the free market at prices above $38 an ounce, and to sell the remainder to the Club at that official price, thereby getting the best of both possible worlds. After 1970 a compromise was reached. In return for South Africa's agreement not to manipulate the free price of gold, the IMF agreed to buy her residual newly mined gold at the official dollar price per ounce, thus providing something of a floor under the free market."[24][25]

And it goes on:

"When you buy a wedding ring, your jeweler pays $60 an ounce, or $70 or $34, whatever happens to be quoted.

Hoarders in the Near East and India can hoard to their heart's content. French merchants and international crime syndicates out to evade taxes, can hide gold in their wine cellars and Swiss bank vaults, etc. [...] But note this: With the price floating above any official floors, speculation and hoarding are now two-way streets. A mid-east sheikh can make a bundle if he buys at $55 and sells at $68, but he can lose his shirt if he buys at $55 and has to sell at $38.50 or as low as $33. [This is quoted from his 1973 edition published at a time when the good professor had no idea that the price of gold would soar to $850 per ounce in 1980 while the dollar lost over 90% of its purchasing power since World War II. –auth.] [...] For the first time in 15 years the international monetary structure has been able to be quite indifferent to the vagaries of hoarders and the ups and downs in the free-market gold prices.

The two-tier system works well, but it is only a halfway house, a stopgap arrangement. The frozen and limited total of official gold would soon put a throttle on the expansion of total world trade were it not for the new plan adopted by the IMF to create 'paper gold' in the form of Special Drawing Rights.

Increasing the price of gold: This position was associated with de Gaulle and his economic advisor Jacques Rueff, Sir Roy Harrod of Oxford, and the Bank for International Settlements at Basel. [Well, at least a few reputable people. –auth.]

What are we to think of this plan? Naturally the South Africans love it. So does the Soviet Union, the other principal gold-mining nation. So do the gold hoarders. So do those nations that were least co-operative in the 1960s in resisting the temptation to hoard gold officially. So do the speculators lusting after quick capital gain.

Most experts regard gold an anachronism. How absurd to waste resources digging gold out of the bowels of earth, only to enter it back again in the vaults of Fort Knox. And why adopt a plan that gives a windfall profit to South Africa, Russia, speculators and private or official hoarders? But the even more important objection to reliance on a rise in the price of gold is this:

Modern mixed economies will not go through the agony of deflating themselves, running the risk of mass unemployment and stagnation, merely to obey the rule of the automatic gold-standard game. And if the gold standard game is not played according to its rules, small disequilibriums will not be prevented from accumulating into major disequilibria with ultimate crisis and breakdown.

Even though the world will not revert to the automatic gold standard, it is a fact that official gold does exist and still is an important part of official international reserves. Hence the new IMF reforms are able, as we shall see, to build around gold and supplement it by new reserve assets. *Gradually gold is to lose its traditional role.*

[...] From the standpoint of economics – jobs, income, interest rates, inflation, lifetime savings – gold has not the slightest importance."[26]

In another paragraph, the professor analyses the gold market as follows:

"In the free tier, jewelers, dentists, organized gangsters and tax evaders, French bourgeoisie and peasants (who do have the legal right to hoard gold) mid-east sheikhs, Swiss speculators – all of them bid up and down the price of gold."[27]

The Gold Buyers

For now, we shall not distinguish between the hoarders, the traders, the speculators, sheikhs, investors, etc., but just look at who was actually buying all the gold. Official circles in the U.S. still considered buying gold a non-event and told people that everything was under control, that the balance of payments would improve for the good and that the dollar was sound. The public, however, did not believe these reassuring statements, and the stock market in 1973 and 1974 was in for a correction that surpassed all corrections in its violence since World War II.

James Dines:

"The price of gold climbed relentlessly and gold mining shares were practically alone on the new high list, although less than one out of 100 financial institutions own a single share of a gold mining company. This clearly shows that not only did the public not understand what was going on but the professionals didn't get it either.

On April 1 (!), 1974, near the end of the first big bull move in gold, Merrill Lynch, the biggest brokerage house in the world, published an institutional study on *South African gold shares* which began with:

'We believe that a portfolio of leading South African gold mining shares could provide high rates of return in the form of high dividend income and capital gains in the years ahead. That opinion is based upon our expectation that the price of gold will continue to rise, reaching levels over the long-term that are likely to be much higher than current prices.'"[28]

In South Africa, the mining companies were dominated and controlled by powerful mining houses that determined policy. The profits of the mines in those days, contrary to the North Americans, were paid out in the form of decent dividends. Thus shareholders did not only see their capital appreciate, but they also received dividends, which is the natural reward for taking risks and investing. During the seventies *The Financial Times Gold Mining Index* went from a level of about 50 in 1968 to around 730 by September of 1980. There were quite a few cases where investors at the top of a bull move received higher dividend payments than what they had originally invested in the shares.

James Dines in *The Invisible Crash* figured out that:

"In order to make the dollar convertible again, there must be enough gold to meet all demands from those who hold U.S. dollars, which comes out to $100 billion right now. Therefore, our current hoard of gold, worth around $10 billion at $42.22, would have to go up in price by around ten times to match our liabilities. That is how we get a figure of over $400."[29]

On December 30, 1974, the price of gold reached $197.25 an ounce and some thought that the price would then explode. The reason for this was that after December 31, 1974, for the first time in 40 years, U.S. citizens were permitted to own gold in any form. James U. Blanchard, who founded the National Committee to Legalize Gold in 1971, started the initiative. Later he called it the National Committee for Monetary Reform. (Blanchard had vast enthusiasm, which is one of the great qualities American people still have. Contrary to Europe, where people for decades have taken government and central bank policies for the gospel truth, there are in the U.S. many more informed and studied minds who are fighting for a return to an honest monetary system.)

After a 40-year ban Americans were, therefore, allowed to buy, sell and own gold in any form. At first the U.S. Treasury opposed the move because it feared speculation would be encouraged, but then it gave in.

Hopes that the price of gold could only increase from then on were soon dashed. Many had bought gold in anticipation of a price increase. Those Americans who understood had bought gold long ago. Instead of sharp rise, a correction of the gold bull market occurred and cut the price of the metal almost in half. The price reached lows of $128.75 in 1975 and of $103.05 in 1976. Meanwhile, gold mining shares dropped even more, e.g., the *Toronto S.E. Gold & Silver Index* went from 1811 (it stood at 247 at the end of 1957 when the bull market started) to a low of 700. While bullion dropped by 48%, the shares dropped even more (62%). But consider what happened before: From a low of 247 at the end of 1957 the TSE Index went to 1811 in March of 1974, a total increase of 633%. In every move, gold mining shares acted as a leading indicator, which means that it was always the shares that started to perform well and rose in price before the metal started to move. It was extremely intriguing that beginning with March of 1974, stock prices started to weaken giving a strong indication that something was wrong. From a market point of view, the metal price should, therefore, always be watched in relation to the gold mining shares. Due to significant producer forward selling, this relationship no longer holds.

In the bear market that followed, the Treasury, with its 'worries about speculation' was quick to realize that this represented a perfect opportunity to give its 'enemy' another push down. On December 3, 1974, the U.S. Treasury announced its first gold sale and then sold relatively small amounts at two public auctions in 1975.

The price of gold bottomed in the Fall of 1976 at $103.05. Three and a half years later, gold rose to $850 in a dramatic bull move in January of 1980. Similarly, the shares measured by the *Toronto S. E. Gold & Silver Index* went from 700 in 1976 to 9,644 in 1995, though interrupted by a series of severe corrections on the way up.

Who Were All Those Hoarders, Speculators and 'Criminals' Who Bought Gold?

The Central Banks

When the Treasury and the IMF auctions took place, a number of central banks bought gold, among them the SNB, whose President Dr. Fritz Leutwiler was a firm believer in sound money, and the Banque de France. But West Germany's Dresdner Bank also was a major buyer of IMF and U.S. Treasury gold. It was assumed that considerable buying was done for Middle Eastern oil money.[30]

Other central banks also bought gold, including Japan, Taiwan, Indonesia, and the OPEC countries (Saudi Arabia, Iran, Iraq, Libya, Qatar, Oman, etc.). Singapore was a big buyer, but it never showed up in official statistics.[31]

Although the demonetization drive by the Treasury and the IMF continued, gold continued to be used in transactions by central banks.[32] Typical examples were swap agreements by the Reserve Bank of South Africa in 1976, when the gold market was weak and the need for foreign exchange high.

In 1974, Italy had a severe balance of payments deficit. Instead of stupidly selling gold, which would have depressed the value of its own reserves, the Italians showed foresight. The Banca d'Italia entered into a deal with West Germany whereby Italy borrowed $2 billion from Germany. The loan was secured by about 16.5 million ounces of gold (at a collateral value of about $120 per ounce). When the balance of payments and the Italian economic situation improved, Italy paid back its loan and still owned the gold. Almost 25 years later, the previously very conservative SNB believes that it has too much gold, or 'excess gold', as it likes to call it. It wants to get rid of a large part of it by 'investing' it, or, in other words, converting it into fiat money such as the dollar or the Euro.

There were other countries that also sold gold, such as Portugal or Costa Rica, but they were in a situation of need. Ever since the era of Salazar, Portugal has been a large owner of gold. Central bank gold reserves have not increased since 1972. It was only in 1980 and 1981 when these institutions, under the influence of the Iranian crisis, became net buyers again. There were also official coins that were minted such as the Krugerrand, the Maple Leaf and coins from countries like Austria, Mexico and even the Russian Tchervonetz.

The Role of Swiss Banks

Swiss banks were the portfolio managers of the world. They operated under a Banking Secrecy Law and they provided the best service. Their staffs were exceptionally trained and multilingual and their managements were conservative. The Swiss had tradition. People from all corners of the world had accounts with Swiss banks, not only the French bourgeoisie and peasants, as Samuelson likes to think.

The typical recommendation of a Swiss bank was that every portfolio should maintain a gold position of at least 10%. There were some banks that recommended as much as 40%. Traditionally, the Swiss themselves were not gold investors because the 100% backing of their currency meant that the Swiss Franc was as good as gold. For the Swiss, therefore, gold was a medium that helped clients from countries with weaker currencies such as the dollar, the pound, and the Italian and Turkish liras.

Also, the portfolio managers were of the generation who had lived through the 1930s, World War II and a number of bear markets. From history, they knew that gold would always survive, and their clients knew that too. This is entirely different from today's situation, where the young, present-day portfolio managers only have experienced bull markets and, therefore, lack the insight of older generations.

It is a fact, however, that the Swiss banks managed a greater part of the world's private portfolios during the late 60s, and, consequently, their bankers' decisions had an overriding effect on the gold market and the price of gold.[33]

The Role of Oil Wealth and OPEC

At the beginning of the 1970s, wage and price inflation soared, leading to lofty energy prices and vice versa. The Arabs were very slow to understand dollar debasement, the currency in which their bills were paid. For a long time they did not understand they had been cheated for years. The paper money they received for their black gold had dwindled in value. In 1973 and 1979, they massively increased their prices to compensate for the increment in the American Consumer Price Index. The sudden quasi quadrupling of the oil price turned many energy producers into megamillionaires in a very short time. In 1973, one barrel of oil bought one bushel of U.S. wheat. In 1980, the same barrel of oil bought nine bushels of U.S. wheat. By the middle of the 1970s, the demand for gold by investors from oil producing countries exploded. Not only individual investors were buying gold, but OPEC nations[34] were also in the market. Timothy Green commented:

> "[the] single most important development in the gold market since 1970 has been gold buying by central banks (or other government institutions) in oil producing nations: Indonesia, Iran, Iraq, Libya, Qatar and Oman have all acquired gold."[35]

The dramatic price increases in 1973 and 1979 delivered considerable shocks to the world's financial systems and economies. The immediate consequence was one of the biggest transfers of wealth in the history of mankind. Had America maintained a stable dollar, there never would have been an OPEC problem.

In his book *The U.S. Dollar- An Advance Obituary*, the late Franz Pick, considered by many as the world's foremost authority on international currencies and monetary affairs at the time, gave an interesting explanation of how one should read government statistics.[36] According to Pick, official price statistics showed only part of the true situation of deteriorating monetary values.

In 1973 OPEC oil exports amounted to 29.5 million barrels per day (bpd). In 1979 exports were only slightly lower with 28.5 million bpd. Revenues, however, jumped from $23.1 billion to $160 billion per year. By applying the official government deflator, OPEC's oil revenues in 1973 amounted to a mere $7.3 billion, based on the 1940 U.S. dollar and rose to only $30.9 billion in 1979. This way, the OPEC price increases looked much more moderate. Pick believed that in order to obtain the true picture, his, unofficial, deflator was more useful. According to him, oil revenues, in unofficial constant 1940-dollars, increased only from $5.1 to $11.2 billion per year.[37]

Because most Arabs did not understand bonds and stocks, they invested their surplus funds in either real estate and/or gold. Since Biblical times, gold has been the best means to keep wealth and to transfer it from generation to generation. Gold, therefore, was the ideal vehicle for them. Furthermore, after their oil reserves are exhausted in the distant future, they would still own gold. And gold, contrary to oil, could never be wasted. A lot of buying by Arab investors passed through the Swiss banks, which they trusted.

Doubtful Computations of Growth or the True Rate of Inflation

In spite of its flaws, the dollar exchange standard of Bretton Woods included a thermometer to indicate the height of fever: the price of gold. It continued to work even if its significance had diminished to a mere fraction of its function under the classical gold standard. The little significance it had, it was still a nuisance for the financial powers in America.

In his *Currency Year Book 1977-1978*, Franz Pick wrote that following the 'golden age' ending with 1914, thousands of full or partial devaluations had taken place.

"Beginning with World War I, and even more since World War II, currency destruction has accelerated and devaluations and depreciations have multiplied, making nonsense out of monetary respectability. – The gigantic economic destruction left by World War II led to inevitable monetary debasement. In the aftermath of the post-war economic recovery and forced expansion, governmental attitudes toward preserving the value of their populations' money have ceased to exist in practically all countries. A more cynical and remorseless interpretation of monetary ethics has become the governmental rule during this generation – all in the name of dubious 'economic growth' and in fear of another Great Depression like that of the 1930s. In the process, the management of currencies has turned into nothing more than expropriation of all those who are unintelligent enough to believe their rulers' propaganda. From Stalin to Carter, currency debasement with subsequent devaluation or depreciation of the unit has become the most doubtful weapon to combat economic slowdown – usually without lasting success.

The real epidemics of monetary demise were generated by the American anti-gold policy that began to ruin the currency systems of the non-communist world. With the establishment of the two-tier gold market in 1968, the world saw a speed-up in the alteration of currency values, including unwanted upvaluations as a defense against Washington's nonstop money printing as well as the beginning of the floating of currencies.........."[38]

Franz Pick believed that America had taken an anti-gold stance ever since 1934 when gold owned by the American public had to be surrendered to the U.S. Treasury at the pre-devaluation price of $20.67 per ounce. Then the gold price was increased to $35.00.

> "America has continued to practice an anti-gold policy – even after gold ownership was made legal at the end of 1974 – to keep people from owning a metal governments cannot master. Whether it has been because of fear or simply not knowing how to handle a gold standard and keep it functioning, or whether the complex was a result of the political illusion that the United States does not need bullion behind its banknote issue, is hard to say."[39]

Pick never minced his words when speaking about currencies. When I mentioned the word 'investment' he would scream at me. To him the word investment no longer existed, because the dollar and all other currencies were doomed. He used to call the dollar a "mini-dollar". In one of the chapters of his book, he spoke about currency circulation, which he referred to as "melting money" and "ghost currency". He complained about people not being interested in the workings of currency and, therefore, not caring to protest the slow expropriation of assets by rising costs of living. [40]

He was a non-conformist in a world that preferred conformists. He said: "Economic expansion and inflation seldom travel parallel roads."[41] Public relations releases via newspapers and television continued to stress the 'growth' of the gross national product without telling the lay masses that, thanks to price inflation, the economy of the country is on a one-way road to annual GNP increases only in nominal terms. The people were not told that all the GNP computations for public consumption, as well as for the so-called "investors" in the stock market, were based on melting monetary values uncorrected to the base year of 1940. Had it been corrected, it would have revealed the extent of the disease and of currency debasement. The reason was simple. The repercussions spreading from a declining economic reputation were taboo in Washington, as they were in Moscow. The prestige of any government would suffer.

Pick thought that the true economic figures were largely masked in official statistics. According to his statistical work, the official figures of the gross national product and the development of personal income did not convey the true picture.

Official personal income per capita showed a healthy increase from 1940 to 1980, but, based on Pick's statistics, it actually had declined.[42]

The sad truth remains that, in spite of all the deficit spending and all the growth in money supply, currency debasement had a negative impact on the much-publicized American standard of living. It actually declined for most, except for those rich enough to be in a position to protect themselves or to benefit from the creation of fiat money. However, he felt that:

> "[The] people of this planet will, in one way or another, continue to survive all the expropriation techniques via inflation that are generated by governments, both elected and non-elected. Whether under such conditions fortunes can be made or conserved still remains one of the most interesting questions of our day. Nevertheless, in the end all paper assets will have lost against gold and silver. The precious metal will have protected purchasing power which the clumsy skills of inept governments have tried to destroy. The official gold stocks of approx. 33,000 metric tons and the unknown, countless metric tons in private hoards will prevail, and could force a return of the yellow metal to its recognized monetary function in the currency system to come."[43]

Now the Whole World Was Buying

The Arabs were not the only clients of Swiss banks. French and German business industrialists, Greek shipping magnates, South American businessmen and politicians, wealthy aristocrats from all over Europe, and small savers belonged to their circle of customers. The biggest buyers of all, however, were the Italians, whose jewelry manufacturers were importing hundreds of tonnes of gold year-after-year, and then transforming that gold into rings, chains, medallions and small bars. These products were then exported all over the world.

By the mid-1990s, Italian gold manufacturing reached approximately 500 tonnes a year. That was about the same volume all South African gold mines were producing annually. Asia, from Turkey to Southeast Asia, was also a heavy buyer. India was a huge market with a prosperous smuggling business existing from Dubai into India. The same was true of Geneva, Beirut and other gold trade centers that were running gold into countries that had import restrictions.

London Fights Back

While the Swiss became the principal destination for physical gold, the situation in London was not all bad. Remembering its traditional colonial ties to every corner of the world, it became the leading gold trading center. Thus London found its new role. Meanwhile, the Swiss were so busy with deliveries that they missed part of the opportunity. It was almost the same situation as in March 1968, when the London bullion houses were too slow to react to the closing of the Gold Pool. London 'good delivery' was of course still, a respected guarantee, but Credit Suisse bars had conquered Asia in the meantime.

It follows that futures trading quickly became a most important activity for bullion houses in the City of London. The London Metal Exchange was soon launching 'products' for trading that made it the magnet of the world, as Timothy Green put it.

The Swiss, however, fought back with another strategy. They started to buy up London brokerage firms to handle part of their international trading business. Later, the Germans, French and Americans entered the scene. So important was the new world of gold that its volume eventually outsized physical volume by far.

The Americans and Their New Approach to Gold

After 40 years of prohibition, Americans were allowed to own gold from January 1, 1975 on. The expected gold rush, for the moment, did not happen. To the contrary, gold was headed for a bear correction that lasted almost two years. Why? Many had bought in anticipation of the American giant entering the market. Americans who understood the circumstances had bought coins, shares and mutual funds, etc., a long time prior. Institutions never bought much.

It was too un-American for people educated at Harvard, Princeton or Berkeley to do such a thing. That was reserved for the fringe. The brainwashing by the followers of such economists as Keynes, Friedman, Samuelson and Galbraith, had left its mark. These men surely knew, or know, the history of sound money. For whatever reasons, they did not pay any attention to its lessons. America was the leading economic power, so why should anybody care? Furthermore, many thought a dollar was still a dollar, although at the height of the dollar crisis, there were a number of instances when American tourists in Europe could not exchange their ailing greenbacks.

Newsletters and investment conferences sprung up everywhere. I went to a few such conferences were I met many well-meaning, patriotic and friendly Americans who had lived through the crisis of the 1930s and the Big War. They were afraid and were, therefore, willing to listen to economic lessons the way they are *not* taught at Harvard, meaning without mathematics and sunglasses, but using common sense. It had become un-American to speak about gold. In Europe the situation was not much different. The older generations of bankers and investment advisors who knew what a gold coin looked like and how it sounded when dropped on a table (it is so much more melodious than aluminum or copper coins), were about to retire.

Another reason why they did not jump on the bandwagon right away was the ailing economy and a stock market that had just gone through a serious bear market. Many stocks lost from 50% to 90% of their 1972 value. The recession that followed, therefore, tended to reduce the public's immediate concern for currency depreciation. In fact, the dollar strengthened.

Temporarily, the public regained some confidence in the dollar. Again, politicians massaged public opinion by declaring that everything was fine. Similar developments took place later in the 1980s, but to a much stronger degree, when, in a disinflationary climate, gold entered a long bear market. Many had also bought for the wrong reason. They bought gold only because they were looking for something that was going up, and that something was not the stock market. Unconcerned as they were about the monetary role of gold in this drama, large purchases were made on margin. Because gold price movements can be very volatile, many were whipsawed or even wiped out with the consequence that they developed an antagonism against gold.

COMEX

Founded in 1933, the New York Commodity Exchange (Comex) is the world's largest metal futures exchange. Its genuine function is to act as a trading arena for buyers and sellers of futures contracts in the metals and financial instruments handled by Comex. It has become the leading gold futures and options exchange ever since its gold futures contract was launched on December 31, 1974. Its volume and worldwide attraction has grown dramatically over the years, but the bulk of the turnover has switched to the over-the-counter market. This is a great danger, because it is much harder to measure volume in such a large market, i.e., there is less public disclosure.

Failure of the Greatest Bear Raid in History

Meanwhile, the U.S. Treasury still thought it was stronger than gold. It announced its first gold auction at about the same time Americans were allowed to buy back what had been taken from them by Roosevelt. In December of 1974, a few days before U.S citizens were permitted to buy gold in any form, official Washington started its historic bear raid. When Nixon closed the gold window in 1971, the U.S. government was afraid of losing more gold. Now, the fear was that an additional appreciation of the gold price would further discredit the fiat dollar.

In the meantime, many Europeans were equally brainwashed and believed in the efficacy of the dollar again. In Europe, it was at least technically possible to buy physical gold. Again, the best-organized market was in Switzerland, where service was perfect in even the smallest branch offices in tiny villages. But there were also many statist hurdles to be overcome in Europe.

In many countries heavy value-added taxes (VAT) were imposed, which discouraged would-be buyers. In America, buying physical gold was not easy. There were so many hindrances that millions of would-be buyers gave up. The bank staff at the teller level was not well trained, but trained enough to discourage customers from buying gold. The public in general had no idea where gold could be bought. Many had never seen a gold coin in their lifetime. In short, buying gold was made very difficult. Even Paul Volcker did not know where to buy gold. One day he asked John Exter, former central banker and director of ASA, "John, where do you buy your gold coins?"

In a publication by the AIER *Why Gold?* by Ernest P. Welker, the bear raid and its failure are very well described:

> "Beginning in 1975, the United States, aided by the principal members of the International Monetary Fund (IMF), began a 'bear raid' on the gold market of the world. It was a raid of unprecedented proportions and duration. The underlying purpose of this raid was to convince the citizens of the major nations that paper currencies are better than gold. Success of the operation would ensure that inflating by excessive issues of paper currencies could continue indefinitely."[44]

Every effort was made to convince the public that gold is a barbaric relic, outmoded by the ingenuity of man in devising new, 'rational' monetary systems.

Some economists predicted that gold would prove to be nearly worthless in the absence of an official demand for monetary purposes. Some observers suggested figures near $25 per ounce as the probable equilibrium price for gold based on non-monetary demand.

Monetary officials had good reason to devise and implement their bear raid. During 1973 and 1974, general prices increased in double-digit rates in most countries, and the price of gold rose more than 200%. There was talk in this period about the possibility of runaway inflation, a flight from currency, and a collapse of international monetary arrangements.

In January 1975, the first gold auction took place. Two million ounces were sold. In June of the same year a second auction took place with half a million ounces sold.

In August 1975, and in a further move to demonetize gold, the Group of 10 (G-10) leading industrial nations and Switzerland decided that official reserves of the G-10 and the IMF should not be increased. To the contrary, it was decided that the IMF gold stock should be decreased by 50 million ounces, of which 25 million ounces were to be sold over a four-year period. The first auction took place on June 2, 1976, and the last on May 7, 1980.

But gold was stronger. After having reached a low of $103.50, it started its historic upward move reaching a level of $430 in September of 1979.

The Dramatic Coup by Dresdner Bank

However, the decisive breaking of the $400 price level occurred when the Dresdner Bank made a bid for the whole allocation at the U.S. Treasury auction in August 1979. This hit like a bombshell and the gold bull market then entered a manic phase. That this would be the final explosion, and from then on the notion that something was wrong with the irrational behavior of the bullion price was confirmed by the warnings received from the gold share market. The gold share market as a leading indicator had already entered a correction phase.

Official Gold Auctions Fail

Even after an increase from 300,000 to 750,000 ounces per auction, the U.S. Treasury could not stop the uninterrupted bull market in gold. Only when the Treasury announced in November of 1978 that it would again increase the amount to be sold in December to 1,500,000 ounces, did the market react with a small correction of the up-trend.

This was, indeed, a war of major proportions. In January 1980, the price of gold reached an historic high of around $850! The public had become fearful about what governments were doing to their money. It took people many years to wake up, and, when they finally did, no force could stop the power of gold.

The Treasury's Retreat

On October 16, 1979, the Treasury announced it would discontinue its regularly scheduled gold auctions. The Treasury never expected the price to soar to $850. At the same time it was announced that the regular auctions would be replaced by 'surprise auctions' whenever the experts in Washington felt there was a need for 'orderly markets.'

In its publication *Why Gold?*, the AIER[45] assumed that the U.S Treasury would always operate in the gold market, directly or through intermediaries, for the purpose of discouraging 'speculators' whenever a marked rise in the price of gold appeared to endanger the acceptability of the fiat dollar. The Treasury had thus operated in the foreign-exchange markets on behalf of the dollar and would presumably not hesitate to act similarly in the gold market.

$850 Gold Was Too High.
The Iranian Crisis and the Hunt Brothers

It would have been far better for the price of gold to settle around a price between $400 - $430. Considering that, at $35 per ounce, gold was undervalued for a long time, this would have corresponded to the loss of purchasing power of the dollar since WW II. Instead it reached $510 by Christmas of 1979, and then a panic hit the market driving gold up to $850 by the second week in January of 1980.

One of the major reasons for the last spike was the Iranian crisis. In late 1979, Iranian student Revolutionary Guards stormed the American Embassy in Tehran taking U.S. diplomats as hostages. At about the same time, religious fanatics temporarily seized the Grand Mosque in Mecca. Both events created fears of another Middle East crisis leading to a new oil crisis.

In November 1979, the U.S. government acted promptly by freezing Iran's gold at the Federal Reserve in New York. While the actions of the Iranians were an act of lawlessness, the American action was no less so. Immediately the central banks of the world realized that their gold at Fort Knox was not completely secure. It was preferable to buy gold and then move it to its own vaults than leaving it within reach of a foreign power. With its assets frozen, Iran became so scared that it started to buy gold in Zurich. Iraq, with its oil wealth, was another major buyer. This was precisely the spark that was needed to get the price of gold over $800 within a matter of a few weeks.

Silver Bonanza

In his book *The Silver Bulls,* Paul Sarnoff wrote:

> "In 1973 the Hunt Brothers from Texas with numerous friends, among them the House of Saud, began stockpiling silver in all its marketable forms and even tried to corner the market. Bunker Hunt's passion for silver paralleled Baron von Thyssen's compulsion to acquire old master paintings. In both cases the mania went beyond the urge to amass ever larger fortunes."[46]

The Hunts are said to have started buying silver when it was around $1.60 per ounce. In the summer of 1980, well after the silver collapse, they had 63 million ounces (*Fortune*, August 11, 1980). The buying led to a vigorous price move and reached its peak in early 1980. The daily setting of new record silver prices not only stimulated speculation in the white metal, but also had an influence on the price of gold. Then the price collapsed dramatically from a high of $48 per ounce down to $10.80 per ounce within seven weeks. In his book *The Restless Metal*, Prof. Roy Jastram points out that silver has been erratic since 1875.[47]

At the top of the market in January of 1980, the Hunts could have liquidated their position for a multi-billion dollar profit. But they did not. The Hunts were struck an almost mortal blow in January 1980, when the Comex changed its rules, barring them and their associates from buying silver by instituting 'liquidation only' trading.

There is no doubt that both events, the Iranian crisis and the silver adventure of the Hunts, greatly influenced the gold market and vice versa, with all the negative side effects that are common to dramas of this kind.

The Wisdom of Eastern People

In the 1970s, people of the East bought a lot of gold. In the Middle East, buying gold has a tradition spanning thousands of years. When the oil shock came, massive hoarding started. Other big buyers were to be found on the Indian sub-continent, Southeast Asia and East Asia. As much as these people loved gold, they were also highly price sensitive. When the West and central banks were still falling over each other to buy gold at the top of the bull market, the East quietly started selling. In the end, however, the dishoarding of gold in all forms reached proportions which were almost impossible to handle, either by the dealers or the refineries, sending the price down to under $600 per ounce in a very short time.

Eastern central banks, however, and contrary to the famous man in the street, did not show as much wisdom. The Bank of Japan and The Bank of Taiwan, with reserves of hundreds of billions in fiat dollars, held only tiny gold reserves compared to the large gold holdings of the Western countries. (Twenty years later this still holds true for Japan and Taiwan.) Thus they were cheated, as were the Arabs when they sold their oil for irredeemable paper tickets.

Perennial Purchasing Power of Gold vs. Paper Money

In his book *The Golden Constant –The English and American Experience 1560 – 1976*, American Professor Roy Jastram demonstrated the impressive qualities of gold as a store of value. Its purchasing power has remained almost constant over hundreds of years. For example, the purchasing power of gold in the mid-twentieth century was almost identical to that of the seventeenth century.

> "Nevertheless, gold maintains its purchasing power over long periods of time, for example, half-century intervals. The amazing aspect of this conclusion is that this is not because gold eventually moves toward commodity prices but because commodity prices return to gold."[48]

In the years after World War II under the system of the gold exchange standard, the annual rise of the CPI (Consumer Price Index) in the U.S. was close to 1% in most years until 1965. Only in 1956 and 1957 did it stray with the CPI rising 2.9% in 1956 and 3.0% in 1957. During the Johnson presidency in 1966, inflation increased greatly as a result of financing the Vietnam War. The CPI went up by 3.4%. In 1970 it rose by 5.5% until it reached a level of 15% in 1980, when things really got out of control under the Carter administration in almost every respect.

It was not surprising that Americans started to vote by buying gold in whatever form they were legally allowed to do so.

End of the 1970s and End of the Great Bull Market in Gold

The rise of the price of gold to $850 in January 1980 was, of course, far beyond any reason. However, after the inflationary 1970s, the world seemed to be on the verge of a disaster with a very uncertain economic future ahead. All of this would never have happened if the world had returned to a gold standard. This is the tragedy of our time that has led to crises and wars. It is the consequence of giving up sound money – of giving up gold.

The 1970s were the decade in which the U.S. government, the Treasury and the Fed tried to defeat gold. It was a bitter war and an unnecessary fight. The damage will one day be described in history books. But, it ended with a victory for gold.

There is another conclusion that one day will be drawn from the monetary drama. Mr. Ray Vicker, Chief European Correspondent of *The Wall Street Journal*, wrote on May 16, 1973:

> "Instead of fighting gold as an evil metal to cut from the monetary system at all costs, America should be examining how to use gold to further its own interests.
>
> [...] It does seem that American policy makers should be paying more attention to how gold could be utilized as an ally of American policy rather than to waste any more time fighting it as if it were a monetary cancer to be removed."[49]

America is the second most important gold producer. The country would clearly benefit from a prosperous gold mining industry; so would many other industries and the economy as a whole, not to speak of the other gold producing countries and, thus, the world.

Part IV: Gold Rush and Gold War

[1] Conversation with author, February 2, 2000.
[2] *"Das Gold ist der Souverän aller Souveräns,"* Democritus, as quoted in Karl Peltzer, *Das treffende Zitat*, 6th edition, (Thun, Switzerland: Ott Verlag, 1976), 291.
[3] Timothy S. Green, *The New World of Gold* (London: Rosendale Press, 1993), 130.
[4] Ibid., 116.
[5] Richard M. Salsman, *Gold and Liberty*, (Great Barrington, MA: American Institute for Economic Research, 1995), 73.
[6] Ibid., 76.
[7] Ibid., 76.
[8] Don Hoppe, *How to Invest in Gold Stocks*, (New York: Arlington House, 1972), 548/549. Extract from the Executive Statement, 15 August, 1971.
[9] John Exter, "The US and the World are ...", *Blakely's Investment Review*, vol. 1, no. 1 (1989), 4.
[10] Richard M. Salsman, *Gold and Liberty*, (Great Barrington, MA: American Institute for Economic Research, 1995), 76.
[11] see various articles:

Steve H. Hanke, "IMF Money Buys Trouble in Russia", *The Wall Street Journal*, 30 April, 1992;
"An IMF Victim", *The Wall Street Journal*, May 8, 1992;
Scott C. Antel, "The IMF's Advice May be Worse Than None at All", *The Wall Street Journal*, April 10, 1997;
William E. Simon, "Abolish the IMF", *The Wall Street Journal*, 24 October, 1997;
"Monetary Leadership", *The Wall Street Journal*, 3 November, 1997;
James K. Glassman, "The IMF Only Gets in the Way", *The International Herald Tribune*, 10 October 1997;
Robert M. Bleiberg, "Good Money After Bad", *Barron's*, 1 August, 1983; also:
Anna J. Schwarz, R. Christopher Whalen and Walker F. Todd, *Time to Abolish the International Monetary Fund*, (Greenwich, CT: CMRE, 1988);
Alan Reynolds, *The IMF's Destructive Recipe of Devaluation and Austerity*, (Indianapolis, IN: Hudson Institute, 1992).

[12] Don Hoppe, *How to Invest in Gold Stocks*, (New York: Arlington House, 1972), 189.

[13] Ibid.

[14] Johnathan R. Laing, "The Next Meltdown? Fears Grow that Derivatives Pose a Big Threat", *Barron's*, 7 June, 1993, 10ff.

[15] Alan Greenspan, speeches at the International Conference of Banking Supervisors, Stockholm, Sweden, June, 1996 and at the Catholic University of Louvain, Belgium, January, 1997.

[16] Carl Menger, *Grundsätze der Volkswirtschaft* (Vienna: Wilhelm Braumüller, 1871), 250ff; English translation: Carl Menger, *Principles of Economics* (New York: NYU Press, 1981).

[17] Carl Menger, "The Origin of Money", *Economic Journal*, vol. 2 (1892): 243.

[18] Antal E. Fekete, introduction to "The Origin of Money", (Greenwich, CT: Committee for Monetary Research & Education, 1984), 17.

[19] Ludwig von Mises, "Wilhelm Roepke, RIP", *National Review*, vol. XVIII, no. 10 (1966): 200.

[20] Wilhelm Roepke, *Die Lehre von der Wirtschaft*, 8th edition (Erlenbach, Switzerland: Eugen Rentsch Verlag, 1958), 77.

[21] John Exter, "The International Means of Payment" in *Inflation and Monetary Crisis*, ed. G. C. Wiegand (Washington, DC: Public Affairs Press, 1975), 137.

[22] Ibid., 137.

[23] James Dines, *The Invisible Crash* (New York: Random House, 1977), 271.

[24] Paul E. Samuelson, *Economics* (New York: McGraw-Hill, 1973), 722.

[25] From *The Pocket Money Book*, (Great Barrington, MA: AIER, 1994).
On December 30, 1969, in a reversal of policy, the 'two-tier' market was established. The IMF announced an agreement to purchase newly mined South African gold—thereby establishing a method for increasing the world's official stock of monetary gold—at $35 per ounce if the market fell any lower than $35. The agreement also provided that the South African central bank could sell gold

on the free market from its official reserves in order to meet foreign exchange requirements, regardless of the free market price.

On December 7, 1973, the IMF terminated its agreement to purchase gold from South Africa at the request of South African officials, so that the country could meet its foreign exchange needs. Presumably, the arrangement had not been used for some time, because South Africa was able to sell gold on the open market at a price higher than the $35 the IMF had promised to pay. (10)

[26] Ibid., 722-724.

[27] Ibid.

[28] James Dines, *The Invisible Crash* (New York: Random House, 1977) 458/9.

[29] Ibid., 403.

[30] Timothy Green, *The New World of Gold* (New York: Walker and Company, 1981), 183.

[31] Ibid.

[32] On July 11, 1974, the Group of Ten decided to permit gold (at market-related prices) to be used as collateral for loans between official institutions. *The Pocket Money Book* (13).

[33] See also the chapter on "The Swiss Portfolio" in Green, *The New World of Gold*, 206/7.

[34] OPEC (Organization of Petroleum Exporting Countries), a trade organization of thirteen oil producing countries headquartered in Vienna, was founded in 1960 to offset the cartel of leading oil companies and to fix a common oil policy.

[35] Timothy Green, *The New World of Gold*, 182.

[36] Franz Pick, *The U.S. Dollar – An Advance Obituary* (New York: Pick Publishing Corporation, 1981), 39.

[37] Ibid.

[38] Franz Pick, *Currency Yearbook 1977 –1979*, New York, Pick Publishing: 1981, page 28.

[39] Ibid., 69/70.

[40] Page 30.

[41] Ibid.

[42] Franz Pick, *The U.S. Dollar – An Advance Obituary*, 33-35.

[43] Franz Pick, *The U.S. Dollar – An Advance Obituary*, 11.

[44] Ernest P. Welker, *Why Gold?* (Great Barrington, MA: AIER, 1981), 33.

[45] Ibid., 33/34.

[46] Paul Sarnoff, *The Silver Bulls* (Westport, CT: Arlington House, 1980), 3.

[47] Roy Jastram, *SILVER: The Restless Metal* (New York: John Wiley & Sons, 1977), 69.

[48] Roy Jastram, *The Golden Constant* (New York: John Wiley & Sons, 1977), 132/189.

[49] Ray Vicker, *The Wall Street Journal*, 16 May, 1973, as quoted in James Dines, *The Invisible Crash*, 118.

Part V: The Not So Golden 1980s

"Though it [paper money] has no intrinsic value, yet by limiting the quantity, its value in exchange is as great as an equal denomination of coins, or of bullion in that coin. [...] Experience, however, shows that neither state nor a bank ever had the unrestricted power without abusing that power; in all states, therefore, the issue of paper money ought to be under some check and control and none seems so proper for that purpose as that of subjecting the issuers of paper money to the obligation of paying their notes either in gold coin or bullion."[1]

David Ricardo, Economist (1817)

Gold Enters a Long Bear Market

A price of over $800 was not sustainable and, while the price of silver was collapsing, gold fell back to $475. For the next ten years, gold fluctuated between roughly $300 and $500. Whenever there was a political or financial crisis, gold would shoot up to about $500, and, when the shock was over, it would settle back to about $300. This level was reached twice, first in 1982 and then again at the beginning of 1985.

The last time gold reached a level of $500 was in December 1987 following the October crash of 1987, but that was nothing more than a rally in a bear market.

Change at the Fed

During the last years of the Carter presidency, the situation deteriorated on all fronts. Inflation was out of control. Then, in 1979, Paul Volcker became Chairman of the Fed. For a while the inflationary process continued, but then Mr. Volcker started to raise interest rates. In the meantime, Ronald Reagan had become President. Within a very short period, Volcker succeeded in limiting the decline in the purchasing power of the dollar. His strategy resulted in more stable prices at home and improved exchange rates in the international currency markets. According to the October 4, 1999 issue of *Barron's,* Volcker had managed to bring inflation down from 14% to the 3 – 4% range before he handed the reins over to Alan Greenspan in 1987.[2] Bond yields also fell sharply, from a peak of about 15% for long-term Treasuries to below 6%, and the prime rate, the base for many bank lending rates, came down to 8% from a peak of 21% in late 1980.

More Conservative World Economic Management

At the end of the 1970s and in the beginning of the 1980s, there were many similarities between the American and the British economies. Both nations seemed to be in for a major decline. Politically however, there was a strong move to conservatism in both countries, or at least there seemed to be. There were striking parallels between the 1920s and the 1980s. Both decades had conservative governments in power. Both decades saw wealth and business glamorized, and politics took a conservative turn with Republican presidents in the White House. In the 1980s it was Ronald Reagan in the United States and Margaret Thatcher in the United Kingdom.

In both decades, the 1920s and the 1980s, major tax cuts extended credit booms by raising the after-tax return to lenders. In the 1920s, U.S. personal income tax rates were cut to 25%. In the 1980s, they were cut from 70% to 28%! In both the twenties and the eighties, consumption spending fuelled by debt was the main engine of growth. As an economic historian wrote about the twenties:

> "The public had gone into debt on a large scale to finance purchases of homes, (and) consumer durables. [...] In both decades, job growth was in services, not manufacturing. Both decades gave rise to the conviction that prosperity was now permanent and even that there might never be another recession."[3]

There were many similarities, but there were also many differences. More from the same source:

"In the twenties, the United States was the world's leading creditor. In the eighties, it was the world's largest debtor. The Federal government of the U.S.A. had a budget surplus each year from 1920 through 1930. From 1980 through 1990, the United States ran massive deficits. The national debt was reduced by more than 33 percent during the twenties. It increased by 342 percent during the eighties. In the twenties, the United States ran a significant trade surplus. In the eighties, it ran the largest deficit of any trading nation in the history of the world."[4]

In many ways the 1980s were a decade of excess. The impact of these excesses worked, and continues to work, itself through the system, particularly in the form of an enormous build up of debt. For many years, debt in the U.S., not to speak of the world, has been rising faster than the GNP. This is particularly serious because the dollar is considered the world's reserve currency.

The U.S. Gold Commission

In 1981, President Reagan, who was a believer in the gold standard, asked Congress to form a Gold Commission. Reagan was worried about the rates of price inflation, interest and unemployment, which had reached unbearable levels. More and more, some people began to ask whether a gold standard could end the financial crisis. The 17-member study group amassed huge files on the workings of the gold standard and the use of gold as a monetary metal. As was to be expected, the composition of the panel was rigged in such a way that instead of studying gold, it decided to ban gold forever from the so-called monetary system. Out of the seventeen members on the panel, only two (Dr. Ron Paul, Congressman from Texas, and businessman Lewis Lehrman) were in favor of gold.[5]

Gold Production in the 1980s

High gold prices and modernized mining techniques resulted in a sharp rise of the Western World's gold production. This occurred at a time when central banks were no longer buyers, and confidence in paper currency was making a comeback. During the 1980s, yearly production rose from 962 tonnes in 1980 to 1,746 tonnes in 1990. In 1980, South Africa was by far the largest producer with 70% or 675 tonnes. Ten years later, its share had shrunk to around 37%, while the U.S. recorded a dramatic eightfold increase to 259 tonnes. Australia, the third largest producer, experienced a more than twelve-fold increase to 197 tonnes, and Canada, fourth on the list, sported a 300% increase to 158 tonnes.

According to Michael Kile in his book *The Case for Gold in the 1990s*, the most remarkable development of the decade was on the demand side in the capacity of international markets – particularly the jewelry and investment segments – to absorb the record production and, thereby, to provide significant price stability.[6] This situation became increasingly important as Swiss portfolio managers started to sell gold in their clients' portfolios until most portfolios contained no gold at all. During the entire period of the 80s, the propaganda claiming that gold was demonetized continued.

Gold as Jewelry and its Significance for the Gold Mining Industry

In his essay "The Near Death & Resurrection of the Gold Mining Industry," Dr. Lawrence Parks of the Foundation for the Advancement of Monetary Education (FAME), New York, came to interesting conclusions. The gold producing industry in its present predicament would do well to heed and to rethink present strategies:

> "The gold-as-jewelry strategy has not helped. The amount of gold fabricated into jewelry is a *contrary* indicator of the well-being of the gold producers. More gold fabricated into jewelry corresponds with a *lower* price for gold, *lower* profits for gold producers, and a *lower* market capitalization of their companies. [...] It is noteworthy that since 1987 (the year when the World Gold Council began operation) jewelry offtake and the price of gold have had consistent and significant *negative* correlations

116

for more than 14 years. Whenever the price of gold decreased jewelry offtake increased, and vice versa. Either way, especially in light of these high negative correlations, the clear implication is that promoting gold jewelry will not be profitable for the producers. [...] When the gold price is perceived cheap, more of it is fabricated into jewelry. If gold demand for higher-value use increases, then the gold price increases, and gold demand for jewelry fabrication falls off. [...] Whatever the higher-value use of gold is, *that* is the market the producers should concentrate on; *not* jewelry fabrication, which, as the data confirms, is a lower-value use."[7]

How did the producers respond to lower gold prices?

Lawrence Parks:

"As the gold price has drifted lower over the past years, the response of the gold producers has been an *engineering* response. The producers have been very innovative in finding new ways to get gold out of the ground ever more efficiently, and they have been very resourceful in finding new reserves. But despite their superb technological and prospecting achievements, they have not been rewarded, and neither have their shareholders."[8]

It seems to me, however, that not all of the jewelry offtake is low-value jewelry demand. A large part of the Asian demand is for high carat jewelry with relatively low workmanship. It is primarily destined for investment purposes.

On December 29, 1989, the last fixing of the year was US$ 401 / oz.

Part V: The Not So Golden 1980s

[1] David Ricardo, *Complete Works*, ed. Piero Sraffa. (Cambridge: Cambridge UP, 1966).
[2] William Pesek, "Happy Anniversary, *Barron's*, v.79 issue 40 4 October 1999, 28-30
[3] James Dale Davidson and William Rees-Mogg, *The Great Reckoning* (New York: Summit Books, 1991), 143.
[4] Ibid.
[5] Ron Paul and Lewis Lehrmann, *The Case for Gold – A Minority Report of the U.S. Gold Commission* (Washington, DC: Cato Institute, 1982).
[6] Michael Kile, *The Case for Gold in the 1990s*. (Perth: Gold Corporation, 1991), 12.
[7] Lawrence Parks, "The Near Death & Resurrection of the Gold Mining Industry" (New York, FAME, 2000). (See www.fame.org)
[8] Ibid.

Part VI: The Gold War of the 1990s

John Law, the Man Who Ruined France, and the 1990s

"He succeeded in reaching the Continent, where he traveled for three years, and devoted much of his attention to the monetary and banking affairs of the countries through which he passed. [...] He soon became intimately acquainted with the extent of trade and resources of each, and daily more confirmed his opinion that no country could prosper without paper money.

[...] Law seized every opportunity to instill his financial doctrines into the mind of one whose proximity to the throne pointed him out as destined, at no distant date, to play an important part in the government.

[...] When Law presented himself at the court, he was most cordially received. He offered two memorials to the regent, in which he set forth the evils that had befallen France, owing to an insufficient currency, at different times depreciated. He asserted that a metallic currency, unaided by a paper money was wholly inadequate to the wants of a commercial country [...] He used many sound arguments on the subject of credit and proposed that he should be allowed to set up a bank, which should have the management of the royal revenues, and issue notes both on that and on landed security...

[...] He made all his notes payable at sight and in the coin current at the time they were issued. This last was a master-stroke of policy, and immediately rendered his notes more valuable than the precious metals.

[…] Every day the value of the old shares increased, and the fresh applications, induced by the golden dreams of the whole nation, became so numerous that it was deemed advisable to create no less than three hundred thousand new shares. […] Law was now at the zenith of his prosperity, and the people were rapidly approaching the zenith of their infatuation. […] People of every age and sex and condition in life speculated in the rise and fall of the Mississippi bonds.

[…] The price of shares sometimes rose ten or twenty per cent in the course of a few hours, and many persons in the humbler walks of life, who had risen poor in the morning, went to bed in affluence.

The warnings of the Parliament, that too great a creation of paper money would, sooner or later, bring the country to bankruptcy were disregarded. The regent who knew nothing whatever of the philosophy of finance, thought that a system which had produced such good effects could never be carried to excess.

[…] One year later, in 1720:

But the alarm once sounded, no art could make the people feel the slightest confidence in paper, which was not exchangeable into metal. M. Lambert, the president of the parliament of Paris, told the regent to his face that he would rather have a hundred thousand livres in gold and silver than five million in the notes of his bank.

[…] John Law was neither knave nor madman, but one more deceived than deceiving, more sinned against than sinning. He was thoroughly acquainted with the philosophy and true principles of credit. He understood the monetary question better than any man of his day; and if his system fell with a crash so tremendous, it was not so much his fault as that of the people amongst whom he had erected it."[1]

What Were the Reasons for
Gold's Weakness in the Late 1990s?

Annual new mine production of gold in 1999 was approximately 2,500 tonnes, or about the same as in 1998, and also as projected for 2000. Demand for gold was at over 4,000 tonnes annually. How is it possible that the gold price weakens year after year when there is a strong and growing demand for the metal?

How is it possible that, over a period of months, if not years, the gold price in New York closes lower than the London fixing of the day? One daily aspect of gold price manipulation is that last-hour and last-minute selling in New York regularly counteracts any price increase overseas.[2] How is it possible that the New York bullion dealers ridicule London bullion houses day after day? When is New York's control over the price of gold going to stop? What will put an end to this peculiar situation?

Was a Booming Stock Market the Culprit?

After an inflationary period that persisted for 36 years, inflation in the U.S. peaked in 1981. Commodities and interest rates hit new highs. Bonds were the buy of a generation. In 1982, the greatest bull market in common stocks began, carrying the Dow Jones Industrial Average from around 800 to over 11,000, representing a gain of about 1,400%.

During this period, a lot of corporate restructuring took place. The trend towards globalization of world equity markets made for a very favorable environment for stocks. Stocks became extremely popular and thousands of new mutual funds were formed. The first signs of a mania, causing the biggest one-day bust in the history of the U.S. stock market, appeared in October of 1987. The setback was, however, short-lived and aggressive monetary policies helped recapture lost ground. From then on, the public came to believe that the deflationary trend would not last forever and that, in order to preserve capital, it was better to allocate one's savings to common stock rather than to any other asset.

These developments were highly unfavorable for precious metal investments – at least until 1999, when most commodity prices bottomed out and began to recover, indicating that there was another inflationary cycle in the wings. This was most apparent in crude oil prices, which bottomed in December 1998 and since have more than tripled.

While a deflationary environment with a booming stock market is certainly not the ideal base for gold demand, it is, nevertheless, hard to understand most of gold's price weakness throughout the decade. Almost all of the reasons that made the stock market go up could also be considered positive for gold. There was ample liquidity in the system, and currency debasement was still with us. A price of $400 to $450 seemed to be justified when considering the loss of purchasing power the dollar had suffered since World War II. Furthermore and contrary to the 1980s, gold demand started to outpace new mine supply in the early 1990s.

The following reasons help explain part of the behavior of the gold price:

1. Portfolio disinvestment, particularly by Swiss banks, until most portfolios contained no gold;
2. A deflationary economic environment;
3. The stock market boom, making stocks a major competitor; and
4. The huge overhang and central banks selling/leasing of gold.
5. A demographic shift in gold ownership. Gold is an older person's investment. When these people pass on, their heirs dump the gold; a development that probably also took place in France.

While the first, the second and the fifth reason are facts, the two other points are unlikely to pass serious analysis. There is, however, no reason why gold should not do well in a period when stock prices are rising, although rising stock markets will always be interpreted as being based on the effectiveness of the fiat money system. Forces that have a positive effect on stocks, such as a lenient money policy and a rapidly growing money supply, should also be positive for gold.

122

This leaves culprit no. 4 – the central banks. This reason is not fully satisfactory. We need to look at it, because the central banks are important holders of gold. However, their percentage of total world gold stock has dwindled and continues to do so. Prior to 1971, all newly-mined gold not worked into jewelry went into the coffers of central banks. From that date on, central banks became net sellers, albeit at a small level.

Yet, the central banks' role as sellers has consistently been exaggerated. Most of their sales, which are usually handled by the BIS, found their way into the coffers of other central banks. Gold sales had a mostly negative effect because of the concomitant damaging media noise, and not because of the amount of gold offered. Central banks were also becoming less and less of a threat, because there had been an important increase in gold ownership in the private sector. Something that still holds true. While 50 years ago 70% of the world's gold was held by central banks, today their share is less than 25%.

Beginning with the early 1990s, my analysis of the gold market has been wrong more often than right, although I always diligently collected all information available. I could not understand why the price of gold, in view of the improved supply and demand situation, did not climb but remained in a depressed state. I, therefore, began looking for an explanation, and it took me a long time until I found what I believe are the new forces at work.

Was It the Central Banks?

On February 6, 1996, I visited J. Aron & Co, a well-established bullion firm in London. It is a subsidiary of the prestigious Wall Street firm Goldman, Sachs & Company. Robert Rubin, its former CEO, was serving as U.S. Secretary of the Treasury at that time. Rubin has since resigned from his post. A Johannesburg stockbroker, Merton Black of Ivor Roy Jones, now owned by the Deutsche Bank group, introduced me to J. Aron & Co. I had a meeting that day with Neil R. Newitt, Managing Director, and Philip Culliford, Executive Director.

Although I had never met these gentlemen before, they knew my name and were very open with me. Culliford saw a strong demand for bullion on the part of U.S. funds, but little demand from the Middle East. Newitt was outright bearish on gold and said that the central banks would stop any increase in the price of gold. Having been active in the gold market since 1968, he was in regular contact with central banks and seemed to know what he was talking about. However, he thought that of the 35,000 tonnes of central bank gold holdings only a small portion, approximately 3,500 tonnes, could be loaned out or sold. The conclusion drawn from the discussion was that there could be no doubt that the central banks were controlling the price.

I left quite puzzled and still wondering why central banks would have an interest in keeping down the price of their only asset of value? Afterwards, I visited Deutsche Morgan Grenfell, where Robert Weinberg told me that the firm of J. Aron was very active in the gold lending business. For this reason they were very interested in forward sales by gold mining companies. Weinberg also mentioned that Newitt was known for being notoriously bearish about the price of gold. This was understandable since he knew what was happening.

After leaving the Goldman Sachs subsidiary, it was still not clear to me why the central banks should want to keep the price of gold low. As sellers, it would appear to be normal to try to sell at the highest possible price. In the business world, it is the buyer who is interested in a low price for goods he wants to acquire.

Because central banks are responsible for managing assets belonging to the people of their respective countries, such irresponsible behavior is hard to understand. One result of my visit, however, was, that I realized that the gentlemen at J. Aron, who were acting for central banks, undoubtedly had better information and advance knowledge that easily could be exploited. What I did not yet realize was that these were the people who actually advised the central banks.

It is Not Only the Central Banks!

And so I found out, unfortunately belatedly, who had the biggest interest in keeping the gold price down, or at least unchanged. It was not the central banks—it was the bullion banks. Commission business had become more important to them than a stable currency system. The bankers are at the horns of a dilemma here. They reap their profits due to volatility of the market. If there were monetary stability, their revenues would decline, at least in this sector of activity. In the end, it is the banks that are in control of the monetary system. They *are* the monetary system.

For years commission-hungry bullion dealers were busy spreading rumors and fear that the price of gold could go only one way—south. Year-in, year-out, bullion dealers predicted lower and lower gold prices in an attempt to capture the producer business. Who knows how big their own short positions were?

Central banks and several big governments make gold unstable

At a conference organized by the World Gold Council in Paris on November 19, 1999, Robert Mundell, Professor at Columbia University and 1999 Nobel Prize Laureate in Economics, made the following remarks during the question and answer session after his speech on the "The International Monetary System at the Turn of the Millennium":

> "Gold is subject to a lot of elements of instability, not the least of which is the attempt on the part of several big governments to make it unstable. [...] If you notice what happened in the past 20 years in government policy in respect to gold, nobody sold gold when the price was soaring to $800 an ounce. It would have been a good deal and it would have been stabilizing if they would have done so. But people sell it when it hits bottom; the British have been selling gold now that it seems to have hit the very bottom. [So do the Swiss! – auth.]. That element – governments selling when the price is low or not selling when the price is high – makes it destabilizing. Governments should [...] buy low and sell high."[3]

125

So what do governments actually want if they are guilty of destabilizing or capping the price of gold? They simply want to maintain the funny money illusion.

Major Changes in Central Bank Activities in the 1990s vs. the 1970s

One purpose of this book is to inform and to draw attention to a number of significant changes and developments in central bank activities and their influence on the gold markets and the world economy. The theoretical role of an independent central bank is to protect the integrity of the currency of its country. At least that is what the public is told. The true role of central banks, especially the Federal Reserve, is to liquify bank balance sheets when they become impaired. They are the so-called 'lenders of last resort' – a bailout facility. Time and again, fiat currencies have collapsed all over the world. The examples of Russia, Mexico, Indonesia, Thailand, South Korea, Turkey and elsewhere have proven that sufficiently, yet the central banks continue.

The late Professor Murray Rothbard explained the crucial role of pro-central bank propaganda for public consumption as follows:

"The official legend claims that a central bank is necessary to curb the commercial bank's unfortunate tendency to over-expand, such booms giving rise to subsequent busts. An 'impartial' central bank, on the other hand, driven as it is by the public interest, could and would restrain the banks from their natural narrow and selfish tendency to make profits at the expense of the public weal. The stark fact that it was the bankers themselves who were making this argument was supposed to attest to their nobility and altruism.

In fact, as we have seen, the banks desperately desired a central bank, not to place fetters on their natural tendency to inflate, but, on the contrary, to enable them to inflate and expand together without incurring the penalties of market competition. As a 'lender of last resort', the central bank could permit and encourage them to inflate when they would ordinarily have to contract their loans in order to save themselves. In short, the real reason for the adoption of the Federal Reserve, and its promotion by the large banks, was the exact opposite of their loudly trumpeted motivations. Rather than create an institution to curb their own profits on behalf of public interest, the banks sought a central bank to enhance their profits by permitting them to inflate far beyond the bounds set by free-market competition."[4]

Under the gold standard of the nineteenth century, there were natural restraints to inflation because of the rules of the automatism. Governments and the business community understood how to live with the fact that the over-creation of money would be penalized with a loss of gold. Gold would start to flow out of the country, leading to an 'automatic' tightening of the money supply and a rise in the price of money until the rules of balanced budgets and sound finance were observed again. Gold acted as a natural curb, and there was no need for central banks.

This makes it evident why not only the central banks, but also the commercial banks hate gold. They dislike gold, because the price of gold is the thermometer measuring the amount of leverage they employ. It indicates when restraint is needed. The gold standard demanded discipline. Under the present funny money system, discipline is not necessary and not really desired because there is always the 'lender of last resort'. This is the reason why politicians and the banking system do not want to return to a gold standard and why central banks want to get rid of gold. It is because the 'lender of last resort' function and the gold standard are not compatible.

Activities of the World Gold Council (WGC)

The WGC has published a number of studies on central bank gold policies and the gold market, providing a good insight into some aspects of the "New World of Gold". Some examples are:

- *The Changing Monetary Role of Gold*
- *Central Banking in the 1990s – Asset Management and the Role of Gold*
- *Derivative Markets and the Role of Gold*
- *The Gold Borrowing Market – A Decade of Growth*
- *Utilization of the Borrowed Gold by the Mining Industry – Developments and Future Prospects.*

The WGC is an organization set up and financed by the gold mining industry to promote gold around the world. While the WGC publishes studies and occasionally organizes public conferences, its motives remain unclear as it promotes gold mainly in the form of jewelry. In essence, jewelry is a low-value marginal use of gold. The jewelry industry has a vested interest in a low gold price.

Since 1987, the year the WGC began operating, it has been promoting gold jewelry. The WGC hardly ever speaks about the store-of-value function of gold and never about gold as money. It seems to me that promoting gold for jewelry at bargain prices is neither in the interest of the industry the WGC is supposed to represent (the gold mining industry and its shareholders), nor in the interest of the gold producing countries. Gold is too valuable to be used for jewelry purposes only. This is what the WGC does not seem, or does not want, to understand.

Both, the WGC, and also the mining industry, should understand that gold's most important purpose is its money function. Even though it is not very apparent at the present, gold is still at the heart of capitalism and will undoubtedly regain its former prominence as long as the world is facing the disastrous consequences of the current catastrophic currency muddle. If this is not understood by the WGC and no steps are taken in the direction of alleviating the situation, then the present activities of the WGC are questionable and the whole effort could be called a mission failed.

For the price of gold, it would be extremely positive if steps were to be taken soon to remedy this unfortunate situation. It would require some rethinking by some members of the mining industry, but that may be an illusion as long as some of the large gold producers want the gold price to decrease, or at least to remain low, enabling them to buy up smaller producers before the price goes up!

Role of Gold in the European Central Bank (ECB) and the Euro

At first, there was a lot of guessing about the role of gold in the new European monetary system. There was some doubt whether there would be a role for it at all. Finally, it was decided that the ECB should not have all its reserves in paper, but hold 15% of it in gold.

Still, what is missing is the link. One cannot run a fiat currency and hope it will be a strong currency. There can be any amount of gold in the cellar without an explicit link; it still remains a fiat currency. But so it was promised to the people of Europe, in particular Germany. It was the first time in history that a currency union was formed before the political union. Oddly enough, the ECB has a president, but Europe still does not have a finance minister. Every country maintains its own finance ministry and central bank. Worst of all, the ECB has no control over the EU banking system that continues to create Euros out of thin air. The Euro is a currency without market justification, prescribed by politicians.

The launching of the Euro on January 1, 1999, was a major event. Its initial weakness during the first year did not surprise considering the manner in which most European countries had to doctor their books in order to comply with the rules of Maastricht.

The new currency does not yet have the desired credibility. It has no record, no history, but is already used as a reserve currency. The SNB had 20 billion Swiss Francs worth of Euros on their books by the end of 1999. The Euro's future is still uncertain. Its credibility would be improved enormously if the ECB would buy gold, thereby opening the possibility of a future link to gold. If it does not chose to do so, the future performance of Europe's fiat currency is not promising as well-informed and critical Bruno Bandulet, publisher of Germany's financial newsletter *Gold & Money Intelligence,* describes:

"The Euro: Who is afraid of Mr. Duisenberg?

Since it was born on January 1, 1999 as a virtual currency, the Euro has been an utter disappointment. The British are far from joining, the Germans detest it, payments in Euros still amount to only 2.4% of company transactions in Europe and – according to a recent report from the European commission – preparations for the final changeover in January 2002 are still very slow and clearly inadequate. No more talk of dethroning the mighty dollar.

What went wrong? Not much, really. It came as it was to be expected. Today, two years later, the Euro is still a stateless, synthetical paper currency without political authority behind it. The European Union is no optimal currency area. You can't have a common monetary policy, which fits Germany, Spain and Ireland at the same time.

The European Central Bank is a multicultural institution, which still has to develop a corporate identity. Compare Greenspan with Duisenberg: Everybody listens very carefully to what Mr. Greenspan has to say, but no forex dealer (who is cynical by profession) is afraid of Mr. Duisenberg.

Thumbs down on the Euro forever? That would be an easy verdict if the dollar were a fundamentally sound currency. Far from it: the US current account deficit is approaching $400 billion per annum, the net indebtedness to the rest of the world will easily have surpassed $2,000 billion when you have read this. The Americans consume and invest much more than they save. They depend on capital flows from Asia and Europe. This can go on for a long time, but certainly not forever. So, a continuous dollar bull market past 2000 would be a bigger surprise than a gradual or sudden decline into the next century, which, incidentally, starts on January 1, 2001.

This does not mean that the Euro will necessarily still be around in ten or twenty years' time. The Euro is an unprecedented and reckless currency experiment of which we have only witnessed the very first chapter: Plenty of surprise and suspense still to come."[5]

Interestingly, the Europeans have no contingency plan if the Euro fails. Whether the currency will still be around in ten years time cannot be answered now. Much of the weakness since its inception seems due to a correction of a previous overvaluation of the major European currencies. It could have happened to the German Mark even if there had been no Euro. However, should the weakness of the common currency continue for too long and be too severe, then this could create a serious problem for the dollar. All this shows again how fickle our non-system of floating exchange rates is and what a danger this represents to economic stability.

The known major official sellers of gold

At the end of 1999, gold reserves of all monetary authorities summed to 33,500 tonnes or about 3,200 tonnes less than in 1975. Consequently, one can hardly speak of a flight out of gold by central banks.

The importance of gold sales by monetary institutions has been so exaggerated that its emphasis can only be seen as part of the war plan against gold. There is overwhelming evidence that the Fed has launched a major PR campaign to discredit gold.

On June 12, 2000, Bloomberg reported that Fed economist Dale Henderson, at the occasion of a luncheon talk at the International Precious Metal Institute (IPMI) in Williamsburg, Virginia, said that the world's central banks had little need to maintain reserves of gold because it had lost almost a third of its value in the past four years. He said that the role of central bank gold is diminishing and that central banks should sell their gold reserves.[6] This was part of a Federal Reserve report prepared by Henderson. It said that speeding up central bank bullion sales and decreasing mining would benefit the individual countries and the users of the metal, such as jewelers.[7]

One conclusion that can be drawn from such far-fetched statements by a Fed economist is that the U.S. Government has entered into life and death combat with gold. If an economist from the Federal Reserve makes an official statement, it is consistent with Federal Reserve policy. No person would dare to make such a statement otherwise. The first time this policy surfaced more clearly was during the Asian crisis. Everything collapsed from stock market to currencies to real estate. Only gold stood firm, as it had done on such occasions in the past. But, it was so noticeable that it did not escape those wanting to elevate the dollar to the *only* world currency. After all, an attack on the dollar was not considered good medicine for the U.S. stock market.

It is part of the anti-gold manipulation strategy that sellers of gold are always made known. In some cases even three times: first, when the sale is announced; second, when the sale actually takes place and, finally, when the sale is completed. The buyers, however, always remain anonymous.

Forty years ago, a formerly very conservative country, Canada, became an important gold seller. Why should she keep all the gold in the central bank's vaults when there is so much more in the ground? The result of this short-sighted policy is reflected in the exchange value of the Canadian dollar, which 40 years ago was valued higher than the U.S. dollar, and at a time when the U.S. dollar was still king.

The same thinking prevails in Australia. It is no small wonder that the Australian miners are among the most aggressive hedgers and forward sellers in the gold mining industry. Under mysterious circumstances, the Reserve Bank of Australia, Australia's central bank, sold 167 tonnes of gold in 1997 for a total of A$2.4 billion.

Two other prominent sellers were Belgium and the Netherlands wanting to 'bring their house in order' before the ECB started operating. Belgium announced that it would use the proceeds of the sale of 200 tonnes to reduce its enormous debt but, according to a high placed-source, actually needed to be jawboned into selling. The socialist Dutch sold 400 tonnes, supposedly to bring the proportion of gold in their reserves in line with Germany. Other sellers in the 1991/92 period were Russia and Iraq, two countries with specific problems of their own. During those two years, approximately 900 tonnes of official gold were known to be sold. Some others were also selling, and all of the gold found buyers!

When Central Banks Sell Gold, Their Currencies Devalue

The Australian and the Canadian dollars are vivid proof of what happens if gold leaves the land. Both are countries rich in natural resources and should top the list of wealthy nations. However, having gold, or anything else for that matter, in the ground does not make a country wealthy. The best example is Russia. Instead, these countries have been driven out of paradise and, concomitantly, destroyed the purchasing power of the savings and pensions of ordinary people by their own doing. Australia and Canada did not entertain wars, yet both countries are loaded with debt. Canada in particular has a debt-load that is frightening. Consequently, their currencies devalued.

The following has to be kept in mind: Even if currencies are no longer linked to gold, it is no accident that certain countries have higher gold reserves than others do. In Switzerland, for example, gold reserves were built up by older generations through hard work and privations, and not through speculation.[8] In countries where squandering away the gold reserves suddenly becomes official policy, we must assume that a fundamental change in philosophy is taking place, a change for the worse.

This is beginning to show in the formerly most conservative country of all – Switzerland. Switzerland has entered the currency war, that is to say the devaluation war. The country's new gold policy can only be seen in this light: Cheapen the currency to support exports. The best way to carry out this policy has always been to sell gold for funny money. And since this also helps to depress the price of gold, the SNB is really killing two birds with one stone. But, most importantly, it is also killing the goose that lays the golden eggs.

The Conspiracy Theory

"Why are the central banks selling gold, or are they playing the hands of the short sellers," asks French chronicler and monetary expert Paul Fabra.[9] He refers to the increasing worries of the public about central bank sales.

In my view, this article is so crystal clear and illuminating that it should have been reprinted it in every newspaper of the world. The author was acquainted with President de Gaulle and monetary expert Jacques Rueff. His conclusion is that by selling gold in order to buy increasingly volatile government bonds, central banks are playing a more dangerous game than ever. Performance is the name of the game on Wall Street. By selling gold (their only asset of value!) to buy somebody else's fiat money in exchange for a meager yield, central banks (which should always be liquid) are risking illiquidity! Paul Fabra asks:

> "Is it still possible to speak of long-term reserves if short-term profitability has priority over safety? No, because in a world where real money is replaced by fiat money and monetary reserves increasingly consist of other countries' fiat money, the monetary system resembles a house of cards."[10]

Fabra continues:

> "Nobody has gone further than the Swiss National Bank, historically known for its prudence. Even before selling their gold, they converted large parts of their foreign exchange (mainly in forms of U.S. Treasury Bills) into foreign government bonds (U.S., German, Japanese and Dutch). In spring of 1999, the Bank of England announced that the proceeds of their gold sales would be used in the same way. By investing in government bonds they are ignoring the fact that bond markets have become dangerous places. That was clearly demonstrated in 1994.
>
> But their worst activity certainly consists of lending gold cheaply, which is subsequently sold by

the borrower and either invested in higher yielding U.S. Treasury Bonds or even in common stocks. By now, this so-called 'Gold Carry Trade' has replaced the 'Yen Carry Trade' where low-yielding yen were borrowed in the market only to be resold immediately and invested in high-yielding US$ or GB£ bonds. Borrowing commodities, never practised since medieval times, has been reinvented, but this time outfitted with all the sophisticated techniques of modern investment banking. Central banks are running a high risk by lending their gold [which is their countries' and citizens' patrimony! –auth.] for a meagre yield of about 1.5 to 1.9% via intermediaries to hedge funds or to gold mines before they have produced the gold. Consequently, by lending their gold, which is then sold forward or short, central bankers are becoming short sellers themselves and, thereby, obviously contribute to weaken the price of their only asset of value – gold! What is just as abominable is that they have been depressing not only the value of their own assets but in addition pushed down the value or price of the savings of millions of people around the globe."[11]

The IMF Folly

One of the worst lies was the proposed sale of some IMF gold in order to help the economies of developing countries. On Monday, March 15, 1999, French President Jacques Chirac opened fire. The next day President Clinton began shooting. On the third day Secretary of the Treasury Rubin, a former partner of Wall Street firm Goldman Sachs, joined in: "The International Monetary Fund will probably sell 5 – 10 million ounces of gold to fund a program of debt relief, but will not disrupt the markets with its sales," he said.[12]

If this is not manipulation, I don't know what is! All three had the same brilliant idea concurrently. That most of these developing countries also happened to be gold producing countries did not matter. A further deterioration of the attitude towards the gold market and a lower price of gold could only do further economic damage to nations such as South Africa, Ghana, Mali, Peru and others.

The IMF proposal was openly criticized as a further act of manipulation of the gold market. Fortunately, the Clinton Administration's proposal met strong opposition in Congress. It was considered misguided and potentially offensive. Congressman Jim Saxton of the Joint Economic Committee said that renewed IMF sales would further distort the market pricing of credit and aid the transfer of wealth from taxpayers to a select few, such as officials of inept and often corrupt and brutal governments, already over-paid international bureaucrats not subject to taxes, and Wall Street fat cats.[13]

This is a prime example of damaging entire nations with the very mechanism that pretends to be helping them. For example, the debt relief proposal was meant to help Ghana, one of the Heavily Indebted Poor Countries (HIPC). The problem was that 40% of Ghana's total exports came from gold. But the price of gold had been forced down by the sale of gold that was supposed to provide the funds for the debt relief program.

Such a move also destabilized South Africa, which is the largest producer of gold in the world. Needless to say, producers of gold in the U.S., Australia and Canada were similarly hard hit. The truth was that this whole manipulation cost the mining industry and taxpayers billions of dollars and ought to be considered a crime.

The biggest blasts against the price of gold certainly were two events, which will be discussed in detail below. They were the proposed sale of Swiss gold and the auctioning of the Bank of England gold.

The Media are Anti-Gold or It Glitters Best that Glitters Last

For decades the media of the establishment have done everything in their power to either avoid the subject of gold or to denigrate it. German Swiss Television stopped reporting gold prices years ago. The *Neue Zürcher Zeitung* is no better. When the South

African gold mining index changed its composition in 1999, it was simply dropped. There are many pages with price quotations of derivatives and options, but the new S.A. gold mining index can no longer be found. Fortunately, the Australian mining index is still reported every day.

Even *Barron's* has changed. There is no more Robert Bleiberg, a great writer and a man who understood gold's function as a monetary metal. The people commenting on gold today have no idea what money is and are better not mentioned. *The Toronto Globe and Mail* ran an editorial on May 11, 1999, under the heading "Gold No Longer Glitters." The article was hailing central bank gold sales as "sensible and long-overdue policy." It noted that Canada sold the vast bulk of its monetary gold reserves over a 15-year period starting in the early 1980s.[14] In a letter to the editor Professor Antal Fekete of the Memorial University of St. John's Newfoundland answered them:

> "How true – and how the Canadian dollar shows it!
>
> During the very same period, the Canadian dollar has lost one third of its value in terms of the U.S. dollar while the latter has lost nine tenths of its purchasing power, which incidentally, was a direct consequence of the U.S. defaulting on its international gold obligations in 1971 – an act your editorial euphemistically calls 'severing the gold link.'"[15]

Golden Scrap or End of the Golden Age

Both above headings are prime examples of the many anti-gold articles that appeared in the monetarily illiterate press. Almost daily there are new ones created to hide the truth from the public. But the prize-winning comment comes from Kenneth Gooding under the title of "Death of Gold." He wrote that "Gold has always been more than a precious metal – men have even lost their lives for it. But no longer. Gold has fallen from grace and is now a mere metal and a bad investment."[16] Gooding is a man who spent most of his working life badmouthing gold, a problem only a psychologist may be in a position to explain.

The Oscar for the Best and Longest Diatribe Against Gold

Peter. L. Bernstein wrote a whole book to prove that the gold standard was no longer of value. Whenever he could, he ridiculed the significance of monetary gold. He even fell back on Prime Minister Disraeli to help him. Disraeli told a group of Glaswegian merchants that

> "it is the greatest delusion in the world to attribute the commercial preponderance and prosperity of England to our having a gold standard. Our gold standard is not the cause, but the consequence of our commercial prosperity."[17]

Politicians have been wrong about money more often than not, and it is a historic fact that Prime Minister Disraeli, who remained a great romantic throughout his life, was not always precise about facts. This was no tragedy because he had a Rothschild as advisor.[18]

Let us, for the purpose of the argument, cite another historian, Sir William Rees-Mogg:

> "The argument that convinced me of the case of gold was that it worked. [...] First of all, one should examine British history. From the restoration of King Charles II in 1660 down to the outbreak of World War I, Britain operated on an unqualified Gold standard. [...] From 1661 to 1913, with the exception of the Napoleonic period, there was full internal and external convertibility into gold, so complete that all other forms of money can be regarded simply as convenient transferable receipts for gold. Gold was money and money was gold. [...] The British price system during this period was not only stable but had a strong tendency to return to an equilibrium point. (...) This long period cannot be dismissed as uneventful. [...] The fact remains that during the whole period of 252 years prices declined 10% from 100% in 1661 to 91% in 1913. In other words: during the whole period where gold was used as money,

prices were stable. (Source: The Economist, July 13, 1974).

One should, however, not look at the British experience alone. In the monetary history of the United States we have shorter runs and more monetary experimentation. From 1879 to 1914, the dollar was convertible into gold at a fixed ratio specified by law and maintained in practice. Chart 62 of Friedman and Schwartz, *A Monetary History of the United States*, shows the high degree of stability of wholesale prices in that period, fully comparable to the stability in Britain."[19]

Bernstein's superficial and untrue statements can also easily be refuted by the German and Swiss examples. The German economic miracle was based on Ludwig Erhard's successful Deutsche Mark (DM). Switzerland would never have become a leading banking center and industrial power with the highest GNP per capita in the world without the Swiss Franc. Bernstein is also refuted by John Maynard Keynes. In his *Tract on Monetary Reform* (1923) Keynes says the following:

"The individualistic Capitalism of today [...] presumes a stable measuring rod of value and cannot be efficient – perhaps not survive – without one."[20]

Furthermore, Bernstein displays another serious weakness when he confuses the gold exchange standard and the gold dollar standard of 1944 with the classical gold standard of the nineteenth century.[21]

Gold and Culture

Over and over again, the question arises: Are the campaigns of disinformation against gold orchestrated by someone or some powerful groups who want to buy all the gold; or is it because politicians and the people who finance their campaigns are trying to make people believe in fiat money and paper fairy tales in order to float more debt? First and foremost, it is the financial sector, and not necessarily government that reaps the highest benefits from fiat money, and, therefore, wants the merry-go-round to keep on spinning. Has the world fallen into this trap or gone astray because mankind has forgotten the monetary lessons of its own history?

At a time when law and order is becoming a thing of the past, is it a coincidence that trade wars and currency wars dominate, and entire nations are politically and economically destabilized? Has the world lost its moral frame of reference at the same time its monetary system broke down? Or did the world just slide into this mess by accident, piece-by-piece at the same time it was losing its moral roots and sense of history? Few history books refer to monetary history. What was the reason for the Renaissance culture and prosperity in overcoming the dark Middle Ages? How did Britain become an Empire? Only by its sword? No, it had the better monetary system and it was based on gold. A second, more provocative question: Why did Britain lose its empire?

The Bank of France On Gold

In a monograph published in May 1997 by the World Gold Council, A. Duchâteau, the head of Forex and Reserves Management Department of the Banque de France, explained why central banks hold gold as a guarantee of prudent currency management. An extract from his statement:

> "There is a major difference between the attitude of financial operators, who treat gold like a commodity, in the same way as oil or other metals, and that of the monetary authorities, who handle gold very cautiously because, in the eyes of the public, gold reserves are one of the elements underpinning confidence in the currency.
>
> Gold reserves are a sign of monetary sovereignty.
>
> Monetary authorities have generally only drawn on their gold during particularly dramatic economic or social difficulties.
>
> The gold reserves of central banks provide insurance against major disturbances in the

international monetary system. In this respect, it is revealing that the last sharp rise in the price of gold, which occurred in the early 1980s, coincided with the fear of a collapse of the banking system as a result of the Latin American debt crisis. [See the case of the German loan to Italy. – auth.]"[22]

Pourvu que cela dure… or let us hope that the French central bank does not change its policy.

Central Banks Are Acting Foolishly

Sentiment and psychology are important in the gold market. When stock markets are booming there is generally not much investor interest in gold. These are ideal times for manipulating the price of the metal. As will be noted later in this book, when the news came out in November 1996 that Switzerland would mobilize its huge reserves of gold, the price of gold was around $386. At that time, holdings of central banks and official institutions, including the IMF and the BIS in Basle, amounted to 34,726 tonnes. At $386 per ounce these official reserves were valued at $416 billion. The next day the price had dropped to $376 corresponding to a book loss of over $11 billion. The gold price never recovered and dropped to a level hovering between $290 – 300, where it stabilized for months. At $300, the value of all official reserves was $324 billion.

When in spring of 1999 the Bank of England announced that it would auction off much of its gold, the price of the metal was around $295, and struggling to overcome the psychological hurdle of $300. The announcement led to dramatically more weakness, which, of course, was magnified by strong selling of speculative funds. When gold bottomed at $250, total official reserves were valued at $270 billion, which represented a loss of $146 billion for the period starting from when the Swiss made their announcement.

Again, another aspect is overlooked completely. There is a large and growing gap between new gold production and demand for gold. In the absence of central bank sales and lending, the gold price would not be so depressed. Because of continued debasement of the currencies, it is safe to say that, in a free market (which we do not have), gold would be valued more highly than it is now. Assuming a price of $500, the value of all official gold would be around $540 billion. This is more than $200 billion higher than if valued at the present level of $270 – $280. This is huge if one considers that central banks only earn about $500 million to $1 billion per annum from their lending gold. By lending gold, they also risk never seeing their gold again should there be a short squeeze.

What Are Central Bankers Really Up to?

No normal businessperson would purposefully act in such a way as to depress the price of his most valuable asset. Hence, central bankers ought to know better. And they probably do know better. They also know perfectly well that their display of fighting inflation is for the benefit of a gullible public. What central bankers are really interested in is the continuing efficacy of their respective banking systems. These arrangements allow banks to garner enormous revenues – about $350 billion net of interest expense in 1999 in the U.S. alone[23] – provided the fiat funny money systems are sustained. To continue this unearned and undeserved bonanza, gold money, which would be the people's choice in a free market, must be disparaged, destroyed and eliminated.

American money manager, Richard M. Pomboy, gave a satisfactory answer in 1997 in an open letter to the *Financial Times* as well as the *Wall Street Journal*:

> "Why do they [the central banks] do this? First of all, they probably record the income but not the loss since many central banks do not record fluctuations in the price of their gold. Nevertheless, the decline in value is real, no matter how they choose to keep their books. Second, some Western central banks dislike gold because it can provide a discipline and a store of value, which is contrary to the prevailing concept that the central bankers themselves know the correct monetary balance to achieve non-inflationary growth. We live in an era where paper assets are unquestioned and confidence in central

bankers is at a high point. The third reason for this gold activity may well be the desire of Western central banks to have gold tarnished as an alternative to government debt issues, which are needed to finance deficits. Finally, central banks and producers are encouraged to sell through bullion dealers who provide a continuously negative view of gold to get this order flow."[24]

A Japanese banker, who did not want to be identified, and whom I met at a Paris conference of the World Gold Council in 1999, told me that Japan is not allowed to buy gold as long as U. S. battleships are cruising in the Pacific to protect their 'security.'[25] The same probably applies to Taiwan.

Such statements are difficult to check, but seem plausible if one considers that recently countries like Kuwait, Sri Lanka, Bangladesh, Uruguay (once so prosperous it was called the Switzerland of South America) and Jordan have been persuaded to lend and sell their physical gold. Lebanon appears to be the next country to follow suit.

Godfathers of Easy Money

In a very lucid article under the above title, an American university professor said that central banks claim to be bastions in defense of their currencies.[26] Instead, they have often been a cause of the crises, which they then take the credit for resolving. When central bankers broke the rules of the gold standard during the 1920s and replaced them with a gold exchange standard, they in effect allowed their banks to create their own irredeemable funny money. This set the stage for the Great Depression. Similar mechanisms are at work today. Central banks are selling their gold or lending it at a time when financial markets resemble a house of cards. This is irresponsible.

From these few statements we can only conclude that central banks are no natural friends of gold; or as previously noted, the 'lenders of last resort', the *raison d'être* for central banking and the gold standard are incompatible.

If central bankers cannot be trusted and are not in a position to handle the patrimony of the people, built up by generations dedicated to hard work, in a trustworthy manner, then they are not the right people for the task. However, I suspect that they may have forgotten the lessons of history. But what is driving the bullion bankers?

Their only motive was to make money. They made legendary amounts of money with the 'Gold Carry Trade'. By borrowing gold from the central banks at a 1% lease rate, then selling the gold (thereby flooding the physical gold market with an artificial supply) and investing the proceeds in Treasury securities at 5%, they were making fortunes. Who can blame them?

It was the Chairman of the Fed, Alan Greenspan, himself who invited them to do so by declaring before the House Banking Committee on July 24, 1998, and again on July 30, 1998 before a Senate Agricultural Committee, that: "[…] central banks stand ready to lease gold in increasing quantities should the price rise." By allowing an unprecedented manipulation of the gold price, the central banks laid the foundation for the biggest money game in history.

Nobody cared that the manipulating (a strong, but truthful assessment) governments, central banks and bullion banks, were completely ignoring the free market process. Greedy bullion banks were permitted to eat away the profits that should have gone to the gold mining companies, their shareholders, workers and last, but not least, the poor gold producing countries. During the last forty years of an openly rigged gold market with the manipulative activities of the gold pool, which continue to this day, none of the gold mining companies' managements ever protested the all too obvious suppression of the gold price.

The War Takes a Turn for the Worse

Let us not forget, we are still at war. Those of us who lived through the unholy experiences of the Gold Pool are in a position to compare. Who were the adversaries and manipulators of gold during this period? It was the U.S. Treasury that mobilized other central banks to cap the gold price. Because of the growing U.S. balance of payments deficits that would weaken the dollar and, therefore, endanger the Bretton Woods system, gold played its historic role as barometer. When the price of gold started to rise, the central banks and national governments did not like it. They openly proposed and talked about selling gold and finally did. Instead of fighting the origins of the malaise, they were destroying the barometer.

The rationale behind the governments and central banks suppressing the price of gold is that gold is a political metal. As long as there has been money, rulers or governments have always intervened. Today, the U.S. Treasury is afraid of gold for several reasons. Gold in its historical role as a currency is fundamentally incompatible with the modern financial system based on the fiat dollar. For thirty years, ever since President Richard Nixon disconnected the U.S. dollar from its golden life support, the depreciation and instability of currencies has been scandalous.

Starting with 1971, no paper currency has been linked to gold, with the exception of the Swiss franc, which only recently lost its tie to gold. The result has been an astronomical build-up of debt. Today, the global fiat money system is based on nothing but faith and the hope that the debt will be repaid one day. The one thing that could seriously shake this faith and, therefore, the foundations of the modern financial system itself, is a rise (especially a sharp rise) of the price of gold in U.S. dollars. The central banks, whether they have a lot, a little or no gold, do not want to see a rise in the price of gold, because they are afraid of the message it would send to the markets. Furthermore, it may have serious consequences for those commercial banks that are short in the gold market.

Should America change the situation? Because of the monetary arrangements arising from the death of Bretton Woods, the U.S. balance of trade deficit has grown dramatically. It is now beyond the point of no return. It is going from bad to worse. Under the present perilous U.S. dollar standard, Americans can buy all the goods of the world with irredeemable paper dollars. Some of the dollars return home to be reinvested by foreigners in U.S. capital markets. Can the country maintain a negative savings rate forever? Have the Americans found a way to turn economic laws upside down? Of course not. It is a frightening situation. The American people can go on consuming more while saving less, year after year, only because our present inequitable international monetary arrangements permit some market participants, primarily the financial sector, to stealthily siphon off wealth from others. It is, therefore, understandable that certain one-world-one-currency big government planners and bureaucrats believe that it would be best if everybody else could adopt the dollar as their currency because this would make things a lot easier.

Ecuador is the first guinea pig to dollarize its economy by adopting the dollar as its official currency. Others may follow at their own risk. As the recent example of Argentina has shown, trying to stabilize the economy by pegging the peso to the U.S. currency can backfire. The dollar's relentless appreciation is tearing Argentina's economy apart.

Barry Riley wrote in the *Financial Times*:

> "Adopting some other country's currency without any mutual agreement on policy is very dangerous. Such a blunder led the U.K. into deep trouble in the early 1990s when Germany, which was overheating after reunification, set the interest rates for the European exchange rate mechanism.
>
> Now we cannot expect the U.S. Government to have any concern for Argentina's economy when it appears to have little regard for its own."[27]

This idea of a world monetary system consisting of a few currency blocks first and later of a single currency for all, seems to have been dreamed up by some government or IMF economist. The entire world would then have the same monetary policy "Made in Washington, DC." This is one of the central reasons behind the war against gold. God protect us from that devouring monster!

The group of master planners wanting to globalize the world as fast as possible for their own short-term self-interest have now become so removed from reality and so arrogant in their overconfidence that they are unable to solve the crisis because they fail to understand gold. They have forgotten that markets always triumph, and that gold is the choice of the free market But, as in every war, in the end there will be many losers, and the winners will be the ones buying the gold.

In the meantime, the arsenal of weapons has been greatly improved. The Gold Pool of the 1960s and the Treasury and IMF auctions of the 1970s are medieval weapons compared to today's sophisticated systems. The old weapons were direct and everybody knew what could be expected. Today's war is a clandestine, cold and remorseless affair. The devastation that the gold mining industry is suffering is in some ways comparable to what is happening to the Chechens or Afghans.

The generals fighting gold are the most experienced and sophisticated the world of finance has ever seen. They are fighting with the help of their powerful army consisting of wealthy bullion and giant investment banks. They even dispose of a 'Foreign Legion' of sorts in the form of foreign central banks. Their modern weapon system, the derivatives market, puts them in a position of being able to unleash an enormous amount of firepower at the stroke of a pen. It is to be hoped that this firepower does not turn into an atomic bomb.

The major disadvantage to this potential atomic bomb is that the generals may not even be in control of it. As a result, there was, and is, a real possibility of a worldwide financial crisis. Chances are that this crisis may turn out to be more destructive than any other drama mankind has witnessed. We may see a financial earthquake of a magnitude that will change the world and its economic and political foundations forever. Wouldn't it be prudent of these sophisticated generals to fight the real danger? Gold is not the enemy. The enemy is the lack of the classic gold standard, a system guaranteeing prosperity.

Dramatic Change in the Gold Markets
of the 1980s and the 1990s

For the last forty years, there has been no free gold market. During the 1960s, the gold market was controlled by the central banks' Gold Pool at the behest of the U.S. Treasury, which wanted the gold price suppressed. At that time, the price of gold served as a perfect monetary barometer signaling the oncoming dollar crisis.

During the 1970s, the U.S. Treasury and the IMF auctions capped the gold price. As we know, all attempts failed. Gold, which was fixed by President Roosevelt in 1934 at $35 an ounce, climbed as high as $850 per ounce during the 1970s. Since 1981, gold has been in a bear market, but the suppression continued with the help of governments' sometimes invisible hands as well as central bank sales.

Because of the negative experiences with failed interventions during the 1960s and the 1970s, it was generally thought that the U.S. would not touch its gold hoard that had shrunk to some 8,100 tonnes. It was thought that the Americans would prefer that the Europeans get rid of their golden treasures. This belief was, however, shaken recently by stories that there never has been an audit of America's gold since World War II. Furthermore, reports that the designations of gold owned by the U.S. Treasury were changed several times in the past two years were beginning to worry analysts.

They suspected that something mysterious might have happened to America's gold. By the mid 1990s, a concerted effort aimed at the price of gold was started by the U.S. government. It was then that the Swiss gold was targeted in earnest. During the last weeks and days of Bretton Woods, Switzerland was among the countries that were 'impertinent' enough to ask for more American gold in exchange for their 'excess' dollars. It was their right to do so.

With 2,590 tonnes of gold, Switzerland had one of the biggest gold hoards in the world. Because of this golden guarantee, it also had the strongest currency. For some of the bigger nations with weaker currencies, this was bothersome. This is one of the reasons why certain people in high places thought it was about time for the old-fashioned Swiss to become more modern by selling half of their gold—and another battle by the enemies of gold was won.

New Allies: Bullion Banks, Investment Banks and Paper Gold

Before gold ownership and futures trading were legalized in the U.S., the Winnipeg Commodity Exchange was the world's first and only gold futures market. With gold ownership in the U.S. becoming legal beginning January 1, 1975, the situation changed and futures markets in the U.S. and London took over. A monster was in the making that eventually would not only dwarf all physical volume but open doors to influencing and manipulating the gold price without bringing physical gold into play.

It is estimated that the volume in the futures market amounts to 800 to 1,000 tonnes a day compared with annual mine production of approximately 2,500 tonnes. The tool, with which it is possible to move the gold price to unrealistic levels without actually owning the physical metal, is called leverage through derivatives. A consequence of the downfall of Bretton Woods is that foreign exchange markets resorted to floating, and floating necessitated hedging. The human mind is very inventive. New hedging schemes (derivatives) were created for the gold war.

The Gold Loans / Forward Sales

As everybody knows, a bar of gold, like a banknote, yields nothing. At the beginning of the 1980s, some creative Wall Street dealers found ways to change this. They invented the gold loans/forward sales business. They sold the idea to some owners of aboveground gold and to those who owned gold still to be mined. Central banks with their large 'unproductive' stockpiles of precious metals loaned their gold at an interest rate, the gold lease rate, which normally ranged between 1% and 2% per annum. The gold would then be lent to mining companies, providing them with cheap loans, usually in the range of 3% to 4%. These rates were so low the mining companies would never find more favorable terms. The mining companies, knowing they could back their loans with their own production, would then sell the gold on the spot or forward market, in which case they obtained instant cash or higher deferred prices.

As can be seen, this new business offered something for everyone: The central banks received a regular cash flow for their gold, and the mines got cash and protection from falling prices. The cash could be used to step up exploration or for new plant and equipment, and the investment bankers garnered hefty fees from both sides of the transaction with a minimum of risk.

Soon, however, the original ideas were pushed into the background. Instead of just hedging, the whole business became an explosive speculation machine with new instruments created in addition to gold loans and fixed forward sales. The new instruments were spot deferred sales, contingent forwards, variable volume forwards, delta hedging, puts and calls. Investment bankers, encouraged by their lucrative profit center, lost no time and missed no bearish argument to build up their clientele steadily and aggressively. The Australians were generally considered the most aggressive by selling, in some cases, yet-to-be-mined gold reserves up to seven years forward.

What neither the central banks nor the gold mining companies realized at first was that this activity turned into a vicious circle contributing to lower and lower gold prices. So, if somebody wanted to manipulate the gold market, he only had to convince the central banks to lend more and the mines to hedge more. Then they could sit back and watch their income from fees grow. That they were undermining the gold price in the process did not concern them.

Who Were Those Players?

Their names were part of the Gotham banking elite: Goldman, Sachs; J. P. Morgan; Chase; the bullion dealers, and big banks such as Deutsche Bank; Société Générale of France; UBS of Switzerland and Crédit Suisse. They were engineering a most profitable new business by acting as intermediaries between naïve central banks, who were receiving negligible interest in return for not only depressing the price of their only asset of sure value, but also for risking to lose part or all of it.

The meager income the central banks received from their doubtful operations (estimated to be between $500 million and $1 billion p.a.) was minuscule in comparison to the hundreds of billions in unrealized book losses incurred with their own monetary gold. The central banks should be asked why they are lending gold that belongs to the people at such low rates instead of lending it at the going dollar rate? Furthermore, they should also be asked whether they are aware of the risk they are taking by lending gold. It makes no sense to loan gold at such ridiculous rates and then risk losing it.

By their actions, central banks are depressing the value of gold assets in any form, be it in people's savings, gold mining companies' profits or, consequently, the price of their shares. The price of gold was depressed for years in a manner that had nothing to do with supply and demand in the physical market. Even if it is argued that gold no longer has any monetary function in the present fiat money system, it still makes no sense to depress its price just for the benefit of greedy bullion bankers and hedge fund managers playing the short side. It is a fact that in times of war gold can always be used for payment when no other medium of exchange is acceptable. Since the end of 2000, gold has played its useful and historical role of balancing portfolios in uncertain times again. From this point of view, the war against gold does not make any sense either.

For some mines this game proved deadly. They went under or had to be closed when they still could have prospered under fair and honest market conditions. Hundreds of thousands of workers who would have had jobs were forced out of work, losing their chance to earn a living in dignity. Their income and spending were lost to their economies, leaving the gold producing countries in worse shape than before. Moreover, these countries wouldn't have had to beg from such organizations as the IMF, which misses no chance to depress the price of gold. It does it either by outright sales or by issuing regular well-planned statements that have the same effect. It is extremely hypocritical to shed tears over the poverty in Africa when the situation could be alleviated substantially by not manipulating the price of gold.

The last central banks to enter the lending business were the Deutsche Bundesbank and the SNB. As the two central banks are also among the five biggest gold holders in the world, the impact of their lending was clearly negative on the gold market.

The Gold Lease Rate

The gold lease rate, a.k.a. interest charged for lending gold is the rate at which central banks are willing to lease or, better, to risk their gold reserves. The lease rate is sometimes, but not always, a good leading indicator for gold price movements, because it somehow mirrors the activities of the various gold market participants. Such was the case when, on September 27, 1999, some central banks decided to limit the volume of gold sales and lending activities for the next five years in their so-called 'Washington Agreement'. The lease rate, which usually fluctuates between 1 - 2%, shot up to 9% within a few hours, reflecting a fundamental change in the market and possibly the beginning of a panic within the lending institutions. On August 11, 1999, market participants and analysts noticed a growing tightness as the 6-month lease rate moved to 4.12%. The gold price was then quoted at $257. The conclusion was that the lending market was losing its attractiveness. But when the central banks decided to limit sales, the gold price jumped to over $330 in a few days, and the lease rate went to 9%, suggesting that a serious crisis was in the making. Obviously, this was the moment of big clouds clearing from the gold market. However, the fact remains that the biggest overhang on the market did not stem from central bank sales, but from central bank lending.

Hedge Funds and Investment Banks
Also Undermine the Price of Gold

It did not take long until the hedge fund industry determined that the gold price would remain under continuous pressure and that shorting represented a speculator's paradise. Positions having no relation to the fundamentals of the gold market were built up. The best example of how wrong funds can be (even with Nobel Prize winners on their board), was demonstrated by the collapse of Long Term Capital Management (LTCM) during the Russian default crisis in October 1998. This company had practiced the art of leverage in its most extreme form. The New York Fed orchestrated its rescue, because LTCM's failure supposedly threatened to affect the international financial system similarly as the collapse of the Austrian bank, Creditanstalt, did in 1931. That clearly revealed how far the world of finance had come.

One of the most miserable and ethically questionable new business profit centers created by the investment banks is the so-called 'gold carry trade', a new version and successor of the 'yen carry trade'. Banks and funds, as well as financial operators, borrowed yen for an extended period of time at almost no interest, sold the yen and bought Treasury Bills instead, thereby cashing in on a higher interest rate. As the example shows, everything went well as long as the price of the yen was subdued, but when the yen turned, a less pleasant scenario presented itself. The 'gold carry trade' was no different. Gold was borrowed, subsequently sold and the proceeds invested in Treasury Bills. Another routine of borrowing gold was even worse. It was sold and reinvested in common stock, sometimes in the high technology sector. To some extent this only spurred the already ongoing mania in the stock markets. As these new banking practices continued, the price of gold came under constant pressure. The greater the bearish mood in the gold market, the more confident the investment banks became.

The Folly of the Central Banks, or Lending Gold Is Selling Gold

Central banks helped to keep this speculative orgy alive by lending more and more gold to bullion bankers. The only aspect the central bankers overlooked is that lending gold is like selling gold. They disregarded the possibility that they might never be able to recover the gold they had lent out – at least not in form of physical metal. The reason is quite elementary: Once the gold is loaned out it is sold and ends up mostly in the hands of jewelry owners. Thousands of tonnes of central bank gold disappeared forever via the leasing route, and estimates on the total short position vary from 5,000 to 16,000 tonnes, or two to six years of production. What were the central banks thinking?

Julian Baring, gold mining analyst and one of the great personages of the gold scene in the City of London, who, unfortunately, passed away in September of 2000, had the following to say on central bank lending:

> "The wisdom of central banks' lending gold to others who then stuff the market with it is debatable."[28]

Central Banks and Investment Banks Are Helping to Cause a Gold Mining Industry Disaster

> "Central banks sales and lending have been by far the largest factor responsible for the bear market in gold. Because gold mining company managements believed in the bearish case for gold (i.e., never ending sales by central banks), they engaged in forward sales and other hedging transactions facilitated by the bullion dealers." [29]

John Hathaway wrote in his 1999 annual gold investment review that without this pressure the gold price could never have been so weak. The mining industry was, therefore, equally shortsighted. They were selling what they had not dug up by borrowing the metal from central banks through bullion banks. Seduced by cheap loans, they started projects that would have been uneconomical under normal market circumstances. The more the gold price fell, the more difficult it became to remain profitable or to limit the size of their losses. Many companies, therefore, resorted to mining higher grade ores just to stay alive. They were selling the precious metal at the most unfavorable price at the most inopportune time, thereby shortening the life of their mines. Also, exploration virtually stopped.

The moment the Bank of England announced its sales program in the spring of 1999, it became even more obvious to some that the price of gold was being manipulated. The mining companies had pushed the price to the lowest level for many years causing a real hedging orgy. Even a traditional non-hedger like Newmont Mining was driven into hedging by some overreaching bullion bank.

By then it had become clear that one day this farce would end. The beginning of the end came in September 1999. The gold markets, after years of speculation and short selling, had been distorted to such a degree that the central banks began to wake up. They saw that in order so save their own position they had to act. In the 'Washington Agreement', fifteen European central banks, including Switzerland, agreed to limit future sales and lending for a period of five years

Irresponsible Hedging is Ruining Mining Companies and Entire Countries: The Tragedy of Ashanti and Ghana

The sudden spike in the price of gold had two immediate mining-business victims: the big African producer Ashanti of Ghana and Cambior of Canada. Ghana is a heavily indebted African country. In 1992, 31% of the population was living in abject poverty, and 27% of the children under the age of five were suffering from malnutrition. Gold and cocoa exports are the country's principal foreign exchange earners. Fluctuations in the gold price have an almost immediate effect on that country's economy. From 1993 to 1997, cocoa's share of export earnings fell from 50% to 30%. Gold's share during the same period went from 15% to 39%, creating hope that rising income from gold would make the country's economy less vulnerable to the sometimes dramatic price fluctuations in cocoa.

Neighbouring Mali, the world's fifth poorest country, is in a similar situation. Dr. Mark Bristow of Randgold Resources (RRL) expects Mali's gold mining to increase from 15% to 18% of the gross domestic product (GDP) by 2001. Apart from Mali's government, the gold mining industry is now the biggest formal employer, and its tax payments account for about 20% of the nation's civil service bill.

The gold riches of the West African countries Burkina Faso, Ghana, Ivory Coast, Mali and Senegal are legendary. Ghana, the country of the Akan nation, was so famous for its goldfields, its highly developed gold producing techniques and superior goldsmithery that the region was called The Gold Coast. In the fifteenth century Portuguese tradesmen already described how a king of the Akan people was covered with gold chains and other gold jewelry.

The kings of Ghana and Mali underlined their noble and dignified appearance with the splendor of their clothing and their gold jewelry. Mansa Musa, a Mali king in 1324 undertook a pilgrimage to Mecca. He traveled through Egypt where he was offered a grand reception. Contemporary chroniclers reported that they were deeply impressed by his enormous gold treasures. There were rumors that when he arrived in Mecca, the gold price turned weak because he literally flooded the market with his gold. When he returned to Mali, it was said that he took Egyptian goldsmiths with him, because he had promised the Sultan of the Mamelukes, Al-Dawadari, to introduce a gold coin system. The destructive influence of the colonial powers and, later, industrialization, caused this feudal culture to die. Fortunately, many of these artistic masterpieces are now in museums and on exhibit as extraordinary witnesses of the high level of African goldsmithing craftsmanship.[30]

It is not surprising that Ghana, Mali and the other countries have high hopes that the prosperity of their respective nations will take a turn for the better with the arrival of modern gold mining methods and foreign capital. In September 1999, however, there was a brutal awakening when Ghana's Ashanti Goldfields Co., Ltd., almost went bust. Oddly enough this coincided with the announcement of the Washington Agreement, an announcement that should have been beneficial to gold producers.

How could this happen? The price of gold, which had been steadily falling since spring, suddenly surged from $269 to $307 per ounce within a week. There should have been much excitement about the sudden increase of the gold price, but there was nothing but despair when it became apparent that for some participants – and in this case it was Ashanti – a rising price meant ruin. Ashanti had entered into thousands of derivative contracts (over 2,500 in all!) with no less than 17 banks, including Goldman, Sachs, Ashanti's main financial advisor.

According to *The Financial Times* of December 2, 1999, Goldman sold a wide range of financial derivatives to gold companies.[31] It was the leading member of the so-called 'big-four' of investment banks with whom Ashanti traded. The others were

Credit Suisse Financial Products, Société Générale of France and Switzerland's UBS.

The result of all this professional 'advice' ended in disaster for Ashanti and Ghana. At the end of June 1999, Ashanti's hedge book had a positive value of $290 million. In early October, it had a $570 million loss, and there were margin calls pending to the tune of $270 million. Later, the banks explained that the hedging transactions were 'client driven'. However, the sad fact remains that one of the world's richest gold mines was driven into ruin by greed, irresponsibility, extremely bad judgment, and a gold market that had lost contact with reality. Subsequently, a three-year moratorium was worked out because nobody could afford to let Ashanti go under. This gave some big industry players the chance to pick up the valuable pieces.

Ashanti's fate was one of the reasons why a number of industry observers believe that the gold price would not be permitted to rise. That would not only completely destroy the company, but would pull down other heavily hedged mining companies as well. Last but not least, many of the involved banks would have been in a precarious situation – not to speak of central banks' outstanding loans.

For the first time in the history of the gold market we had the absurd situation that almost none of the major producers wanted a higher gold price, at least not for the moment. The exceptions were the holders of bullion or coins and the shareholders of companies such as Agnico Eagle Mines, Harmony Gold Mining Ltd. and Goldfields Limited. A lot of guesswork was done on how Barrick might extricate itself out of this situation because it was considered the mother of all hedgers, the top holding company of the remaining gold mining funds and number one on almost every buying list for gold mining shares. However, the tragedy is that fate had hit the people of Ghana hard.

Hedging or Speculation?

The dictionary meaning of "to hedge" is

a) a means of protection or defense, b) to protect oneself from losing or failing by a counter balancing action, c) to protect against risks from price fluctuations, d) to protect oneself financially as by buying or selling commodity futures as a protection against loss due to price fluctuation.

The dictionary meaning of "to speculate" is:

to assume a business risk in hope of gain, especially to buy or sell in expectation of profiting from market fluctuations.

In its purest form, hedging enables managers of productive businesses to safeguard their enterprises against unpredictable price movements. However, as financial markets internationalized, newly developed financial instruments reflected the new situation in the market. It is safe to conclude that the astonishing growth in the trade of gold-linked financial instruments had more to do with rapid money-making schemes than with the containment of risk. Because of the very low lease rate, it paid to hedge. If, as shown in the cases of Ashanti and Cambior, price fixing for future production protected against downward price moves, but threatened the producer's existence if the gold price increased, then it certainly cannot be called "hedging". It is pure speculation.

A Glittering Future?

In June of 1999, the World Gold Council published an informative report highlighting the situation as it presented itself for some of the poorest countries in the world:

> "One of the overlooked consequences of the recent gold price has been a setback to the development of some of the world's poorest and most heavily indebted nations.
>
> Of the world's 42 Heavily Indebted Poor Countries (HIPCs) more than 30 are gold producers with at least 12 producing in excess of 3 tonnes a year. Production is rising in a number of HIPCs and

the group's total output is likely to be around 200 tonnes, on cautious estimates, in the year 2000, generating at the price prevailing in mid-May 1999, more than $1.6bn in export revenues.

In 9 HIPCs, gold accounts for at least 5% of export revenues with around 5 countries likely to join this group in the near future, and possibly more in the medium term. In some countries – Ghana, Guyana and Mali – gold accounts for more than a fifth of export revenue; Guinea and Tanzania are likely to join this group shortly.

Sub-Saharan Africa, which includes 33 of the 41 HIPCs, currently produces 25.1% of the world's gold. Three-quarters of this – 18.5% is produced by South Africa but the share of global output of the remaining has doubled since 1990.

Gold earns sub-Saharan nations almost $7 bn a year in foreign revenue.

The damaging effect of the fall of the gold price on these countries goes far beyond the immediate impact on export revenues. Gold-mining's multiplier effects [which also applies to U.S.A., Canada, Australia and other gold producing countries – auth.] bring additional jobs, wages and taxes for the governments. Mining facilitates the growth of legal, physical and financial infrastructure.

Gold mining is sometimes one of the few available channels for diversifying a country's exports and production, which in turn is often a critical stage in the development process.

The paradox is that the future growth of these nations is being undermined by precisely those who wish to proffer a helping hand – The IMF and the governments of some well-developed countries.

With the threat of gold sales from the IMF, Switzerland and the U.K., the price of gold has fallen sharply. Key members of the IMF have said they wish to see it sell as much as 311 tonnes of its gold to fund debt relief. [This was history by the time of writing – auth.]

> Sales and the threat of sales by central banks and the official sector are the single biggest factor preventing a price recovery. This represents a major obstacle to the expansion of gold mining in underdeveloped nations, and thus diminishes opportunities for genuine, long-lasting and sustainable economic growth in gold producing HIPCs."[32]

The example of South Africa, the biggest producer as such, merits a closer look at what happened to employment in recent years. In 1987, the gold mining industry, according to the S.A. Chamber of Mines, had a total work force of 564,000. By 1996, when the Swiss threat of sales began, that total had diminished to 345,000 employees and has been reduced by another 100,000 since. While part of the employment reduction is a result of greater mining efficiency, most of the reduction is a consequence of the low price of gold. If one considers that, on an average, ten to twelve people depend on an African miner for their livelihood, then one can conclude that millions of people were negatively affected. Only by taking the multiplier effect into account, one arrives at the real cost of this irresponsible gold war. Does it surprise anyone that crime is on the increase in an otherwise peaceful nation?

Will Hedging Kill the Goose that Lays the Golden Egg?

Julian Baring had the following comment to offer:

> "You would have thought that if forward sales by mining companies was as beneficial to shareholders as the mining companies say they are, their shares would go up every time a forward sale was announced. But that has not been the case."[33]

A closer look at hedging reveals that in many cases hedging has turned into speculation. Antal Fekete, professor at Memorial

University of St. John's, Canada, describes some present-day hedging practices as follows:

> "The 'Hedging Revolution' started in 1985. Barrick Gold (then called American Barrick) was one of the pioneers. Hedging was a most brilliant idea when it was first conceived at Barrick. It put the gold mining industry in a category by itself as the only segment of the economy that could pull itself out of the debt-morass by its own bootstraps.
>
> Barrick's hedging policy as described in the company's annual reports (see in particular those for 1994, 1995 and 1996) is not, strictly speaking, an exercise in hedging, but an exercise in speculation. Barrick is betting that the gold price will never again be able to repeat the feat it has performed several times since 1968, namely to break out on the upside, never again to fall back to those old prices. Should it try, Barrick and others would promptly club it down with their persistent short selling. This was a revolution, indeed. The gold miner cut a strange figure, indeed, showing him as gold's worst enemy. He made every budding rally abort through unilateral hedging. The result of Barrick's innovation was competitive, industry-wide short selling. This was very demoralising to the market, certainly on the supply side but no less on the demand side. The industry as a whole suffered: everybody wanted to sell before everybody else. But it was even more demoralising to potential buyers and all long-term holders of gold. The market perception was that the industry was being led down the primrose path to ruin. While selling gold short, these so-called hedgers were ultimately ruining their own market. At the very least they would kill the upside potential. But, more ominously, there was also a bearish element in the picture. The powerful speculative following of the gold market has been chased away from the long end

en bloc, and was forced to join Barrick on the short end of the market.

But even from Barrick's own point of view, unilateral forward selling appears to be a short-sighted and, in the long run, self-destructive policy. It throws all conservative principles to the wind in the aggressive pursuit of short-term profitability. Whatever the short-term benefits may be, the policy ultimately shortens the working life of Barrick's gold properties. This appears to be undermining Barrick's economic strength in the medium to long run. The declining gold price devours payable grades faster than exploitation through a most wasteful resource utilisation could. Barrick reportedly had to close down operations at five of its ten working sites, due to the disappearance of payable grades at those sites – not through extraction, but through the falling gold price. *It is for the first time in history that productive gold mines were forced to close down in peacetime – not through the attrition but in consequence of the collapse of the gold price.* These mine closures reflect an enormous destruction of capital represented by the abandoned milling plants and other equipment. Nobody could predict the fiasco – least of all the officers of Barrick. How could it have happened? Most observers stress the fact that while there is a physical limit on the production of cash gold, namely milling capacity but, there is no limit on the "production" of futures contracts, its maturity dates are allowed to be pushed ever farther in the future. Barrick's anti-conservationist mining practices and aggressive short selling policies were the equivalent of inundating the market with an unlimited amount of gold futures contracts."[34]

Barrick's cost of producing its top grades of gold may well be reduced to $150 per ounce – but how long will these top grades last?

"Thanks to unilateral hedging, gold and paper now fall together." [35] says Fekete.

In his view the only solution to the dilemma is bilateral hedging. Bilateral hedging means that the policy of forward sales is compensated by a policy of forward purchases of gold. At the time, every rise in the price of gold was countered by forward sales – but nothing was done to counter the fall.

"If one understands this, that in the case of a gold mine, neither forward sales nor forward purchases need to involve speculation but are what they are – namely hedging in the interest of the company and its shareholders."[36]

In the fall of 2000 I asked Professor Fekete whether his position regarding Barrick had been revised? He said that he had not changed his mind at all, quite the contrary.

"You may want to add the very serious charge that [Barrick] knowingly misleads shareholders, creditors, and the general public. For several years in a row, in its Annual Reports, at its shareholders meetings, and press conferences, Barrick has been reporting consistently higher profits, attributing it to its ability to realize higher prices for its newly mined gold than prices that were bid in the market during the entire year in question. These reports of higher profits have been duly certified by reputable accounting firms, and they have never been questioned by academia, let alone the financial press.

We all know what academia and the financial press would have to say if a company with publicly traded shares would announce that it is manufacturing and marketing the 21st century version of 'perpetuum mobile.'

Barrick boasts that it could accomplish this miracle of consistently selling gold at a price higher than the market has ever bid during the entire year by the sophisticated tool of 'hedging'. Why not share this 'secret' with the American farmer? Would it not be wonderful if they, too, could consistently realize higher wheat prices than the market is willing to bid? Where are the farmers' organizations to demand that they should also be told the secret of turning the stone into bread?

Barrick could not share its secret with anybody because the 'miracle' can only be accomplished by fraud. If one wants to be charitable, one would assume that the accounting firms do not understand what they are certifying. Otherwise they would not give their good name to this chicanery aiming to mislead the public. Unfortunately, there are signs that suggest otherwise. The accounting profession may be a full accomplice in this conspiracy to defraud.

It is not, has never been, and will never be possible to sell gold forward at a higher price than the highest price bid by the markets during the year under review, any more than it is possible to turn lead into gold profitably.

Here is what Barrick is doing. It sells gold, borrowed for long-term at a low rate of interest, and invests the proceeds into high-yielding U.S. Treasury paper. Then it recalculates its revenues boosted by the interest income (owing to the positive spread between the yield on the Treasury paper and the gold rate) as if it had been received through a higher sale price on gold per ounce. Why is this a clear fraud? Because the transaction remains incomplete, and profits are only 'paper' profits, as long as all the deals have not been closed out and the borrowed gold returned to the owners. It may never be possible to realize those paper profits. It is quite conceivable that these forward commitments can only be closed out at hideous losses. For such a scenario, nothing more drastic needs to happen than for the price of gold to return to a higher level where it has already traded for years or decades—before the entire deal is closed out and the borrowed gold returned.

Barrick simply assumes that 'what goes up must come down.' If the gold price goes up, say, $200 per ounce, then it is duty-bound to come down at least that much in due course. Those with financial staying power, such as Barrick considers itself to possess in good measure, will be able to ride out any storm caused by temporary spikes in the gold price. They can roll over all futures contracts showing a loss, several times if necessary, until the gold price comes down again. Barrick and others will, therefore, always be able to close out their deals at a profit.

The truth remains, however, that all Barrick has accomplished is to have swept margin calls on its gold-borrowings under the rug, thereby concealing the potential liability from its shareholders and creditors. Therein lies the fraud, which SEC and other watchdog agencies of the U.S. government should uncover and expose. Instead, they adopt the 'hear no evil, see no evil' attitude.

Barrick wasn't around in 1968. But suppose, for the sake of argument, that it was. Assume further that Barrick had sold borrowed gold at $38 per ounce (which may have appeared as an incredibly smart thing to do that year to the gold producers of the day). In that case Barrick would still be rolling over its gold loans in the forlorn hope that the price of gold will be good enough to drop below $38 an ounce, in order to enable Barrick to unwind its losing position with a profit. But in fact, after 1968, the year the U.S. Treasury defaulted on its obligation to pay its creditors (foreign central banks with short-term dollar holdings) in gold at $35 an ounce as contracted, the price of gold took off never to come back again. Barrick could still be holding the bag of losses, and keep reporting huge profits, because the conspirator bullion banks allow it to roll over its short position in gold at $38 an ounce. It may be pointed out that today the position of the U.S. Treasury vis-à-vis its foreign central bank creditors is far inferior to its position in 1968.

It has happened any number of times in history that the gold price took off; never ever to come down *to the level it has started from.* For this reason, any accounting assumption that a commitment to deliver gold at a future date can be closed out profitably in the future (if only one is willing and able to wait long enough) is simply fraudulent. It should never be allowed in a society with self-respecting legislators making meaningful contract laws. And the fraud should be exposed by self-respecting accountants and other watchdogs of fair play.

Just as grain elevator operators are not allowed to treat, in their balance sheets and income statements, the long positions they have in the wheat futures markets in the same way as they treat wheat physically present in their elevators, - gold mines should not be allowed to calculate and report profits on the sale of borrowed gold in the same way as they calculate and report profits on the sale of newly mined gold. There is a contingent liability on the long positions of a grain elevator; for the stronger reason, there is a contingent liability on the short position of a gold mine. Until and unless these positions are closed out, there is no profit to report. As the proverb says, 'there is many a slip between cup and lip.'

It is to the eternal shame of our civilization that it allows this unsavory conspiracy between the bullion banks, the gold mines, the accounting profession, and the government (with academia and the general public looking on) to defraud the general public through the hocus-pocus of 'hedging' and forward selling.

Such blatant and ongoing abuse of trust is possible only under the regime of irredeemable currency. A most powerful argument in favor of the gold standard is precisely the one asserting that it will not tolerate the perpetuation of abuses of trust in dealings among upright men."[37]

The Possibility of a Mining Industry Disaster

Gold mining companies were selling what they had not dug up yet by borrowing from central banks and bullion houses. They then sold the obtained gold and pocketed the cash in return for a promise to the lender to replace the gold that they had borrowed out of their future production. Then they used the cash to invest, upgrade, lower costs or buy back shares; but somewhere down the road, they will have to dig up the missing gold and replace what they originally borrowed and sold.

This deadly game became popular first in Australia where companies started to sell gold forward in 1982. The examples of Ashanti and Cambior clearly demonstrate where all this can lead to. Let us hope that these two casualties are not just the proverbial tip of the iceberg. It is clear that the industry has worked itself into a situation that could not be worse. Ted Butler astutely noted:

"Because so much future production is already sold, there will be weeping and gnashing teeth in the mining world, when there should be joy."[38]

Lawrence Parks came to the following conclusion on 7/18/ 2000:

"If present trends are allowed to continue, in five years the industry may well be a memory; the mines closed, the employees out of work; and the shareholders wiped out. Business as usual will not do. It is urgent that the producers rethink their predicament and embark on a new path. Old concepts, assumptions and strategies, which have demonstrably failed, must be discarded."[39]

The study ends on a hopeful note with the prospects of a resurrection, but only if gold producers take certain actions that will revive the industry.

> "At the end of the day, to revive the fortunes of the gold producers it is necessary and sufficient to restore gold as the choice of free markets and free people all over the world as money that does not depreciate at home or abroad; as money that is steady as the stars; as money that is as faithful as the tides, or, as the American Federation of Labor put it at the turn of the century: 'Gold is the standard of every great civilization!' That is the salvation of the gold mining industry; gold as the standard of every great civilization! [The big guns in the industry are well advised to start thinking along these lines before it is too late. –auth.]"[40]

Gold and Gold Mining Shares in the 1990s

American Investors Services, Inc. summarized recent developments in the gold market as follows:

> "The dollar price of gold averaged $278 per oz. during 1999, 5.3% less than it averaged during 1998. The 1999 average was the lowest in 20 years.
>
> Mine production in 1999 was more than 2½-times its level 20 years ago, but growth has slowed markedly. Looking ahead, output could decrease, as low prices have put the brakes on many projects. Net fabrication continues to exceed [new] mine production by a substantial margin, which has been mainly made up from sales of official stocks. Announcements of such sales, and related hedging activities, appeared to be the cause of the gyrations in the gold price during the year."[41]

During much of the 1990s, the bullion price was in a trading range. However, it is clearly visible from any chart that the real weakness coincided with the threat of Swiss sales. Switzerland was knowingly (or innocently) fooled into what I would call the biggest bear raid of the 1990s because it had one of the biggest gold hoards. The Swiss threat was the Sword of Damocles hanging over the market for years, enabling the short-sellers to make billions while the mining industry and savers lost billions of dollars. The blow-off to the downside was reserved for the Bank of England under the influence of its own (Labour) government.

The American Investment Services conclude that any sustained increase in price from its recent trading range will probably only occur when Western investors return to the bullion market. They were the major buyers in the 1970s when the gold price increased from $35 an ounce to $850 within ten years.

During the last few years, gold mining shares moved up and down in a roller coaster fashion, reaching a low at the end of 1997 and the beginning of 1998. The South African mines in particular made every effort to streamline and reduce costs to help compensate for the reduced price of gold. The Randgold & Exploration Company Limited started a real revolution. This is unique in the annals of gold mining. In the past, the South African gold mining industry had been operating a costly system with outmoded management contracts. The parent mining finance house received dividends and charged fees for services from the individual gold mines in the group until the ore bodies were exhausted.

Randgold & Exploration was the first to end this arrangement. In a successful attempt to reduce costs and increase efficiency, they made the mine managements responsible for both the operating and financial success of their respective mines. Over the next five years and through a dizzying series of mergers, acquisitions, reorganizations and spin-offs, Randgold emerged as a holding company. Its primary asset at present is its 61% stake in Randgold Resources, a company active in exploration in West Africa, and which, recently, has successfully developed the Morila mine project in Mali. Randgold & Exploration also holds an interest in the refurbished mega-mine Durban Deep and in a package of mineral rights throughout Africa.

Randgold & Exploration, which came out of Rand Mines, has given all its mines, including Durban Deep and Harmony, their independence. This was extremely successful in saving the 100-year-old moribund mines. It restructured many of the mining operations and sent them on a successful exploration and development program in several West African countries. In Mali, Randgold Resources, under the leadership of Roger Kebble and Mark Bristow, made the richest discovery of the decade at Morila, now a joint venture with AngloGold, the biggest gold mining company in the world. Durban Roodepoort Deep Ltd. (DRD) founded in 1895, was a dying company and about to be closed when the new owners and management started a successful modernization and expansion program.

Since then, DRD, under the leadership of Roger Kebble, has increased its production almost sevenfold to over one million ounces a year by building a sound South African production base through acquisition and restructuring. The company also gained interests in Australasia and is on the way to becoming one of the world's top ten gold producers. The modernization of the country's gold mining industry soon embraced all of the other groups such as AngloGold and Goldfields Ltd. They made decisions concerning field exploration, modernization and mergers that will guarantee their survival even under the most adverse of industry conditions.

Who are the Winners and the Losers of the Gold War?

History has shown that wars invariably leave more losers than winners. However, the winners never win as much as the losers lose because in a war there is destruction. The gold wars are no different. An overview shows that there are practically no winners:

Parties involved	Winners	Losers
Gold mining companies		X
Gold mining shareholders, owners		X
Ordinary working people everywhere		X
Gold producing countries		X
Central banks		X
Savers		X
World economy		X

World employment situation		X
Taxpayers of the world		X
Investment banks, bullion banks	X*	X
Gold speculation, e.g., hedge funds, short sellers	X**	
Gold buyers, e.g., jewelers	X	

* Investment banks are mainly interested in fees and the present fiat money system has provided them with a bonanza, which they intend to maintain as long as possible. If there was a sound gold mining industry, their fee income could benefit, because there would be all kinds of new corporate activities. But it is the economies of all the gold producing countries that would benefit the most from increased volume in the gold business and associated multiplier effect a sound mining industry has on business activity in general. In addition, there would be no danger of a gold derivative banking crisis.

** Hedge funds are also allowed to go long in bullion or may buy gold mining shares for capital appreciation. Permanently shorting the gold market is extremely dangerous at this stage. From experience, we know that there is no fever like gold fever.

The only group to benefit long-term, the only winners today and tomorrow, are the gold buyers, most prominently among them the jewelry industry, because they are buying gold at unnaturally depressed levels. The ones to benefit most financially, however, are financial entities such as Goldman, Sachs, etc., who are on the other side of the gold industry's short and forward sales. When the price finally explodes, these same houses, which have profited from the fiat money arrangement, are most likely to own most of the gold and, possibly, the gold mines.

The groups that are worst off are the mining companies, their employees and their shareholders in particular, due to billions of dollars in lost revenue, lost dividend income, and, especially, lost market capitalization. Meanwhile, the gold company executives still receive their salaries regardless of the mortal danger facing the industry. In a business that is known to be a high-risk, there should be commensurate rewards for the real risk takers: the shareholders.

When there are none, shareholders vote with their feet and leave the sinking ship. This is not only visible in the price of gold mining shares around the world, but it is also a bad omen for the future because mines always need new equity capital to replenish plant, equipment and reserve funds. Because exploration has virtually come to a stop, reserves are not being replenished. If the current trend continues, the industry will exhaust the mines in a few years and then shut them down.

On the loss of specialist gold investors, Julian Baring had the following to say:

> "The body of professional gold mining investors has become so emaciated that it can no longer be looked upon by the mining industry as a serious source of capital. The mining industry will have to look elsewhere for investors, but those investors don't know our 'rules.' Little do they know or care about 'market cap per resource ounce.' [...] They will want to see a return on their money which compares favourably with what they expect to get elsewhere."[42]

South Africa Could Win the War

South Africa, a major producer of gold, needs to become aware of the other dimensions of gold, its symbolic significance, and the practical side of the metal. Gold has been the best money for almost 3,000 years. It became the world money under the gold standard of the nineteenth century when national currencies were defined as a weight of gold. It was this use of gold as money that represented an ingenious automatic mechanism, which guaranteed an integrated payment system, stability, prosperity, freedom and economic growth. And as we know from bitter experience, no alternative system has come even close to the perfection of the gold standard. A free, international and multilateral world economy requires a global currency. Gold is the free market choice for that currency, because it is the most efficient form of money. Equally, there cannot be the slightest doubt that there is no way to rebuild a full potential world economy without gold. To restore a global currency system, or a new financial architecture as it is now called, without gold is not only difficult, it is impossible.

This is what South Africa (and Russia also) needs to understand. It has to realize that it is producing the most precious product that will serve as the indispensable basis for the coming global currency reform. If the country can get accustomed to this thought, then it should realize that it will have to fight for its product against the unholy alliance that is determined to ignore or even destroy it. It has to familiarize itself with the symbolic dimension of gold during the 5,000 years of civilization in the making.

South Africa should acquire a higher consciousness of the role of gold and the part South Africa plays in this arena. It should fight for gold and not let it be ridiculed and denigrated by those who pretend that it is a thing of the past. Every cheese producer fights harder for his product. It should finally adopt a forward strategy and become the leading force in the gold question. Together with a consortium of equally open-minded and forward-looking gold mines, it should launch a public relation campaign to reinstate the world's interest in gold and the gold standard.

All major African gold producing countries ought to be interested in joining this campaign. South Africa should also remember how America, as a pioneer country, managed to become the biggest economic power in the world without foreign aid or the help of a World Bank or IMF. America did it on its own with the occasional help of gold loans.

A lot of financing was done by issuing gold-backed bonds. This is what South Africa, Russia and other gold producing countries need to learn and put into practice: Financing growth by issuing gold-backed bonds instead of squandering wealth by giving away precious gold at bargain prices. This is what these countries rich in natural resources ought to do. It is their only chance at economic revival and future prosperity. Switzerland may serve as a model, a shining example of a country that has achieved the highest standard of living in the world without possessing any natural resources to speak of. South Africa has the advantage of owning resources and space.

Gold as money prevents inflationary policies and corruption. Gold is a precondition for a free society. It is the most liquid product, the best store of value, the best insurance and nobody else's liability. Only by anchoring the economy in the principles of natural law will we be able to find a long-term solution to the problems of South Africa and the world as a whole.

Part VI: The Gold War of the 1990s

[1] Charles Mackay, *Extraordinary Popular Delusions and the Madness of Crowds, Money Mania – the Mississippi Scheme 1719 and 1720.* (London: Richard Bentley, 1841), 1 ff.
[2] On October 6, 2000, Bill Murphy of GATA reported in his Midas column at *LeMétropoleCafé* that in the Far East and Europe, gold traded higher in the morning 40 out of 42 times, only to be shoved back down on the COMEX shortly before closing. Furthermore:
  1. Under the heading of *"Evidence of Gold Manipulation on the COMEX"* published on December 6, 2000 at Reginald Howe's *Gold Sextant*, Michael Bolser presented a thorough analysis entitled *"Anomalous selling in COMEX gold, 1985 to November 2000."*
  2. In his complaint filed on December 7, 2000, in the United States District Court for the District of Massachusetts in Boston against the Bank of International Settlements, Basle, Switzerland, several government and central bank officials, and certain large bullion banks, U.S. lawyer Reginald H. Howe alleges manipulation of the gold price from 1994 to the present by a conspiracy of public officials and major bullion banks. This manipulative scheme appears directed at three objectives: (1) to prevent rising gold prices from sounding a warning on U.S. inflation; (2) to prevent rising gold prices from signaling weakness in the international value of the dollar; and, (3) to protect banks and others who have funded themselves by borrowing gold at low interest rates. They are short of physical gold and in danger of suffering huge losses as a consequence of rising gold prices. See annex.
[3] *Gold and the International Monetary System in a New Era*, World Gold Council Conference, Paris, November 19, 1999. (London: World Gold Council, 1999), 47.
[4] Murray N. Rothbard, *The Case Against the Fed*, (Auburn, AL: Ludwig von Mises Institute, 1994), 83.
[5] B. Bandulet, "The Euro: Who is afraid of Mr. Duisenberg", *Ambiance Magazine*, Special Issue Private Banking, Zurich, September 2000, 27.

[6] Dale Henderson, talk at the Conference of the International Precious Metals Institute (IPMI), Williamsburg, VA, 12 June, 2000. Retrieved from www.LeMetropoleCafe.com, 21 September, 2000.

[7] Federal Reserve report by Dale Henderson and economists at the University of Chicago and Amherst College, May 2000. Retrieved from www.LeMetropoleCafe.com.

[8] In 1934, the U.S. private gold was stolen from the people who 'deposited' gold in banks and received certificates that were to be redeemable in gold. The gold was confiscated and the notes were defaulted. Beginning in 1963, the redemption promise was no longer printed on the U.S. paper currency. (Paragraph IV, article 34 of the complaint of Reginald H. Howe vs. the Bank for International Settlements, Civil Action No. 00-CV-12485-RCL, registered at the U.S. District Court in Boston, MA).

[9] Paul Fabra, "Les banques centrales jouent-elles à la baisse de l'or?" *Les Echos*, (Paris, 16 May, 1999).

[10] Ibid.

[11] Ibid.

[12] "IMF Folly." *The Northern Miner*. (Don Mills, Canada), 29 March – 4 April 1999, 4.

[13] Statement from U.S. Rep. Ron Paul. "Clinton Administration Proposal that IMF Sell-off Gold Holdings", www.house.gov/banking/31799pan.htm, 17 March 1999.

[14] Editorial. *The Globe and Mail* (Toronto), 11 May, 1999.

[15] Letters to the Editor. *The Globe and Mail*. (Toronto), May, 1999.

[16] Kenneth Gooding, "Death of Gold", *Financial Times*, London, 13/14 December, 1997, I.

[17] Peter L. Bernstein, *The Power of Gold* (New York: John Wiley & Sons, Inc., 2000), 258.

[18] Robert Blake, *Disraeli* (London: Eyre & Spottiswoode, Publishers Ltd., 1966).

[19] Sir William Rees-Mogg, *The Reigning Error* (London: Hamish Hamilton Ltd., 1974), 68-71.

[20] John Maynard Keynes in Tract on Monetary Reform (1923) as quoted in Sir William Rees-Mogg, *The Reigning Error*, 258.

[21] Peter L. Bernstein, *The Power of Gold*, 68.

[22] A. Duchâteau, *Central Banking and the World's Financial System*, (London, World Gold Council, May 1997), no. 15, 52 – 54.

[23] $350 billion representing gross revenue less interest expense.

[24] Richard M. Pomboy, "An open letter to central bankers, gold mining companies and gold investors." Advertisement in the *Financial Times*(London) and *The Wall Street Journal*, 9 June, 1997.

[25] See also Paul Volcker and Toyoo Gyohlen, *Changing Fortunes* (New York: New York Times Books, 1992).

[26] "Godfathers of Easy Money", *Financial Times*, London, 21 October, 1998.

[27] Barry Riley, "", *Financial Times*, London, 14/15 July, 2001, 20

[28] "Julian Baring, 1935 - 2000", *World Gold*, vol. 3, no. 10 (October 2000), 14.

[29] John Hathaway, *Gold Investment Review – Annual Review 1999*, Tocqueville Asset Management, L.P., 11 January 2000.

[30] Timothy F. Garrard, *Afrikanisches Gold* (Munich: Prestel Verlag, 1989).

[31] Lionel Barber and Gilliam O'Connor, "All things to all men", *Financial Times* (London), 2 December 1999.

[32] World Gold Council, *A Glittering Future? Gold Mining's Importance to Sub-Saharan Africa and Heavily Indebted Poor Countries*, (London, June 1999), 4.

[33] "Julian Baring, 1935 - 2000", *World Gold*, vol. 3, no. 10 (October 2000), 14

[34] Antal E. Fekete, *Gold Mining and Hedging*, (St. John's, Canada, Memorial University of Newfoundland, 1998), 2/3.

[35] Ibid, 3.

[36] Ibid, 4.

[37] Antal E. Fekete, e-mail to author, 3 November, 2000.

[38] Ted Butler, *Gold Digest*, www.Gold-Eagle.com, 16 August, 1997.

[39] Lawrence Parks, *The Near Death & Resurrection of the Gold Mining Industry*, (Woodside, NY: Taylor Hard Money Advisors, Inc., 2000), 1.

[40] Ibid, 9.

[41] *Gold and Mining Investment Guide,* American Investment Services, Inc., (Great Barrington, MA: 31 May, 2000), 34.

[42] "Julian Baring, 1935 - 2000", *World Gold*, vol. 3, no. 10 (October 2000), 14

Part VII: Betrayal of Switzerland

"When we assign the production of money to government, we should expect inferior money."[1]

Lawrence White, economist

"The art of war is of vital importance to the state. It is a matter of life and death, a road either to safety or to ruin. Hence, it is subject of inquiry, which can, on no account, be neglected by any of us today ...and tomorrow."[2]

Sun Tzu (China about 500 BC.)

"The price of liberty is eternal vigilance."[3]

Wendell Phillips (1811-1884)

"In the Old *Testament*, *Genesis* tells us that gold is a valuable asset. It cannot have been its monetary charm that attracted our biblical fathers – and, at that time, central banks were not running the show. Hence, no charm, no harm! Something that has enjoyed unique esteem for thousands of years is not going to melt down in the space of a few years."[4]

Jean Zwahlen (1995)

Tragic Turn of the Gold War

In the nineties, the gold war entered what may be its last and most tragic phase. Gold-rich Switzerland became the main target. War preparations are often made a long time before actual hostilities begin. The groundwork was laid many years ago when it was suggested that neutral Switzerland join more international organizations. The battle for Switzerland's gold opened when the country became a member of the IMF in 1992.

177

A few years later, in 1996, the SNB radically changed its gold policy. Almost a quarter of a century after Switzerland's central bank started floating its currency in January of 1973 under the leadership of Fritz Leutwiler, another historic shift took place. This time the change was more dramatic. Very few realized what an impact it would have on Switzerland's future as a sovereign nation. The same goes for its position as a financial center or the long-term effects on its economy. For decades neutrality and the strength of the country's currency were at the base of the world's confidence in Switzerland's banking system. The reason was quite simple: The Swiss Franc was 100% backed by gold and, therefore, considered as good as gold.

Late in 1996, the Swiss government, in co-operation with the SNB, came to the surprising conclusion that, in today's world, a 40% reserve backing of its currency was no longer necessary. These were the sensational findings of a joint study group, which had been formed to work out a plan for eliminating this 'old fashioned' proviso without excessively shocking the prudent Swiss citizens. To many, there is still no doubt that the 40% reserve requirement, which was anchored in the constitution, was one of the cornerstones for the worldwide respect given the Swiss Franc and the Swiss banking center.

According to the 1995 SNB Annual Report, gold reserves only covered 43.2% of notes in circulation. That was down from 46% in 1990. Since notes in circulation were increasing every year, a change was needed. The legally determined gold price of SFr 4,595 per kilo was totally unrealistic when the market price was around SFr 15,000. (Five years later, at the time of this writing, the gold price is still around SFr 15,000.) The best possibility for a quick and clean solution would have been to increase the official price of gold to market-, or to near market-level, as the French and Italian central banks did. This would hardly have been more difficult to handle than Leutwiler's historic decision.[5] In 1996 the scenario of simply adjusting the price upwards had become unthinkable because Switzerland had joined the IMF in 1992. Under the IMF's Articles of Agreement, linking a currency to gold is prohibited.

178

For decades the SNB had been considered as solid as the rock of Gibraltar. Not that its record was impeccable, to the contrary, it blundered repeatedly. But, it had in its coffers 2,590 tonnes of gold representing the golden guarantee. It was the fourth largest gold reserve in the world, equivalent to 8% of total official gold, or almost as large as the reserve of Germany, a country 10 times larger than Switzerland.

The Swiss National Bank Decides to Give Up its Independence Because of its Own Blunders

Things were going to change. In the early 1990s, the Swiss economy was not doing well, and unemployment was uncharacteristically high. The SNB knew that the most expeditious tool to weaken the franc was to drop the golden link, i.e., to reduce monetary discipline. The golden link had to be eliminated anyway because Switzerland had surrendered to the rules of the IMF by becoming a member. That did not seem too extraordinary. President Lyndon B. Johnson had done the same in March of 1965 when he promised 'guns and butter' to his country. LBJ weakened the link between gold and the dollar, and Congress removed the requirement that the Fed maintain a 25% reserve of gold certificates against member bank deposits.

Chronology of the Swiss Monetary Drama

1992

Switzerland joins the Bretton Woods Institutions

"All Warfare is based on deception."[6]

Sun Tzu (China, 500 BC.)

"The Swiss National Bank has no intention of selling any gold."[7]

SNB Board member, June 20, 1992

The end of the Swiss Franc's historic tie to gold was brought about in 1992, and not in 1996 or 1999. The decision was taken when Switzerland joined the IMF. According to IMF Articles of Agreement (2b, paragraph IV) adherence to a gold-backed currency was prohibited, and Switzerland fell to its knees under the leadership of its Federal Councilors EU-favorer Flavio Cotti and the social democrat Otto Stich. The only ones who did not know what was going on were the Swiss people. They were never told the truth.

In recent years the government and its growing bureaucracy built up a powerful PR machine for the purpose of direct intervention. It is now the order of the day that before each plebiscite this opinion-making propaganda machine is deployed, and heavy pressure is put on citizens to follow government proposals. The whole exercise is not only illegal, but it is done at taxpayers' cost. This is no longer a democracy.

Before Switzerland joined the Bretton Woods institutions, its government propaganda machine relentlessly 'sold' the issue to the public as a better form of foreign aid. The nation that founded the Red Cross always had an understanding for humanitarian aid. Despite the heavy pressure, the outcome of the vote was quite close. Only 55.8% voted in favor. Not an overwhelming result, particularly if one takes into account that the majority, including most well-informed people, had no idea about what the IMF did and still don't know to this day. The only major force opposed to joining the IMF was the Swiss People's Party (SVP).

The IMF

Alan Reynolds of the Hudson Institute, stated the following in March of 1992:

> "In July 1944, at an international conference held at Bretton Woods, New Hampshire, the United States and Britain joined with other major economies to found the IMF. Its purpose was to promote exchange stability. On August 15, 1971, when President Nixon suspended gold convertibility of the dollar, the central concept on which the IMF was founded was gone. Still, no one proposed closing

down the IMF. Instead, bureaucrats in the IMF sought a new reason for their existence. The IMF's Articles of Agreement were thus revised to legitimize the new, more flexible system. In the succeeding years, the IMF substantially expanded its activities in financing payments – in an apparent effort to justify and redefine a continued role for itself."[8]

The essay came to the conclusion that the IMF generally has not played a positive role. Already in August of 1983, Robert M. Bleiberg commented in *Barron's* that ever since Bretton Woods, the Fund has compiled a near perfect record of failure. Former U.S. Secretary of State, Henry Kissinger, and former U.S. Secretaries of the Treasury, George Schultz and William E. Simon, were all for abolishing the IMF. On October 24, 1997, William Simon wrote in the *Wall Street Journal* that the IMF is ineffective, unnecessary and obsolete. He concluded:

"The House and Senate now have a golden opportunity to force the long overdue elimination of the IMF. There is no longer any reason to burden tax payers with the expenses of this outdated institution."[9]

Alan Reynolds found that if the IMF has a positive role to play, this role has yet to be defined.

In a monograph published by Committee for Economic Research and Education (CMRE), distinguished economist, Anna J. Schwartz, along with R. Christopher Whalen, then Director of Investment Banking at Prudential Securities Inc. in New York and Walker F. Todd, formerly an attorney for the Federal Reserve Bank of Cleveland and economic consultant, found that, based on the IMF's failures, it was time to abolish the IMF and the Treasury's Exchange Stabilization Fund.

Beginning with 1992 and thanks to the fateful decision taken by an uninformed Swiss government, the Swiss taxpayer was unnecessarily burdened with the cost of joining the IMF.

Helvetistan

From then on, Switzerland was referred to as 'Helvetistan' in IMF circles. The *Neue Zürcher Zeitung* (NZZ) reported in November of 1992 that the countries with which Switzerland was grouped together were possibly off to a difficult start.[10] It was not hard to disagree with this opinion. In order to secure a seat on IMF's Board, Switzerland was forced to join a group of countries with which the Swiss had little or no economic or political relationship, not to speak of cultural or historical ties. They were all central Asian republics and formerly part of the Soviet Union: Azerbaijan, Kirghizia, Turkmenistan, Uzbekistan, and Tajikistan. It is interesting to note that, at the time of this writing, Switzerland's seat on the IMF Board is not as secure as it appears, due to the next quota revision.[11]

How could Switzerland sacrifice its uniqueness and surrender to an organization, which had lost its *raison d'être* after the collapse of Bretton Woods? Joining the Bretton Woods organizations in 1992 signaled the end not only for Switzerland's unique currency, but in the long run it also posed a threat to its prominent position as one of the world's big financial centers. It is the *classe politique* that, if it had its way, would eventually and carelessly sacrifice Switzerland's sovereignty. Again, either the public was not given the real reasons for joining the IMF, or then the government did not understand what it was doing.

Both situations are true. There was no reason why Switzerland should have joined the IMF, and the reasons that were given to the electorate were simply not serious. In spite of Switzerland's neutrality, the government was consistently pursuing a strategy of internationalizing Swiss politics. We need to "be part of the international community" or "we cannot stay out" were, and still are, the arguments of the Federal Council and the Nationalbank.

Regardless of the fact that Switzerland had already spent billions of Swiss Francs in tax money and continued to play an important role in developmental aid, the Federal Council wanted the country to join every international organization. Because Switzerland is a small country, it would not have much influence. Years of observing Swiss politics, Swiss political life and having contacts with high-ranking politicians have lead me to believe that in monetary matters the Swiss government has no idea what it was (or is) doing. I am convinced that there are very few members of the present parliament who understood the deeper significance of joining the IMF. Not one person may realize that it is Switzerland's political and economic suicide in slow motion.

How was it possible that the banks of a small country and the Swiss banking institutions became some of the most powerful financial organizations in the world, handling a large percentage of international investment portfolios? It was only possible because the gold backing of the Swiss currency provided confidence. After the downfall of Bretton Woods, the Swiss franc was the only currency in the world that was still tied to gold. It was this unique attraction and guarantee of soundness that made the Swiss franc the focus of the envy of the proponents of a dollar standard. The Swiss franc had an attraction the dollar did not have. Its tie to gold could no longer be tolerated by the masters of a future new world order.

How could the Swiss be lured into giving up their gold standard? The easiest way was to let them join the IMF. Why? Because the IMF, although it pretends to be in favor of strong currencies, explicitly states in its Articles of Agreement that member countries are prohibited from tying their currencies to gold. They can tie their currencies to anything else, to Special Drawing Rights, etc., but not to gold. The best solution, therefore, was to make Switzerland join an organization that was against gold—the IMF. That is how the Swiss franc lost its unique status. And that is why Swiss banking will gradually lose its powerful position.

It was a sensational triumph for the manipulators. They had finally achieved what they wanted for so long: the complete abolishment of gold's monetary role. From there it was only a short step to convince Switzerland to sell its gold, thereby pushing the price of gold further down into the abyss. The switch was thrown and the manipulators only needed to wait. The gold wars were entering their most decisive phase.

1995

World Gold Conference – Swiss National Bank keeps its gold reserves

On June 19, 1995, Jean Zwahlen, one of the three members of the Governing Board of the SNB, said on the occasion of the World Gold Conference in Lugano that he does not believe in selling or mobilizing Switzerland's gold reserves. During his opening speech, he defined gold as ultra-reliable and said:

> "To state it bluntly, the Swiss National Bank has no intention whatsoever to sell or mobilise its gold reserves. There are several reasons for this. Our monetary constitution, admittedly a leftover from the 'good gold days', prevents us from downsizing the gold stock or from actively managing it. Reserve diversification does not automatically require the sale of gold. In the past, diversification was primarily achieved by increasing foreign exchange reserves. [...] Moreover, the gold that serves as cover for our banknotes must be available in coins and bars, thus precluding gold lending. Moreover, gold lending would expose us to a credit risk that we could not leave unsecured. Beyond the legal framework, that will be updated sooner or later, there are also economic and strategic reasons for hoarding. Gold, although almost fully demonetised, remains a money surrogate. Not that I mistrust the current monetary system that is based on fiat money: Paper money, including book money and electronic money, is perfectly reliable. My point is that gold is ultra-reliable. Gold reserves are the last resort of the lenders of last resort. At the end of the day, gold is the only reserve item that is not someone else's liability. Consequently, the cost/benefit analysis of gold reserves must be a very broad one. That accounts for low probability events, by which I mean worst case scenarios. But common human nature should be factored in as well. For thousands of years, gold has

stood for wealth and status and for confidence and reliability. The Swiss National Bank's loyalty to gold undoubtedly enhances its reputation and credibility."[12]

A well-known gold expert who attended the Lugano conference told me privately that he saw how representatives of major bullion firms tried to talk Zwahlen into gold lending and how he resisted.

The gold price in Zurich on June 19, 1995, at 4 p.m.: $391.

Jean Zwahlen retired from the bank at the end of 1995.

The Enemy from Inside

For years, the leftist media, socialist politicians and mainstream economists put pressure on the SNB to manage its assets more efficiently and profitably. There was an endless discussion of whether the legal requirement for partial gold backing of the currency had lost much of its original economic function, namely as a means of restricting money creation by the central bank. Some of the strongest attacks came from a university professor of foreign origin (Why doesn't he teach his wisdom in his own country? Its currency became worthless twice during just one century.). He thought it unjust that the Swiss had to tighten their belt due to the SNB's inability to achieve better results with the country's savings. He reckoned that the SNB could have earned billions of francs with it instead of sleeping on the gold treasure. All these prophets, whether they were part of the media, academia, the political or financial sector, proved to be the enemy from inside, because they stupidly, or intentionally, wanted to change a proven policy that had acted as a sure confidence builder for over a century.

1996 - 2000

What does Swiss gold have in common with Goethe's Faust?

The new generation of SNB officials went into action. They had a different view of gold. They may have heard of the gold standard, but they did not understand it. They had not lived through a crisis such as the one of the 1930s, nor had they experienced a 'grand daddy' bear market. Most were born after the war and had been brought up to believe in the stock market. Today, investment bankers generally hold a mostly negative view about gold. Many may have never seen a gold coin in their life. The only gold they have seen belongs to their wives. Gold has been in a bear market for 20 years. Everybody has come to believe that common stocks are in an everlasting bull market because of the wonderful 'liquidity' around. It does, therefore, not surprise that in the future gold should play a lesser role in the minds of the new generation of bankers

The ball started rolling in April 1996, when outgoing Chairman Markus Lusser, a lawyer by training, described the 40% gold backing of Switzerland's currency as 'a relic of the past'. The previously conservative Zurich financial press tuned into the growing anti-gold trend and joined the increasing number of critics of the central bank's portfolio management. They claimed that 'mismanagement' had lost billions rightfully belonging to the people. The leftist boulevard press, politicians and economists, who had been attacking the SNB for not running their assets more professionally, were of no help to the pitiable central bankers.

In November of 1996, legal council of the SNB and head of a joint work group, Peter Klauser, announced the main findings of the group and concluded:

> "Today money depends exclusively on the trust in authorities issuing it. Gold has become a commodity [...] Gold is demonetised."[13]

Klauser started his lecture by borrowing from Goethe's drama *Faust I* where Margarete says: "Everyone seeks gold – and everything depends on gold."[14] Unfortunately, Klauser did not continue. In *Faust II* Johann Wolfgang von Goethe eloquently describes the 'virtues' of paper money.[15] Goethe, one of the greatest philosophers/writers of all times had closely followed the paper money experiments of John Law in France as well as the Assignat scandal during the French Revolution. He understood the workings of a paper money system.

Here is further proof of his astute knowledge about things economic.

"Chancellor

> In my old days my happiness how great!
> Hear, then and see this fateful scroll, for this
> Has turned our woe and wailing to bliss.
> 'Be it to all whom it concerneth known,
> This not is worth a thousand crowns alone,
> And for a guarantee, the wealth untold,
> Throughout the empire buried, it hath hold.
> Means are on foot this treasure bare to lay.
> And out of it the guarantee to pay.'

Emperor

> Crime I surmise, some monstrous fraud.
> Oh shame!
> Who dared to counterfeit the Emperor's
> name?"[16]

"'A few strokes of thy pen, and so thou'lt seal,
This revels crowning joy, - thy people's weal!'
These strokes thou mad'st, which were ere morning-tide.
By thousand hands in thousands multiplied.
That all alike the benefit might reap,
We stamped the whole impression in a heap;
Tens, thirties, fifties, hundreds, off they flew –
You can't conceive the good they were to do.
Look at your town, - t'was mouldering and half dead –
Now all alive, and full of lustihead!
High as thy name stood with the world, somehow
T'was never looked so kindly as now.
The list of applicants fill to excess;
This scrip is rushed at as a thing to bless."[17]

But, back to the SNB and Klauser: Before all this happened, Klauser, whose report sent tremors through the gold markets, was a total unknown to the financial world. But there is a spicy detail to his career: Klauser also serves as chairman of the board of a reputable listed Swiss company by the name of Orell Füssli AG. It just so happens that this company is the leading banknote printer of the country and the SNB is a major shareholder. Under such a constellation, the stock of the company seems to have only one way to go—up!

On November 25, 1996, shortly after the news of the Klauser report was announced, gold tumbled and *Barron's* commented in its Commodity Corner column:

> "Gold prices fell to a 29-month low Thursday, near $ 376 an ounce, amid news of possible Swiss gold sales and technical selling."[18]

The day before the gold price was at $386. The fall of $10 an ounce represented a loss of around $10 billion for all central bank holdings in one day, not to speak of the total losses to all the world's savers. The traders rejoiced. On November 27, 1996, a trader in the service of UBS had the following to say in his daily recommendation sheet, which he cynically titled "Precious Thoughts":

> "Herr Klauser can hardly claim he was misquoted, this [report] will run and run.... and run gold into the $ 360s? Short, horror story: Thursday's near 11,000 rise in COMEX open interest during $2.50 fall suggests another historic day of building new, bigger, better short positions..."[19]

In December, Samuel Schmid, National Councilor and member of the so-called Gold Commission came into my office and asked for my opinion about the Klauser Report. (Samuel Schmid has been elected to the Federal Council in the meantime, and he is now one of the seven members of the Swiss government.) After having studied the paper, my conclusion was that the foremost duty of a central bank is to protect the integrity of the currency, and that, in my view, the proposed changes to the Nationalbank Act would not guarantee that. Quite the contrary, the new policy, if adopted, would contain a number of risks. I advised the head of the parliamentary commission to oppose the changes. Gold lending was a bad policy and exposed the lender to risks no central bank should take. It was not only risky, but also stupid.[20]

The powerful Deutsche Bundesbank and the SNB were talked into 'gold lending' at a later stage of the gold bear market. I wrote to a Member of Parliament that a projected annual profit of SFr 50 million on its lending activities, or an interest rate of a little over 1%, was not worth putting the nation's patrimony at risk. Furthermore, the action would depress the value of the country's own gold stock and with it all of the world's patrimony thereby creating a serious problems for the gold mining industry and the economies of friendly nations.

A little over a year after Jean Zwahlen had spoken out so strongly in favor of the bank's gold reserves, the SNB, in obscure bureaucratic language, welcomed the proposed removal of the gold reserve requirement in its 1996 Annual Report.[21]

Unfortunately, the discussions that took place between the group of 'wise men' at the SNB and the parliamentary commission were never made public. Two questions arise here. If these people are dealing with public funds, why isn't there public disclosure? What are they trying to cover up with all the secrecy? This procedure is not consistent with democracy.

A few details did leak out. It became known that the group wanted to abolish the 40% reserve requirement in one sweep. Why fuss over something that could be handled in one swift move? Not surprisingly, this was decided in 1992, the precise moment the country joined the IMF. National Councilor Samuel Schmid, a fast learner, had enough presence of mind to block legislation. He told the government and SNB people that they could either have a partial revision right away or wait for another year and a half until Switzerland's new constitution was up for popular vote. They were told to take it or leave it! They took it, and by early March 1997 the partial revision of the Nationalbank Act passed. Switzerland's National Bank could finally enter the game of lending gold and depressing the price of gold. A look at the charts tells the story at a glance.

The financial press of March 18, 1997, announced how a study group of the Swiss Department of Finances and the SNB had worked out proposals for a more profitable management of the Bank's currency reserves, in other words, they had graduated to the modern central bank portfolio theory.[22] In its 90th Annual Report closing December 31, 1997, the SNB gives an absolutely unsatisfactory explanation for lowering the gold reserve requirement. It said that the reduction to 25% was necessary because otherwise the gold lending activities would have compromised the SNB by violating the legal limits.[23] Such a justification is hard to believe, but what is even harder to believe is that the SNB should resort to such a bogus explanation.

For me, a Swiss citizen whose family is Swiss on both parents' side for as long as there are written records, this was betrayal. It was completely against Swiss traditional thinking and behavior. We Swiss have always been slow to adopt new foreign procedures, and, in particular, revolutions of such a fundamental nature. Of course, there was the constant lamenting and influencing by a destructive media. There is no doubt in my mind, however, that the main instigators for the change of mind came from overseas. Some foreign master planners with great experience and full of brilliant tactics must have suggested this course of action to Swiss central bankers, making this caper the envy of Clausewitz or Sun-Tzu had they been alive. For the foreign manipulators, the last gold-backed currency, the Swiss Franc, was the only remaining obstacle to be removed from the path to the fairyland of a global fiat currency. Who needs a small country in the middle of the Alps to have the impertinence to own all that gold and to have the best currency? The treasure in the mountains had to be taken by an unusual maneuver.

When reading the following paragraphs, one should keep in mind that the main arena in which these events took place remained to be the war against gold. There is nothing else that worries the would-be masters of the world more than the power of gold. These powerbrokers were not interested in the Holocaust and in the destiny of the poor, innocent people who were killed during World War II. They were not interested in nations' individual history, their languages and cultures. They only have one culture, the dollar culture. Throughout history there were many ambitious politicians who wanted to become the master of the universe. Today this dream still prevails in some arrogant minds. In order to create a world with one government, one central bank and one currency, the biggest and most important obstacle in the path of attaining that goal must be destroyed, and that is gold.

However, and as said before, the war against Switzerland, or the battle for the Swiss gold, was already won 1992, when the country joined the IMF. That was the decisive moment when the usually prudent and historically solid Swiss did not pay attention. What was to follow could be achieved relatively easily by the powerbrokers. But the weapons used were sordid and scandalous. The country could still have kept its dignity had it not been for the big banks.

Over the years, big Swiss banks were very successful in their expansionary drive and opened branches all over the world. Today, almost half of the business of the big banks is done in the U.S. However, in more troublesome times, when law and order are beginning to disintegrate, this is not a clever policy. Because of their heavy foreign commitment, Swiss banks are at risk of becoming victims of blackmail. Possibly, they should never have opened offices in big and powerful countries such as the U.S. or Germany. Maybe, the Swiss banks should have stayed home. Perhaps they ought to have resisted the trap of quick money. Our country [Switzerland] would be in a much better position now.

The Gold War Against Switzerland as a Financial Center

The war activities were started with accusations about Switzerland's role during the war. Sensation hungry U.S. Senator from New York, Alfonse D'Amato, began to question Switzerland's role during World War II. He accused Switzerland of collaborating with the Nazi government. The fact that D'Amato was head of the U. S. Senate Banking Committee left no doubt about the actual target. It was Switzerland with its banking secrecy laws, center of banking and its gold treasure, which was under attack. Per capita, the treasure was by far the largest in the world. As a comparison, at the end of 1996, the Swiss gold stock at market prices for gold amounted to 115% of the currency in circulation versus a mere 21%

coverage for the U.S. dollar and only 20% for the Deutsche Mark. This was the reason why the currency was so greatly respected abroad.

It was a case of modern Conquistadors this time not raiding the gold possessions of the Mayas of Mexico, the Incas in Peru and the people of Colombia, but the vaults of the Swiss. This war was not a war by the sword, but by a much more dangerous weapon – the media, foreign and, unfortunately, also Swiss. The St. Gall private bank Wegelin & Co. declares in its *Investment Commentary*:

> "Special interest groups, backed up by a publicity conscious U.S. senator and the support of the media, systematically increased the pressure on Swiss banks and our country as whole. The mood was further intensified by a class action suit brought before a New York court against Switzerland's three largest banks, seeking compensation of over 20 billion Swiss francs."[24]

The orgy of accusations grew larger with every day.

Totaler Krieg[25]

On July 19, 1999, Jane H. Ingraham wrote the following:

> "The *New York Times* and the *Washington Post* launched an avalanche of shockingly vituperative accusations against the highly respected Swiss banking industry using the suffering of the Jewish people as a bait. The charge: Swiss banks still hold gold deposited by Jews who became victims of the Holocaust. Spearheaded by the fabulously rich Edgar Bronfman (member of the influential Council of Foreign Relations), owner of the multinational liquor company Seagram and president of the World Jewish Congress, the 'funds without heirs' quickly mushroomed into a 'humanitarian' rescue mission for 'abused' Jews who had had bank doors 'slammed in their faces' when they tried to collect. Nowhere in

this sustained propaganda was there a semblance of proof of any 'unclaimed assets'"[26].

According to *The Jewish Bulletin of Northern California,* E. Bronfman announced at a meeting in California on March 10, 1998, that it was time to declare 'total war' on Switzerland.[27] In order to help bring Switzerland to its knees, Bronfman borrowed a vocabulary reminiscent of a propaganda minister who spewed out such verbiage some 60 years ago to attack the enemies of the Third Reich.

What had been overlooked was that in the 1950s and again in 1962, Swiss banks had formally investigated the dormant accounts of persons who may have died in the war, and the banks paid out tens of millions to survivors and Jewish causes. As an executive in a prominent private bank that was owned by a Jewish family, I am a witness to this action and confirm the seriousness with which this investigation was carried out in every bank in the country. I also can confirm that each member of the staff voluntarily contributed a sum of money to Jewish causes.

In spite of this, the pressure was so intense that the Swiss government was forced to agree to convene an independent commission made up of eminent persons to audit the banks' records again. The commission's chairman was none other than Paul A. Volcker, former Chairman of the Federal Reserve, famed and powerful member of both the Council on Foreign Relations and the Trilateral Commission. The *American Spectator* revealed that this was nothing but a fraud and quite transparent:

> "Unfortunately, no reliable study exists, nor can one be undertaken sixty years later, even by eminent persons, that can verify from where and how money came to Switzerland during the 1930s."[28]

Meanwhile, Switzerland's *Journal de Genève* reported an astonishing warning issued by Bronfman:

> "Edgar Bronfman estimates that if the Swiss bankers do not seize the unique opportunity to re-establish their reputations the end of Switzerland as one of the world's great banking centres can be

foreseen, for every essential mark of confidence will have disappeared. The free world may well end up finding such a banking system reprehensible."[29]

Goliath against David

Jane Ingraham continues:

"The shocking truth is that the American/European insider cabal has the power to carry out this extraordinary threat. That the threat was perfectly understood by the Swiss Federal Council was soon apparent. First came the announcement of a Swiss Humanitarian Foundation endowed with seven billion francs, interest from which would be used for the needs of 'persons' in grave financial stress. This vague wording was necessary since nothing whatsoever about Jewish assets had yet materialised. In short, the seven billion had nothing to do with 'funds without heirs'. Yet Bronfman and others who were attacking the banks were jubilant, and with good reason."[30]

Switzerland Drops to its Knees

"Switzerland Drops to its knees" is the English translation of the title of a carefully researched book, *Der Kniefall der Schweiz,*[31] by Luzi Stamm, a Swiss lawyer and conservative Member of Parliament. Based on his analysis of the situation, he came to the conclusion that this capitulation was only possible because of a serious consciousness crisis in Switzerland, resulting in disorientation. The author and many Swiss vehemently disagree with the statement that an American/European insider cabal could have forced Switzerland to its knees. Nobody in the world could have forced Switzerland to do anything, particularly since it, of all European countries, had one of the cleanest records during World War II.

Switzerland was in position of strength, which was foolishly sacrificed by weak and shortsighted leadership. Unforgivably, the Swiss government did not even listen to its own Ambassador in

Washington, Dr. Carlo Jagmetti, who warned the government in Bern about what was brewing inside and outside Switzerland. America would have respected strength. After all, even Moammar Ghaddafy, Saddam Hussein or Milosevic gained respect.

At the time, Switzerland was a large owner of U.S. Treasury securities. To convert just a little of this paper into gold would have sent a clear message. Furthermore, Switzerland has always given high priority to a good relationship with the U.S. Proof of this good relationship is Switzerland's representation of U.S. interests in Iran since the crisis. Switzerland could not have been bullied into paying if its government, the parliament, the SNB and the big banks had understood why this campaign of lies was undertaken in the first place.

In addition to the unforgivable weakness displayed day-after-day by official Switzerland, there lurks a huge internal enemy. It is the incredibly short-term thinking on the part of today's opinion leaders, most politicians and a large section of the media. The Swiss paid and unnecessarily lost a lot of credibility built up by earlier generations.

In February and March of 1997, the Swiss Banks, Swiss industry and the SNB paid 270 million Swiss Francs into the so-called Holocaust Fund. On August 12, 1998, under the joint attack of a few U.S. lawyers and the World Jewish Congress, the Swiss banks were ready for an 'all-encompassing global solution' by paying $1.25 billion out of an unfounded fear of sanctions!

Had the Federal Government and the SNB followed the advice of one of the country's most influential bankers, former National Bank and BIS President Fritz Leutwiler, this outcome could have been avoided. Months before, Leutwiler had been involved in the establishment of a special fund for Holocaust victims. He was mediating between Swiss banks and industry on one side and the World Jewish Congress on the other. Behind the scenes, he convinced the big banks to make SFr 100 million available, and industry signaled that an additional contribution of SFr 50 million would be made to the fund.

When the U.S. confronted Switzerland with boycott threats, Leutwiler contacted the SNB. He suggested that the central bank should make another SFr 200 million available. SFr 100 million were to be earmarked for the central bank's own potential obligations resulting from this affair, and SFr 100 million were to be put aside as an advance for payments by the Swiss Confederation. It was his firm conviction, based on his contacts with top-level representatives of the World Jewish Congress that SFr 350 million would be enough to satisfy Switzerland's critics.

Winston Churchill on Switzerland's Role During the War

> "Of all the neutrals, Switzerland has the greatest right to distinction. She has been the sole international force linking the hideously sundered nations and ourselves. What does it matter whether she has been able to give us the commercial advantages we desire or has given too many to the Germans, to keep herself alive? She has been a democratic state, standing for freedom in self-defense among her mountains, and in thought, in spite of race, largely on our side."[32]

A Wall Street Banker and Friend of Switzerland

A well-informed Wall Street Banker had the following to say:

> "Someone should remind the solons at the Swiss National Bank that a nation of four million totally encircled by the Wehrmacht had no choice but to trade with Germany. At least the older generation had the good sense to insist on payment in gold, rather than accepting Reichsmarks."[33]

Harry Schultz gets right to the point:

> "Ethical aspects aside, it seems no accident that governments are zealously using the Nazi gold issue to discredit and unduly pressure Switzerland to compromise its banking secrecy."[34]

A Central Banker as Fund Raiser

The president of the SNB, Hans Meyer, a colonel in the Swiss Army, is known to be a very cautious man. His speeches are not particularly electrifying and his comments on the economy and his forecasts are not particularly insightful or accurate. But between Christmas 1996 and New Year 1997, while walking his dog in the central regions of Switzerland, he had a sudden inspiration: The Solidarity Foundation! Switzerland would re-value its gold and pay seven billion francs into a fund for humanitarian purposes. He commented to the popular press that when his inspiration struck him, it was as if a light had gone on. He felt Switzerland needed to take a great leap forward. As an advisor to the government he had to propose the idea to Federal Councilor Kaspar Villiger, whose family has its own particular past in World War II.

More Swiss Monetary Chronology, Very Briefly

February 26, 1997: The Federal Council decided to launch a Solidarity Foundation

March 5, 1997: President of the Federal Council, Arnold Koller, announced a proposal to set up a Solidarity Foundation for those "who suffered severe hardship through no fault of their own,"[35] and the concept of financing it through revaluation of gold reserves. It later became known that the whole idea was only crudely planned and lacking serious design in spite of the fact that it represented a decision with unknown implications and, possibly, explosive effects.

Reuters reported at 10.09 GMT the same day: "Swiss plan to sell gold..."

Three days prior, the same Federal Councilor had announced that the family silverware (i.e., Switzerland's gold treasure) would not be sold foolishly.

Prices of gold mining shares, which had increased 20% since the beginning of the year, suddenly dropped like a lead balloon.

March 6, 1997: NZZ of Zurich:

Plans of gold sales hit nervous markets: "It is as if McDonald's would step out of the Hamburger business."[36] Bullion dropped to $354.85 or $5 below the previous day's close of $359.85, as correctly forecasted by UBS traders.

March 17, 1997: Message by the Federal Council on the revision of the Swiss Nationalbank Act, proposing to reduce the gold reserve requirement from 40% to 25%.[37]

March 25, 1997: Fritz Leutwiler assailed the gold fund. Leutwiler, one the world's most respected central bankers, retired president of the SNB and of the BIS, said the proposal was badly 'thought through' and raised questions about the Bank's independence. He was concerned that what had been regarded as one of the world's most independent central banks would come under pressure to use its gold reserves for politically motivated projects.[38]

As the World Gold Council reported, Leutwiler believed the central bank should not let the state touch its "hitherto-sacrosanct reserve". Because of this "ill-thought out" proposal, the central bank had "lost its innocence."[39] Others, such as former Finance Minister Otto Stich, criticized the proposal as a "magician's trick."[40] Publicly and privately, Leutwiler said that on several occasions he had tried to get in touch with the SNB and that he was disappointed by the spinelessness of Hans Meyer.

The powerful SVP president, Christoph Blocher, was totally against the Solidarity Foundation, and former Deputy Chairman of the SNB, Leo Schürmann, stated that launching the Euro would represent an acid test for the Swiss Franc.[41] In times of currency turbulence, Switzerland had always been able to rely on its gold and, therefore, should not sell it.

June 19, 1997 the partial revision of the Nationalbank Act passed the Council of States (Switzerland's equivalent to a Senate).

November 1, 1997: The new SNB legislation took effect.

The Last Obstacle to SNB Gold Sales: The Swiss Constitution

Talking to Swiss people, it appeared that everybody believed there would be a popular vote to decide the fate of the country's gold reserves. This was not the case. At least not in the minds of the Federal Council and of the SNB officials who were permanently looking for ways to reach their final goal of 'freeing' the Swiss gold without involving the populace in the process. The last serious obstacle remaining was the Swiss Constitution.

On October 10, 1997, well-known National Councilor, Dr. U. Schlüer, conservative member of the SVP party and the Swiss equivalent of the U.S. House of Representatives, came to my office. He was a member of the parliamentary commission in charge of the new Constitution. He seemed completely disgusted because, when the new draft was presented to him and the commission, he noticed that the gold reserve requirement was simply left out. Even the word gold had disappeared. When he asked for the reasons for the change, the reply was that it was no longer possible to have that in the Constitution because Switzerland had pledged to the IMF in 1992 to drop gold coverage altogether.

Again, the Federal government's propaganda machine set in, and hundreds of politicians were telling the public why they should vote for the new Constitution. The public had to make up its mind quickly. Never in the history of Switzerland were the Swiss citizens given so little time to decide on such an important issue with immense and incalculable future implications. The government spent years preparing and the voters barely had three weeks to study this vicious document. Although the majority voting for the government proposal was not overwhelming, very few came to the conclusion that this act would abolish the gold link and that it would change Switzerland forever. The only major party voting against the new Constitution was, again, the Swiss People's Party (SVP).

Goodbye Sovereign Switzerland

This was the title of Jane H. Ingraham's article in the *New American*. Her conclusions were that the citizens of Switzerland had voted away their financial stability and independence, setting the stage for total absorption by the EU.

The article starts as follows:

"With scarcely a murmur of dissent, the seemingly impossible was accomplished. Lacking understanding, the Swiss people voted this spring to end the unique soundness of their currency as well as their country's financial power and independence. Oblivious to the consequences of abandoning the Swiss franc's tie to gold, the people of Switzerland – the world's only direct democracy – approved a new constitution that abolishes the traditional gold convertibility (gold reserve requirement) that for generations made the Swiss franc literally 'as good as gold'.

In the past, Swiss citizens had always been allowed as much as a month to scrutinize and debate a single constitutional change; this time they had to decide very quickly, without debate, on more than 100 articles containing profound modifications to their mode of government, their military and their culture. Obviously haste was necessary to prevent the Swiss from realizing that their laws, rights, and customs were being subsumed under international edicts and mandates, including a perfidious attack on the traditional family.

In short, this incredible document dismantles the most natural parts of community life such as liberty, national identity, family, and privacy. In their place are socialist objectives such as the 'right' to a job and the 'right' to housing. Further steps are inevitable as the dials are set for Switzerland's total absorption into the European Union." [42]

One can only compliment Jane Ingraham for this precise analysis. Whether it was the accomplishment of some unknown insiders will probably never be known, although the consequences will be felt. The federal government and the SNB still need to answer the questions: Who has done this to the people of Switzerland? Who, inside and/or outside the country? Who were the powerbrokers that wanted to downsize the Swiss financial center, then abolish the banking secrecy laws and depress the price of gold?

According to American sources it is an open secret. Nobody was present, of course, when these discussions took place. As the rumor goes, two prominent American figures talked the Swiss authorities and bankers into believing that selling gold was the perfect gesture to show the world that the modern Swiss are coming to terms with 'their mixed past' and, therefore, should disassociate themselves from their reverence for gold. For who needs gold in a globalized economy? In conclusion, the assault on Switzerland must be seen as a perfidious attack against freedom. Because Switzerland, like no other nation, upheld the banner of freedom, retained its institutions such as the banking secrecy laws and maintained its strength in the form of a high gold reserve, it could not be tolerated any longer in a world where the proponents of big government were ever increasing their interference in the private lives of citizens.

The Purpose of this Book

The intention of this book is to inform the public that we are in the middle of a tragic currency, monetary and, therefore, gold war. It is not the purpose of this book to discuss the so-called *Volcker Report* and Switzerland's role during the war. If the accusations against the Swiss during World War II are mentioned briefly, then it is only in context with the 'Gold Wars,' and to show the reasons why and how Switzerland got involved in the 'Gold Wars.'

The aim of the Volcker-Commission authorized by the Swiss Bankers Association on May 2, 1996, had, however, a double function insofar as it was aimed at the banking secrecy laws of Switzerland and, consequently, against Switzerland as a banking center. Similar tactics are used by non-elected EU-officials in Brussels.

The immediate cost of the commission to the Swiss banks is estimated to run into several SFr 100 million if not over SFr 1 billion. However, the long-term effect by far exceeds the monetary loss. The cost may be a lot higher because it damages Switzerland's prestige and reputation as well as the confidence placed in

Switzerland. Finally, it is a direct threat to the Swiss economy and an attack on its freedom to decide for itself.

Another reason is to show how much falsehood and ruse is used as weaponry in this war. Most unforgivable is that the raiders were using the sorriest weapon of all: the miseries of millions who died in Nazi camps. Barrick Chairman Peter Munk, himself a Jewish refugee in Switzerland during the war, demanded publicly that this 'orgy of accusations' against Switzerland be stopped. As several respected Jewish personalities also confirmed, this post-World War II attempt at regurgitating the past is beginning to resemble a giant fund raising event.

In his book *Between the Alps and a Hard Place*, Angelo M. Codevilla reveals how the true history of the Swiss in World War II has been buried beneath a modern campaign of moral blackmail. Switzerland has been accused of secretly supporting Nazi Germany and sharing in the culpability for the Holocaust. The campaign set a terrible precedent, whereby a powerful domestic interest group—and major donor to the Clinton/Gore administration—harnessed the power of the U.S. government to grossly distort history and to secure a financial windfall. Codevilla says that, in the process, the larger interests of the United States were subverted for the sake of a favorite domestic constituency of the ruling party. It resulted in the shameful constituency of the ruling party. He also documents how the anti-Swiss campaign offered no evidence for its shocking claims, but still managed to shake down two of the largest banks of a friendly power for $1.25 billion.[43]

One of the most aggressive accusers and slanderers of Switzerland, former Under Secretary of State and friend of former President Clinton, Mr. Stuart Eizenstat, has recently adopted a much more moderate stand regarding Switzerland's war role. He now feels that it is completely wrong to lump Switzerland and Nazi Germany together. The Swiss bi-weekly *Schweizerzeit* feels that Eizenstat's new posture may be explained by his new and apparently very lucrative job. His new firm, Covington & Burling, has good and friendly contacts with the biggest Swiss bank, UBS.[44]

SNB Gold Sales Could Be the Financial Marignano for Big Swiss Banks and the Swiss Economy

The name of Marignano is significant only to the Swiss. There is a small town outside Milan with the Italian name of Melegnano. The traveler on the highway or the railroad will barely notice it. But to Swiss people it is the culmination of their history lessons at school, because it marked the end of a glorious period during the 14th and 15th centuries when Swiss soldiers were considered invincible.

The freedom-loving Swiss were the best soldiers of the period. They had driven the Austrian House of Habsburg out of their territory, beaten Duke Charles of Burgundy in three decisive battles and, in doing so, conquered Lombardy, including Milan. As Switzerland's geography consisted mainly of mountains and the country's economy was, therefore, very poor, most young people had no chance of making a decent living at home. Thousands of young men went abroad every year to serve (and die!) as trustworthy mercenaries for Europe's kings and popes.

To this very day the Vatican keeps the tradition of a Swiss Guard for its protection. It is a relic of the times when popes relied on Swiss mercenaries to enter into wars and conquer territories for them. In the famous battle of Marignano in 1515, a small army of 20,000 Swiss infantry was beaten by the artillery of the French King Francis I who had almost as many Swiss mercenaries as soldiers of his own. It marked a turning point in Switzerland's history as a military superpower. After that defeat, the Swiss decided to become neutral and to abstain from all foreign policy adventures in future.

A similar condition prevails today. The big Swiss banks are active in every part of the world and, therefore, exposed to increased risk and vulnerable to blackmail by jealous competitors. The Swiss were successful in the past, but they probably grew too big. There used to be three big banks, now there are only two. Two of the 'Big Three' merged for no apparent reason. Cash rich Union Bank of Switzerland (UBS), formerly a very successful triple-A bank, was taken over by the smaller Swiss Bank Corporation (SBC) in need of the cash![45]

Size is not everything. Banks do not necessarily have to be big. They must be solid, offer good services to their clients and be profitable for their shareholders. That's all.

Switzerland's unique gold reserve gave the currency and, consequently, the banking industry the necessary respect it needed to build the confidence of its international clientele. With half of this treasure dissipated, a part of this respect will have evaporated. Switzerland's role in international banking will not be the same. As long as the Swiss economy is doing well, and as long as there is enough unrest in the world, there is always enough work to keep Swiss bankers busy even if other banking centers catch up. But the uniqueness and outstanding reputation as a banking center were gambled away unnecessarily by the Federal Government, the SNB and the big banks.

Short-term thinking has become the rule with both the SNB and the big banks. What does the SNB get in exchange for the gold it is selling now? All it has received for its gold are electronic blips representing a potential claim on uncertain values. However, the question really asks for the winners and the losers in this new Swiss gold policy? It certainly was not the Swiss people. They were betrayed.

An even more extreme change can be seen at the big banks. They are primarily looking to maximize their fee income. What would the shareholders say if they knew that 'their' banks were among the leading members of the so-called 'big-four' investment banks who advised Ashanti on its hedging and derivatives policy before it nearly collapse in 1999? In other words, the banks were part of the syndicate that helped ruin Ashanti and Ghana. Is this the future role of Swiss banks? If this is so, what are they going to do as a follow-up? In which far corner of the world will they strike next?

Last Annual Meeting Before Gold Sales Begin

The SNB lost no time. In June 1999, a law designed to permit gold sales was defeated. In spite of this, 1,300 tonnes of 'excess' gold were included in the Washington Agreement of the European central banks of September 26, 1999.[46] They were included, although the Coinage Act, authorizing the SNB to sell gold, had only passed in parliament in late December, three months after the Washington Agreement.

Furthermore, there was still the possibility of a referendum whose time limit did not run out until the end of April 2000. This raises the question of who gave the SNB the right to include the 1,300 tonnes in the Washington Agreement before due process came to an end. This is further proof of the Federal Government and the SNB's blatant disregard for the Swiss people and for the concept of democracy.

During 1999, the SNB stepped up its gold lending activities from 187 tonnes in 1998 to 316 tonnes, showing that it had learned nothing from the near-bankruptcy of LTCM whereby UBS lost approximately SFr 1 billion. By the end of 1999, gold loans valued at SFr 4.7 billion were outstanding. The spoils of this newly found 'profit center' were a meager SFr 57.8 million or only SFr 15 million more than in the previous year, 'yielding' a little over 1%. While the SNB's total profit of SFr 4.4 billion in 1999 was mainly due to the higher value of its U.S. dollar holdings, the outlook for 2000 looked a lot bleaker, because, by the end of 1999, the SNB had a new position on its books of over SFr 20 billion in Euros. If the SNB considered its gold positions a risk, it would soon find out that there lies a much greater risk in fiat money.

Weak Gold Price due to the SNB and the Neue Zürcher Zeitung (NZZ)

Since no referendum had been taken, the SNB announced at its annual meeting that the sale of gold would begin the following day. The day before, the *NZZ*, loyal to the party line, published an article titled "Gold hardly glitters as an investment."[47] It stated that gold producers were on the defensive and that, due to the media, masses of information on alternative investment opportunities were available, making gold very unattractive to investors.

During the week, gold fell by several dollars down to the low $270s. If there ever was any uncertainty about the SNB's and government-loyal *NZZ*'s position in this unholy crusade against gold, then it was removed now. The SNB can be accused of mismanaging the country's gold assets, but the *NZZ* must be taken to task for hiding the truth, or, worse, knowingly misleading the public. The alternative is that the editors didn't know any better, but that is as unlikely as their innocence.

How misleading the *NZZ* reporting concerning SNB matters is, was proven again on January 5, 2001 in an article entitled "Gold Boon for the National Bank – 25.4 billion francs net revaluation profit."[48] The SNB had done nothing else than revalue the price of gold on Labor Day (May 1 in Europe) in its books from the antiquated price of Fr. 4,595 per kilo dating from 1971 to the current market price of SFr 15,291. In other words, the leading Swiss newspaper lauds the fact that the SNB (with a delay of almost 30 years) made an accounting profit while it is widely known that the very same national bank in conjunction with the Bank of England is busily helping the U.S. Treasury and the gold cartel to manipulate and, thereby, depress the price of gold.

The hypocrisy of the newspaper goes even further. Only at the end of the article does it mention that the SNB suffered a foreign exchange loss of SFr 1.1 billion in 2000 compared to a profit of Fr. 4.7 billion in 1999. This comes as no surprise as 'solidarity fund raiser' Hans Meyer had been talked into buying over Fr. 20 billion in euros the year before by the smart President of the European Central Bank, Wim Duisenberg. This move by Meyer out of gold and into the euro happened at a time when it was clear to many that the euro would deteriorate in the foreseeable future and remain a weak currency.

What is to be expected of 2001? In view of the Bush administration possibly having another agenda for the dollar, and because Greenspan & Co. will deliver the necessary Fed stimulus to remove the obvious stress in the banking industry, the possibility of a weaker dollar that might bless the SNB with a renewed loss in 2001 is rather high. The long-term outlook for the euro is not promising either.

Designed to be weak from the beginning, and, given the present intentions of opening membership in the European Monetary Union to former communist nations who are not known for their monetary discipline, the Esperanto currency will ultimately resume its decline. Under such circumstances logic unequivocally speaks for gold. This, of course, is not recognized, but eventually will be. Surprisingly, there is no mention in SNB report about any particular success in last year's lending activities. In the meantime, the SNB continues its gold sale at give-away prices.

According to the *Bible*, a prophet is not without honor but in his own country and among his own kin and in his own house. Let us, therefore, refer to a comment from Federal Reserve Chairman Alan Greenspan regarding international gold sales by central banks. Greenspan was speaking on May 20, 1999 at a House Banking Committee hearing on the international financial system and had the following to say:

> "It's fairly evident that central banks are acutely aware that if they announce they're going to sell gold that the price will go down and they'll get a lower price. No self-respecting trader would ever think of doing that sort of thing."[49]

Strong Gold Price Due to the SNB?

Another doubt has been eliminated. What the SNB ultimately had in mind all those years and deliberately sought was a weak Swiss Franc, even if it had to sacrifice the nation's savings. That was the most important reason why gold had to go. How much pressure the export industry put on the SNB will probably never be known, and it really doesn't matter. A weak Swiss Franc may help some exporters in the short run, but in the long run, such a policy is a national disaster.

Central banks know that we are living in a world of constant currency devaluations and ongoing currency wars. In such situations, gold is the last line of defense. Central banks know that an overwhelming number of people support gold's continuing role as a reserve asset. A survey done for the World Gold Council found a large majority of people interviewed in France, Germany and Italy believed that their country's central bank should maintain or increase its current level of gold reserves.[50]

Already speculation is under way that almost none of these Swiss gold sales will result in actual physical supply reaching the market. On his website, American lawyer and investment advisor Reginald Howe wrote on April 16, 2000 that it is his suspicion that this gold will most probably replace gold that was previously leased into the market by Euro-area central banks, allowing them to bring their physical gold stocks to the same levels as their officially stated gold reserves by procuring

"[...] sufficient physical gold to cover outstanding gold loans on the books of Euro-area central banks, to which it can be directly channelled through the Bank for International Settlements. The Swiss sales obviate the risk of embarrassing defaults that a rising gold price would otherwise bring, particularly in a gold market that is net short by two to four years of annual production. And by removing this risk, the Swiss sales leave the Euro-area central banks, collectively the world's largest holders of monetary gold, with many reasons to cheer – and no strong reason to oppose – rising gold prices.

At the end of 1999 the Euro-area countries as a group reported total gold reserves of 12,457 tonnes [...] putting their total outstanding gold loans in a range of 10 - 12 percent gives estimates of 1,250 to 1,500 tonnes. [...] In these circumstances, final approval for the Swiss gold sales could put the last block in place for a workout of all or most outstanding gold loans on the books of both the Euro-area central banks and the SNB. The essence of the plan would be to allow the leased gold on the balance sheets of the Euro-area central banks to be replaced by gold purchased from the Swiss, and leased gold on the SNB's balance sheet to be replaced by gold purchased from the Dutch and Austrians. [...] the plan would also allow to rescue bullion banks and commercial banks through paper instruments from threatening insolvency in the event of much higher gold prices."[51]

Who Put the Holes in the Swiss Cheese?

The secrecy with which the gold issue was handled at the SNB and the Finance Department is only possible in a country where cronyism runs rampant. In Switzerland, you'll find the same people—mostly politicians, bankers, military officers and other insiders—sitting on the boards of larger companies. There is a club-like atmosphere, but it really borders on incest, and we all know what incest can lead to! Recently, it was said that a seat on the board of a major corporation or bank is more valuable to a Swiss than a title of nobility. The danger of this is that bad news or deteriorating situations are often kept secret until the crises become blatantly obvious. A recent example is Swissair. It clearly shows how a formerly successful business can be run into the ground in a very short time by a negligent board of directors unfamiliar with the industry. Zurich Insurance is another example, and the list of calamities continues to grow. Fortunately, men like Christoph Blocher and Martin Ebner are crusading against these encrusted structures and are placing renewed focus on shareholder value.

If ever light is shed on the real reason why the SNB is parting with half of the country's gold, it could easily turn out to be the most tragic event in Switzerland's history. On LeMetropoleCafe's website, in an essay "Who Put the Holes in the Swiss Cheese?" Professor von Braun speaks the unspeakable:

"The decision of the Swiss National Bank to sell half of their reserves in the final stages of a very long bear market in precious metal has, to this observer of the gold market, always been a tad suspicious. It was one of those announcements that seemed to be rather rushed, since approval was sought in very short order. The Swiss banking industry has been around too long to have engaged in rushed decisions on not other than what has been a cornerstone of its soundness, bullion, secrecy of course being another. Although it's fair to say that the secrecy thing is not quite what it used to be. But selling half of one's gold reserves, well that's a different story altogether.

209

What did the SNB know that the Swiss politicians did not is a question that comes to mind. Could it be that they needed access to a large amount of physical metal for some purpose other than what they told the gullible Swiss public: the new legislation allows them to sell gold as they see fit.

Could it be possible that they needed access to such a large amount of physical metal to allow certain Swiss banks to cover derivative positions held by their bullion trading divisions? Was this exposure a threat to the Swiss banking system, and could it only have been covered by the national reserves?

The Swiss have of course been playing in some rather large ponds in recent times what with a host of mergers and acquisitions such as Credit Suisse and First Boston. Then there was the rather rapid merger of Swiss Bank Corporation with UBS, a case of a smaller fish swallowing a bigger one it seems, along with several UBS heads been given the rapid 'goodbye'. We never did hear what actually happened there, but it is safe to assume that rapidly announced bank mergers, especially when a smaller bank takes over management of larger one, usually mean that a balance sheet may have needed some help.

What was at risk in that merger one has to ask? Could it have been the exposure to gold? Even the merger by Chase Manhattan with J. P. Morgan was done in a rather rapid time frame, Goldman Sachs apparently was J. P. Morgan's first choice but after some initial due diligence, they said thanks, but no thanks. Both J. P. Morgan and Chase Manhattan have considerable exposure to the gold market as well, as does Deutsche Bank, another J. P. Morgan suitor that withdrew quickly, perhaps with some help from the Bundesbank. Who knows what goes on behind central bankers doors these days, apart from waffling.

Did the LTCM shake out give the SNB something to think about when it came to their own 'local' bank positions? Approval for the Swiss sale was given in April after being announced in 1999. Fancy that."[52]

U.S. stockbroker Joseph J. Cacciotti of Ingalls & Snyder in New York offers the following interpretation in his investment letter:

"Of particular note are the strange sequence of events leading to the merger of Chase Manhattan and J. P. Morgan & Co. These two outfits hold by far the largest positions in gold derivatives. Supplies of gold to support these activities have begun to dry up, which will make continuation of this game increasingly difficult, even if it does not threaten the integrity of existing derivatives. On Thursday, September 7th, JPM's CFO and guiding light of the bank's derivatives strategy, Peter Hancock, suddenly resigned to 'pursue entrepreneurial interests'. On Monday, September 11th, the Chairman of CMB and JPM met for five minutes to agree to a merger. Five minutes!!?? Was someone present at this meeting holding a shotgun? There is a certain urgency about this whole affair, which leads me to wonder whether the Fed arranged this union. When something has to be done in such haste, there must be a problem. Hancock's resignation implies a problem in the area of derivatives. If my deduction is correct, it makes sense that the Fed might want to get the huge derivatives positions of these two banks lodged together under one roof in the event that a rescue operation becomes necessary. Both from a practical and a political standpoint, it would be easier to achieve and justify a bail-out of one Wall Street 'fat cat' rather than two."[53,54]

Professor von Braun continues:

211

"The worldwide derivatives market is estimated
to be $100 trillion, a mind boggling number, one
which serves to remind us that such a large derived
amount is required to keep the game going, a game
which sees the underlying real asset representing only
a small portion of this amount. Isn't that interesting.
What would the players in the derivatives game use to
pay off their commitments if things went sour?"[55]

No More SNB Gold Sales through BIS

On March 24, 2001, Swiss media informed that the SNB
would sell its 'surplus' gold directly through first-class institutions
with which it already had working relationships. It previously had
sold via the BIS and would sell another 100 tonnes until the end of
September.

A surprising move at first sight, but at second glance, it may
not be so surprising at all. Basel-based BIS, often called the central
bank of the world's central banks, has come under attack in recent
months. It plans to buy back 13.73 per cent of its shares from its
private shareholders. The shareholders are strongly objecting
because the price offered is far too low. Consequently, on December
7, 2000 (the anniversary day of the attack on Pearl Harbor), a
lawsuit was filed in the U.S. District Court in Boston by Reginald
Howe, accusing the BIS, five elite investment houses and top U.S.
Treasury and U.S. Federal Reserve Board officials, including Alan
Greenspan, of conspiring to suppress the price of gold.

It is also alleged that the BIS is not only involved in the
business of central bank gold lending, but also in the business of
lending IMF gold. This demonstrates once again what a disastrous
role the IMF continues to play. One of the greatest coups against
gold happened in 1987 when U.S. gold on deposit with the IMF was
sold through the Bank of England. That drove the gold price down
by $100 an ounce in one day.[56]

The Gold Anti-Trust Action Committee (GATA), which was
created in January 1999, is an organization that has systematically
followed every move in the gold market for the last several years. It

believes that the SNB decision to sell gold may have been taken to help their own bullion banks climb out of their short gold positions. Moreover, GATA said that it believes with good reason that the BIS is now very much an instrument of the gold conspiracy cabal that is trying to suppress the price of gold, e. g., the group named in the Howe lawsuit. GATA suggests that the Swiss may have made the decision to stop selling through the BIS because it is like selling it through the gold cartel. Or, as Bill Murphy of GATA said: "Maybe the Swiss (via the BIS) were sending the gold to the desperate English instead of to the Swiss banks."[57]

Time will tell if any of these scenarios are right. The public will probably never be told unless something happens that will force the true reasons to come to light. An event that could trigger that is an explosion of the gold price. We know from the defunct Gold Pool that gold is a powerful and formidable foe. When the time is right for it to rise, it will expose this scandal of the century with a vengeance. This may happen at a time when leading stock indices like the Dow Jones Industrial or Nasdaq retreat to lower levels. The traumatic and long-lasting effect of these developments are going to have on public confidence is foreseeable. Meanwhile, the Swiss are continuing to give away their gold at the lowest price in 21 years.

Counting on the Franc

The *Financial Times* already asked in 1999:

"Has the Swiss franc lost its reputation as a safe haven currency? [...] It has only managed a modest strengthening against the poor old Euro. The Swiss National Bank has also made clear that it does not intend to repeat the mid-1990s mistakes, which plunged the Swiss economy into its deepest recession since the 1930s. However, the SNB is steering a tricky course."[58]

French economist and monetary expert Paul Fabra:

"*La BNS se met au goût du jour. L'institut d'émission hélvétique est entré à son tour dans la danse. Il est devenu un acteur actif non plus*

213

seulement des marchés monétaires, mais des marchés financiers en pleine frénésie." (The SNB is adapting to the taste of the day. The Swiss monetary institution itself has entered the dance. It has become an active player not only in the monetary field but also in the financial markets in full frenzy.)[59]

What does this all mean? The SNB has lost its good reputation. Fabra thinks that the SNB completely changed its policies three years ago, and that the change was not for the better.

In June of 2000, Fabra wrote that in reality the stock market had replaced the functions of the central banks.[60] This would explain a recent statement Chairman Greenspan made to House Banking Committee member Dr. Ron Paul, during the question and answer session following his testimony. Mr. Greenspan said that he could not define and could not manage the nation's money.[61] Fritz Leutwiler made a similar comment some years ago. When Leutwiler retired as president of the Bank for International Settlements in 1984, he spoke to reporters about his thoughts for the future. They may be prescient. He feared that the growth of transactions by computer would make it difficult to "allow any proper examination" of whether a commercial bank was solvent, thereby making it practically impossible for central banks to measure the amount of money in circulation.[62]

Taking a step back and focusing on the forest, Robert Landis, comes to the following conclusion:

"[…] the Swiss [were] bullied into surrendering their gold for the benefit of a one-world apparatus operated for the benefit of the Fed. Switzerland is certainly not alone; the list of casualties of the US/IMF machinations is extensive. But among the developed state victims, it is unique. Britain made its Faustian bargain more or less knowingly; the Swiss were defrauded."[63]

The Bank of England's Monetary Dunkirk

The announcement by the U.K. Treasury on May 7, 2000 that the Bank of England was going to sell 415 tonnes of its gold reserves led to a public outcry. According to the World Gold Council, the people of Britain were 5 to 2 against selling the nation's gold.

In the days and weeks prior to the sale, the gold price had started a timid rally and almost overcame the $290 mark, which some analysts considered a crucial technical hurdle. The market had gotten used to endless noises about Swiss gold sales and IMF gold sales programs 'in order to aid developing countries.' Slowly, confidence was returning as the underlying supply and demand for gold suggested that prices should be rising more strongly. However, the U.K. move was a bombshell. The price of gold dropped immediately by $8 to less than $280 a troy ounce. On July 20, gold slipped to a 20-year low of $252.80.

The *Financial Times,* known for its anti-gold stance, commented in its Lex Column on May 9, 1999:

> "The Gold rush has started – but in reverse. With their decision to auction more than half of the U.K.'s 715 tonne gold reserves, the Treasury's boffins are dashing for the exits ahead of other central banks' bears. It is entirely rational for the U.K. to seek to maximise the value of Britain's gold, currently an unjustifiable 43 per cent of net reserves. Trailing a series of knock-down auctions, rather than quietly selling into a liquid market, may appear to be a crude way to go about it. But transparency should pay in the end, if it neutralises fears of secret, unquantified selling.
>
> For that reason it is odd the U.K. government is keeping 300 tonnes. At 18 per cent of net reserves, it will represent a heavy position in a low-returning commodity that has proved to be a lousy investment in recent years, even if it may still serve as a partial store of value in [times of] global crises.

So having already unnerved the
markets, the Treasury might as well have
gone the hog and planned to sell the lot." [64]

As a result of this surprising U.K. action, shares of gold mining companies came under heavy pressure, forcing mining management into a torrent of new and potentially disastrous hedging commitments at a moment that could be a long-term bottom of the gold market. Gold producers such as AngloGold and Goldfields accused the Blair government of taking totally unsuited action because it would encourage speculation, depress the price of gold and destabilize the gold market. South African Prime Minister Thabo Mbeki protested that the decision would have a "potentially disastrous effect" on South Africa. [65]

Chancellor Gordon Brown was said to have been surprised and mortified by the reaction of Mr. Mbeki. When a delegation led by South Africa's mines minister, including senior trade unionists, wanted to meet him in London in order to stop the gold sales, Brown did not have time to see them and left it to junior ministers and officials to meet with them.

On June 3, 1999, HM's Treasury, in a letter, gave the following reply to a worried City banker whose firm's daily bread, amongst other things, is dealing in mining and natural resources shares:

"Sir, like other countries, the United Kingdom
needs to keep under review its official foreign
currency and gold investments. In the sixties gold was
at the centre of the international financial system but
since then the financial markets and the world
economy have moved on. As a result in recent years
its special status has waned. The Government
considered it makes sound financial sense to lower
the proportion of the country's net reserves held in
gold. – The aim of the restructuring is to achieve a
better balance in the portfolio by increasing the
proportion held in currency."[66]

A few weeks later, on July 11, 1999, Chancellor Brown of HM's Treasury told colleagues that the plan to sell off more than half of Britain's gold reserves was not his idea.[67]

In my position as a member of the Carlton Club in London, which is close to the Conservative Party, I wrote the following letter to the President of the Carlton Club's Political Committee, the Rt. Hon. Peter Finlay, MP, on June 3, 1999:

> "Dear Sir, Personally I feel that the Conservative Party could earn considerable credit and merit if it did oppose these probably foreign induced gold sales. Why? First of all: The people of Britain are overwhelmingly opposed to selling the country's gold reserves. Secondly, from history we know that the British Empire was built on the basis of the gold standard which lasted for 250 years until the outbreak of World War I. During this period prices fluctuated but were, in general, mostly stable as they always returned to the equilibrium point, with an index of 100 in 1664 and 90 in 1914. We know what happened to the Pound and currencies in general when the world went off the 19th-century gold standard at the beginning of the war. It is my conviction that had Britain and its politicians known more about gold, England would still own its empire."

His reply was that the leader of HM's Opposition Party, Mr. Hague, shared my views regarding the sale.

In the parliamentary debates in the House of Commons, contrary to the mediocre debates in the Swiss parliament, there were at least some high level discussions to be heard, particularly the speech by Sir Peter Tapsell. He said that he regarded the decision to sell 415 of the 715 tonnes of gold as a reckless act, which goes against Britain's national interest. The sale of that crucial element of the United Kingdom's reserve assets will weaken its scope to operate independently, reduce its influence in international financial institutions, and *weaken the United Kingdom as a world financial power.* [Emphasis added.]

"1. The Lord Chancellor's announcement has so far cost this country's taxpayers over £400 million, which is more than the cost of the Kosovo war to the United Kingdom.

2. The decision reduces Britain's monetary independence. For a country to hold gold is always seen and interpreted as an affirmation of independence and monetary sovereignty.

3. The decision smacks of short-term interests. Governments and their central banks are supposed to act in the long-term interest of their countries.

4. The decision is a threat to the London gold market, because it reduces the Treasury's ability to act as what is known as a swing lender in the market. Many market participants believe that, after the sales have been completed, the Treasury will not have enough gold to fulfil its function as a swing lender and to retain the centre of the world gold market in London.

5. About 20% of the proceeds are to be invested in yen – so the Treasury tells us...

6. The concept of reserve management that lies behind the decision is deeply flawed. After the sale, the U.K.'s gold reserves will be only 7% of its gross reserves, which is slightly less than those of Albania."[68]

In line with the growing world-wide freedom of the press, it was impossible to find media reports on Britain's gold debate. U.S. businessman Bill Murphy of GATA felt that most market participants now believe that there was an orchestrated effort by certain officialdoms to suppress the price of gold:

"As Swiss plans and IMF deliberations have not been sufficient enough to hold the price of gold down, the U.S. puppet Britain was the quickest route for an immediate dumping."[69]

American investment advisor James Turk, editor of *Freemarket Gold & Money Report*, is quoted in *Barron's* on May 31, 1999:

> "For months it has been my contention that central banks are manipulating the gold price. More proof came on May 7th with the announcement of the British government. [...] This downward pressure of the gold price dovetails nicely with the other reason that central banks are motivated to manipulate the price of gold. Gold is the barometer by which central-bank management of a country's currency and economy is being gauged and evaluated. A rising gold price is a sign that monetary danger lies ahead, such as inflation or banking problems. A falling or low-and-steady gold price is taken by the market as a sign that all is well with the national currency and the economy. Clearly, central bankers would rather not have gold looking over their shoulders at their every move. So the central bankers have been at war with gold."[70]

So far, British auctions have been oversubscribed every time. In some cases big mining firms purchased the gold to reduce or eliminate their hedge positions.

Investment advisor and lawyer, Reginald Howe, winner of the 1992 Bank Lips AG Award, on February 29, 2000 wrote about a British monetary disarmament and draws parallels to World War II when the British had to leave Europe, but were able to return with the help of the U. S. But with its gold down to unsustainable levels, Prime Minister Blair's government might not have enough gold to join the Euro-area, especially if the entry fee is doubled. In such a case Britain might logically look westwards to other allies – namely NAFTA. Or, as Sir Peter Tapsell said correctly:

> "When you sell gold then you ultimately loose your independence and monetary sovereignty."[71]

Ominous Parallels Between the
Destiny of Two Financial Centers

In the preceding paragraphs I tried to explain how, as a result of the SNB's new gold policy, there would be one prominent loser, namely Switzerland along with its banking industry, its position in the financial world and its economy. Only time can tell how soon this forecast will come true. The same seems to apply to London that once was the financial capital of the world. When Britain was under the gold standard, the 'Old Lady of Threadneedle Street', as the Bank of England was called, was the world's most powerful central bank.

In the end it is all a matter of confidence. As long as gold is respected, confidence runs high. Both the Swiss and British central banks used to be highly regarded and were solid examples of sound central banking. However, when central banks start to sell off their gold, they are replacing it with depreciating paper money that has been created out of thin air. In such an environment uncertainty becomes the future.

In its heyday, London was at the center of the world's merchant banking. Over the years all the formerly glorious names in banking have disappeared, as they either merged or were taken over by giant and aggressive American, German and Swiss banking firms. After Schroders went to Citicorp at the beginning of 2000, and Robert Fleming sold out to Chase a few months later, there is only one historic merchant bank left – N.M. Rothschild. Another famous name, Baring, once called the 5th Power, disappeared within a few weeks some years ago due to 'unauthorized' speculation in derivatives by one of their traders.

Fed Chairman Greenspan 'Strongly' Opposes Central Bank Gold Sales, but…

There may be no central banker in the world today who has such a thorough understanding of the gold standard and the monetary role of gold as Mr. Greenspan. His historic essay "Gold and Economic Freedom" became world famous. It is one of the best descriptions ever written on how gold and economic freedom are inseparable.

From time to time Chairman Greenspan dropped nostalgic remarks about how much better and safer a gold standard would be than the present non-system. Mr. Greenspan warned, again and again, about the existence of "systemic risk," which, in his opinion, could turn into a calamity at any time. However, and also according to Mr. Greenspan, this drama could never happen under the discipline of a gold standard. He, therefore, may feel that central bankers who are selling their gold are acting foolishly. The following comments he made after the Bank of England announced its sale of gold are typical:

> "The U.S. should hold on to its gold stock. [...] Gold still represents the ultimate form of payment in the world. Germany in 1944 could buy materials during the war only with gold. Fiat money, in extremis, is accepted by nobody. Gold is always accepted."[72]

Unfortunately, in the last three to four years, his views are less clear when it comes to lending gold, for he also said:

> "[...] nor can private counterparties restrict supplies of gold, another commodity whose derivatives are often traded over-the-counter, where central banks stand ready to lease gold in increasing quantities should the price rise."[73]

This statement says nothing else than that Mr. Greenspan is not against manipulating the gold price. Because, according to him, central banks practically guarantee that the price will be capped if need be, there can be no better invitation to short sellers, speculators and manipulators of all kinds. It is also in sharp contradiction to Mr. Greenspan's earlier convictions published in his essay *Gold and Economic Freedom*, in which he favored free markets.[74]

The stage was now set for the manipulation of the gold price and the beginning of the biggest money swindle in all history. If one had let the gold price float freely and unmanipulated, most stock prices in the world's bourses would probably never have reached the unsound and lofty heights they had reached by the beginning of the year 2000.

It also meant something else. Since the U.S. never seemed to sell any gold of its enormous gold stock[75], it was foreigners, such as the Bank of England or the SNB, who were expected to hold the price of gold down. Such statements also cause the price of gold to be under constant psychological pressure. Fewer people buy when highly placed officials warn day after day that a specific asset will go down in value. Central banks do this even at the risk of lowering the value of their own assets. Never mind the savings of millions of people around the globe. In the meantime, the gold mining industry and entire nations go to the poorhouse. Millions are losing their economic basis, as unemployment and misery unnecessarily spread throughout the mining communities.

Harry Bingham of Van Eck Global, wrote on June 7, 1999:

"Only 23% of the world's gold is now held by central banks, compared with 70% when gold suppressing efforts began. The total gold of central banks now account for less than thirty days' trading volume, meaning the effect of their sales in the market will be transitory at best. During periods of low confidence in central banks, official gold sales were counterproductive to their own purposes, regardless of how the gold distribution pattern changes, whoever has the gold has the money."[76]

In the meantime, the SNB and the Bank of England are continuing their clearance sale. Parallel to their mindless and reckless handling of gold, the international respect for both nations is on the decline. The United Kingdom, once the respected and admired empire, has been in a long and relentless decline since World War I. Now, it is the turn of Switzerland. Its formerly strong Calvinistic ethic that preserved the country's moral and physical independence has become so eroded that it is literally becoming the prey of almost any arrogant organized pressure group, nation, or group of nations that want to blackmail it. No wonder the man in the street is uneasy and unhappy and feels that people in high places are taking him for a ride.

Things are changing at the SNB too. In the fall of 2000, in an ugly political maneuver, Jean-Pierre Roth was chosen to replace

Hans Meyer, who leaves the ship before his time is up. The SNB Board had chosen Bruno Gehrig as the successor but was later overruled by the Federal Council. In the past, Roth repeatedly expressed the opinion that the Swiss gold hoard represented a risk. The *Neue Zürcher Zeitung* sees him as having distinguished himself by the way he handled the Swiss gold file.[77] What he had done was nothing else than excel at dissipating the nation's patrimony.

In conclusion, it can be said that Switzerland's beginning to sell off its gold reserve still eludes reason. Many authorities on the subject hold this opinion.. On April 24, 2001, during a luncheon at Rothschild's[78], Robert Guy, who acted as chairman of gold fixing for many years, told me that the *market participants* never understood why the Swiss were selling their gold.

Part VII: The Swiss Money Revolution

[1] Lawrence White, *Free Banking*, (Brookfield, VT: Edward Elgar Publishing, 1993), as quoted in Richard M. Salsman, *Gold and Liberty*, (Great Barrington, MA: AIER, Economic Education Bulletin, 1995), 87.

[2] Sun Tzu, *The Art of War*, reprint (London: Hodder & Stoushton, 1981), 15.

[3] Wendell Phillips abolitionist, orator and columnist for *The Liberator* in a speech before the Massachusetts Antislavery Society in 1852, paraphrasing Mayor of Dublin John Philpot Curran's speech upon the right of election in 1790.

[4] Jean Zwahlen, member of the Governing Board of the SNB at the World Gold Conference in Lugano, Switzerland on June 19, 1995, during his opening address.

[5] See *75 years Swiss National Bank*, 1982, p. 162: "The conflict between article 19 and 22 could be solved in the short-term by authorizing the SNB to value its gold holdings closer to the market price. A long-term solution would, however, require an all-encompassing revision of Swiss monetary law."

[6] Sun Tzu, 17.

[7] Andrew Smith, *The Swiss Revolution*. "Central Bank Gold: The Picture of Less Reserve" (Zurich: UBS Ltd., 18 April, 1997), n. p.

[8] Alan Reynolds, *The IMF's Destructive Recipe of Devaluation and Austerity* (Indianapolis: Hudson Institute, 1992), 4.

[9] William E. Simon, "Abolish the IMF", *The Wall Street Journal*, 23 October 1997, A18

[10] "«Helvetistan» vor der Bewährungsprobe", *Neue Zürcher Zeitung*, 31 October/1 November 1992, 33.

[11] Richard Gerster, "Ist der Schweizer IMF-Sitz in Gefahr?" *Neue Zürcher Zeitung*, 21 August, 2000, 13.

[12] Jean Zwahlen, "Gold – Always a Topical Subject." Opening Address, *Financial Times* World Gold Conference, Lugano, 19 June 1992.

[13] Peter Klauser, "Geld und Gold, zur Reform der Schweizerischen Währungsverfassung." Lecture given at the University of St. Gall, Switzerland, on 19 November, 1999.

[14] Johann Wolfgang von Goethe, *Faust, der Tragödie erster Teil.*

[15] Johann Wolfgang von Goethe, *Faust, der Tragödie zweiter Teil.*

[16] Johann Wolfgang von Goethe, *The Tragedy of Faust*, Part II, Theodore Martin trans., p. 283/4.

[17] Ibid.

[18] "Commodities Corner", *Barron's*, 25 November, 1996.

[19] Andrew Smith, Union Bank of Switzerland, internal daily recommendation sheet for traders, November 27, 1996.

[20] At the time, I was still naïve enough to believe that the Swiss central bankers were motivated by a patriotic interest in the value of the nation's money. I was wrong. All they wanted was to debase the currency. Throughout the world, central banks are engines of inflation, and they have very little interest in sound money. In fact, and especially in the U.S., the central bank is a creature of the banks. They conceived it, lobbied for it and, de facto, control it. The purpose of the central bank is not to protect the currency, but to protect the banking system.

[21] Schweizerische National Bank 89th Annual Report. (Bern, 1997), 36.

[22] "Hoffen auf höhere Nationalbank-Ausschüttungen – Reduzierte Gold Deckung." *Neue Zürcher Zeitung*. 18 March, 1997, 13.

[23] Schweizerische National Bank. 90th Annual Report. (Bern, 1998), 34. "Weil die Nationalbank mit der Ausleihe von Gold Gefahr liefe, die Golddeckungsvorschrift für den Notenumlauf während der Pensionsdauer nicht mehr einhalten zu können, wurde zudem der Golddeckungssatz für den Notenumlauf von 40 Prozent auf 25 gesetzt (Art.19 Abs. 2 NBG)."

[24] Wegelin & Co., St. Gallen, Investment Commentary No. 179, 4 April 1997, 2.

[25] William L. Shirer, *The Rise and the Fall of the Third Reich – A History of Nazi Germany*, (New York: Simon & Schuster, 1960, reprinted by Crest Books, 1962), 357: "General Ludendorff, in his book *Total War (Der Totale Krieg)*, whose title was mistranslated into English as *The Nation at War*, published in Germany in 1935, had stressed the necessity of mobilizing the economy of the nation on the same totalitarian basis as everything else in order to properly prepare for total war."
Erich Ludendorff (1865-1937) was a general and politician during World War I. The use of the expression 'Total War' was later also attributed to the Third Reich's Propaganda Minister Joseph Goebbels. At public appearances toward the end of the war, he asked fanatic crowds. *"Wollt Ihr den totalen Krieg?"* (Do you want total war?)

[26] Jane H. Ingraham, "Goodbye Sovereign Switzerland," *The New American* 15, no. 15 (1999), at www.thenewamerican.com/tna/1999/07-19-99/vol15no15_swiss.htm.

[27] Luzi Stamm, *Der Kniefall der Schweiz*, (Zofingen, Switzerland: Verlag Zofinger Tagblatt, 1999), 245.

[28] Jane H. Ingraham, "Goodbye …"

[29] Ibid.

[30] Ibid.

[31] Luzi Stamm, *Der Kniefall,*9 – 12.

[32] Ibid., Stamm refers to Winston Churchill, *Memoirs*, vol.VI, part 1, 437.

[33] Joseph J. Cacciotti, personal letter to the author, 12 August 1999.

[34] Harry Schultz, *The International Harry Schultz Letter*, 24 February 1997, 6.

[35] Full content of the declaration by Federal Councilor Arnold Koller in *Neue Zürcher Zeitung*, 6 March 1997, 15.

[36] "Die Schweiz und die jüngere Zeitgeschichte, Erklärung von Bundespräsident Arnold Koller vor der Bundesversammlung", *Neue Zürcher Zeitung*, 6 March 1997, 15.

[37] Schweizerische National Bank, *90ᵗʰ Annual Report* (Bern: 1998), 34.

[38] "Leutwiler Assails Gold Fund", *The Financial Times*, London, 25 Mar 1997, 2.

[39] "Leutwiler gegen Stiftung aus Goldreserven" and "Der Tabubruch", *Neue Zürcher Zeitung*, 24 March 1997, 7.

[40] "Otto Stich gegen Stiftung" *Tages Anzeiger*, 10 March 1997, 1.

[41] "Noch eine Stimme gegen SNB-Goldveräusserungen", *Neue Zürcher Zeitung*, 10 April 1997, 23.

[42] Jane H. Ingraham, "Goodbye Sovereign Switzerland."

[43] Angelo M. Codevilla, Preface to *Between the Alps and a Hard Place: Switzerland in World War II and Moral Blackmail Today*, (Washington, DC: Regnery Publishing, Inc., 2000).

[44] U. Schlüer, "Stuart Eizenstats Mässigung", *Schweizerzeit*, 13 July, 2001, 8.

[45] Union Bank of Switzerland was one of the big losers in the fall of Long Term Capital Management. The bank, once the best managed among the big three Swiss banks, was in the process of ruining itself with all kinds of derivative exposures. The $700 million write-off was the largest in Long Term's spectacular drama. (See also, *Roger Lowenstein, When Genius Failed – The Rise and Fall of Long-Term Capital Management* (New York: Random House, 2000).

[46] Under the Washington Agreement on gold, fifteen European central banks have announced that they will limit their official sales to 2,000 tonnes over the next five years, and that they will cease net new gold lending over this period.

[47] "Gold glänzt kaum als Anlagemittel", *Neue Zürcher Zeitung*, 28 April 2000, 33.

[48] "Goldsegen für die Nationalbank – Netto 25,4 Milliarden Franken Aufwertungsgeswinn", *Neue Zürcher Zeitung*, 5 January, 2001, 17.

[49] Bloomberg, 20 May 1999.

[50] "Gold Reserves and Public Confidence" (London, New York: World Gold Council, 1999).

[51] Reginald Howe, "Gold Unchained by the Swiss; Ready to Rock", www.goldensextant.com, 16 April 2000.

[52] www.LeMetropoleCafe.com, 20 February, 2001.

[53] Joseph J. Cacciotti, Newsletter, 31 October, 2000.

[54] See also "J.P. Morgan ends not with a bang but a whimper", *Financial Times,* 23/26 December, 2000, 1, where on the occasion of the 'once venerable' investment bank's last shareholders' meeting some shareholders expressed their disappointment about the miserable and unceremonious end of the House of Morgan: "Bill Smith, an elegantly dressed young man who identified himself as a consultant, asked why a bank that once was big enough to rescue the finances of the U.S. government should now be sold. 'In the last several years—what shall I say—we have weakened.' Another shareholder Ms. Evelyn Y. Davis expressed her sorrow as follows: 'I am dressed in black—Chanel black—because I am mourning.' Ms. Davis predicted that—rather than rolling over in his grave—the bank's founder J. Pierpont Morgan would rise from the dead to curse the merger."

[55] www.leMetropoleCafe.com, 20 February, 2001.

[56] Robert Chapman, "Gold Potpurri", *The International Forecaster*, 26 March, 2001, @www.gold-eagle.com.

[57] Jay Taylor, www.gold-eagle.com.

[58] "Lex Column", *Financial Times,* London, 3 July 1999, 22.

[59] Paul Fabra, *Les Echos,* 3 July 1999, 52.

[60] Paul Fabra, "Chronique: La vraie banque centrale, c'est la bourse!", *Les Echos,* 16/17 June, 2000,

[61] U.S. House Committee on Banking and Currency, *Hearings on* . th Congress, th session, 17 February 2000, page.

[62] Fritz Leutwiler, *The Economist,* 14 June 1997, 110.

[63] Robert Landis, private letter to the author, 6 April, 2001.

[64] Lex Column, *Financial Times*, London, 8/9 May 1999, 24.

[65] "Gold Sales Not My Idea, Says Brown" *The Sunday Times*, London, 11 July 1999, 45.

[66] John Kidman, HM's Treasury, Debt and Reserve Management Team, letter to A. R. Mahalski, 3 June, 1999.

[67] "Gold Sales Not My Idea, Says Brown" *The Sunday Times*, London, 11 July 1999, 45.

[68] Sir Peter Tapsell, Parliamentary Debates (Hansard) Commons, Wedn. 16 June 1999, vol. 333, col.104.

[69] www.LeMetropoleCafe.com

[70] "Barron's Mailbag" *Barron's*, 31 May, 1999.

[71] Parliamentary Debates (Hansard) Commons, Wedn. 16 June 1999, vol. 333, col.104.

[72] Alan Greenspan, testimony before the U.S. House Banking Committee on July 24, 1998 and before the U.S. Senate Committee on Agriculture, Nutrition & Forestry on July 30, 1999.

[73] Ibid.

[74] I had my own particular encounter with Mr. Greenspan. It happened when I was a managing director of the Rothschild Bank AG, Zurich, and Mr. Greenspan was still with his consulting firm of Townsend-Greenspan. I was so fascinated with his

226

essay "Gold and Economic Freedom" that I showed it to all my clients. For one of them, a very wealthy German industrialist, who did not speak English, I translated it into German. Some time later, a U.S. brokerage firm sponsored a speech by Mr. Greenspan in Zurich. At the prestigious Hotel Baur au Lac, he spoke on the U.S. economy to the Zurich financial community. A representative of the U.S. brokerage firm and a friend of mine, introduced me to Mr. Greenspan in the hope he would be pleased to hear that a Swiss banker had taken the time to translate his essay into German. To our surprise Mr. Greenspan did not seem happy. He grimaced, turned his back on us abruptly and briskly walked away without saying a word.

[75] Recently, there has been growing doubt whether the U.S. is still in possession of its 261,5 million ounces it declared to be held in trust by the Department of the Treasury. Firstly, there has never been an independent audit of the U.S. gold reserve since 1955. Secondly, in September 2000, a strange reclassification was made in the Treasury Report. Over 54 million ounces of gold were switched from the category of "Gold Bullion Reserve" to "Custodial Gold Bullion" without as much as an explanation. Even more mysterious is the May 2001 Treasury Report (available at http://www.fms.treas.gov/gold/index.html) where "Reserve" and "Custodial" gold have been entirely eliminated and are now labeled as "Deep Storage Gold". Thus far, the Secretary of the Treasury, Mr. Paul H. O'Neill, has not responded to any questions put to him about the matter by politicians and citizens.

[76] Harry J. Bingham, *Weekly Gold Market Uptdate*, Van Eck Global, 7 June 1999.
[77] "Wahl Roths zum SNB Präsidenten," *Neue Zürcher Zeitung*, 19 February 2000, 218.
[78] N. M. Rothschild & Sons, London, is where the gold fixing takes place. It began In 1919, and is held twice a day, at 10:30 a.m. and at 3 p.m

Epilogue

"Since the days of Homer, gold has been the undisputed yardstick to which all monetary transfers in foreign trade had to measure up. Since 1971 and under American influence, a widespread 'demonetising of gold' has occurred, and the 'worthless', i.e., its value is not clearly defined, U.S. currency has taken the place of the precious metal."[1]

Erich Leverkus

"Because a large part of mankind trusts gold more than government prescribed paper currencies, western central banks felt compelled to artificially undermine the faith in gold at the end of the millennium. They encouraged major speculators to sell the yellow metal short and then were willing to supply the missing amounts out of their own stock at time of delivery. This seemed to be the safest method to suppress the price of gold, at least for the time being. Furthermore, several central banks—among them the Bank of England—sold large parts of their currency reserves at sinking rates and with as much publicity as possible, in order to make sure investors lost their preference for the precious metal. It was an attempt to send the metallic currency, proven over millennia and with its origins deriving from the Sumerian celestial gods of the sun and moon, packing at the end of its career."[2]

Erich Leverkus

The Trade Deficit or
The Richest Country in the World is living on charity

The worst example of what happens when gold is ignored is the U.S. trade deficit. Blanchard Economic Research painted a gloomy picture:

229

"During the decade of the 1970s in which the economy and stock market suffered under the weight of Washington, D.C.'s impact, the price of gold increased from $66 per ounce to just over $800 an ounce in January 1980.

Bill Clinton is leaving the United States the largest trade deficit we have ever seen. More economists are coming to the realization that this 'forgotten' deficit is neither desirable nor sustainable. Since Clinton took office in 1993, the deficit has significantly increased every year. In 1992 it stood at $39 billion. In 2000 it was at $360 billion—an increase of nearly 1,000%."[3]

Blanchard quoted a comment by Mr. David Wyss, Chief Economist of Standard & Poors:

"This cannot go on forever. In the long run you cannot borrow $400 billion a year from abroad. It may not be a problem for the next two years, but it is probably a problem in the next five years. We're basically selling off the country to foreigners."[4]

That is one way to look at it, but it is the wrong way, because Mr. Wyss overlooks the fact that foreigners are sending real wealth to the U.S. in return for irredeemable fiat money. History shows us that such a thing never would have been possible under the classic gold standard.

Blanchard Economic Research continues:

"The reason that we have been able to sustain the trade deficit as long as we have is because foreigners, who have made a lot of money selling goods to Americans, have then invested much of that money into U.S. stocks and Treasury securities. But the bear market in stocks and an approaching 'hard landing' may change all that and foreigners become less attracted to our sluggish markets. This will only exacerbate the bear market in stocks. Worse yet, large foreign holding of our Treasury securities put our entire financial system at risk. Among the foreign holders of Treasuries are foreign governments and central banks, including Red China. The Red Chinese consider America an enemy and they are the third largest holder of our Treasury securities in the world with over $100 billion in holdings. This leaves our financial system vulnerable in the event of a dispute."[5]

In the words of Ernest H. Preeg of the Hudson Institute, also mentioned in Blanchard's article:

"Foreign governments increased official dollar holdings from $432 billion in 1989 to about one trillion in 1999. At some future point, large dollar holders such as Japan and China could threaten to sell dollars, or shift them into Euros and other currencies, as bargaining leverage against the United States related to trade or national securities issues. One Japanese prime minister has publicly spoken of the temptation to sell dollars, and Chinese military strategists have published studies about integrated warfare with the United States, including financial markets."[6]

Representative James A. Traficant (D), Ohio, speaking before the House of Representatives on December 5, 2000, is also cited:

"Mr. Speaker, America's trade deficit for September hit $35 billion for one month, $35 billion. America is heading for a $420 billion, 1-year trade deficit. Unbelievable. If this continues, America will have a crash that will make 1929 look like a fender-bender. What is even worse, China is now taking $100 billion of cash out of our economy, buying missiles, and pointing them at us. Beam us up, all of us. We must be stupid. Ronald Reagan almost destroyed Communism, and the Clinton administration has reinvented it, is now subsidizing, and it is now stabilizing it."[7]

The conclusion of the Blanchard Economic Research leaves no doubt about the outcome:

> "Should foreigners stop buying U.S. stocks or, worse yet, start selling them off, the bear market in stocks will be longer and more intense than otherwise. If foreigners sell off U.S. Treasuries, the impact would be even worse. The dumping of U.S. Treasuries would result in a steep rise in interest rates, a collapse in the bond market, a dive in stocks, a rapidly sinking dollar and monetary inflation. In other words, a financial crisis. Investors need to be prepared. Gold is the most negatively correlated as (to) the U.S. dollar, therefore, the investment risks posed by the trade deficit are to be mitigated by a suitable position in gold."[8]

A crash, under these circumstances, seems a distinct possibility. Out of it, gold will emerge supreme, demonstrating that gold can only be pushed so far. In the long run, it does not pay to fight gold.

American Courage

The EU in Brussels has become a centralist colossus with absolute and despotic powers. Decisions are being made by an army of non-elected bureaucrats and, in many cases, corrupt officials. Europe is now undergoing the broadest experiment in planned economics since the decline of the Soviet Union. As the EU's disciplinary actions against Austria in 2000 have shown, the freedom of nations, particularly of smaller nations, not to speak of the individual citizen, is a thing of the past. In this new feudal system, everybody is supposed to keep their mouth shut and follow party line. The recent sanctions against EU-member Austria are the most striking examples of what can happen to smaller countries if they do not please the non-elected oligarchs in Brussels.

Many years ago, Archduke Otto von Habsburg wisely foresaw the direction the EU was taking and made it plain in his noted essay *Ethics and Morality of Money*:

"[The EU] is developing a form of new-feudalism that possesses all the weaknesses but none of the virtues of earlier feudal systems. Everything belongs to collective groups, whose bureaucratic administrators make use of it as they see fit."[9]

Not so in the U.S., where, in spite of its concentration of huge financial and political powers, one still finds courageous men ready to speak up for honest business practices and freedom. Such people are Bill Murphy and Chris Powell, who set up GATA. Their goal is to restore gold to a free and transparent market. Another remarkable organisation is the AIER that was set up by the late Colonel E. C. Harwood in Great Barrington, Massachusetts. Harwood, whom I had known for a long time and met several times, told me, among others things, that he was convinced that:

"A modern industrial society cannot be maintained without a sound accounting unit with which to calculate long-term depreciation schedules for business and long-term contracts of all kinds, and to record savings, life insurance and pension funds in real rather than fictitious values. The tremendous capital investments required for a modern industrial society cannot be maintained, replaced, and enlarged without correct instead of erroneous and false accounting. Accounting in terms of paper units has become a fiction incapable of providing the information essential to operation of large-scale and long-lasting enterprises. [...] Of all the possible accounting units that men have used, gold has proven to be by far the best."[10]

The same line of thinking is represented by Lawrence Parks of The Foundation for the Advancement of Monetary Education in New York. FAME is a not-for-profit foundation whose mission is to educate people about the benefits of honest monetary weights and measures, as opposed to arbitrary – and fraudulent – (fiat) money which all of us are compelled to use.

Parks commented in a recent interview as follows:

"Fiat monetary systems always collapse because greed and the lust for power know no limits. Those who possess the ability to create and benefit from money created out of nothing always overreach. The result is generally a move towards more statist government to 'remedy' the collapse and 'control or regulate' the economy to help prevent future collapses. Those who create the fiat money are usually left in charge and with greatly expanded power."[11]

Elizabeth Currier's Committee of Monetary Research & Education (CMRE) in Charlotte, North Carolina, was originally located in Greenwich, Connecticut. Over the years it has published over 50 monographs by eminent scholars and sound money advocates. CMRE has organized conferences offering sagacious economic thinkers, most of them not mainstream, a chance to get together.

GATA

The men who set up the Gold Anti-Trust Action Committee, Inc. (GATA) did this on their own initiative. The Chairman, Bill Murphy, an experienced former commodity trader who knows all the tricks of the business, and Chris Powell, a newspaper editor in Connecticut, have set up the organization with the goal to restore gold to a free and transparent market.

The alleged gold manipulators they continuously attack on the Internet include Goldman Sachs, Morgan, Deutsche Bank, sometimes Barrick, and last, but not least, Gold Fields Mineral Services. In their opinion, Gold Fields Mineral Services does not report the true size of the market in their statistics. Consequently, they are seen as belonging to the camp of the gold manipulators. On May 10, 2000, in a meeting in Washington DC with the Speaker of the House and other officials, Bill Murphy distributed his report *Gold Derivative Banking Crisis*[12] to leading politicians. It informs about the seriousness of the situation in the gold market and its potential implications on world financial markets as a whole.

GATA was founded in 1999 as a Delaware Corporation "to advocate and undertake litigation against an illegal collusion to control the price of gold".[13] The founders of GATA moved in response to actions and admissions by major Wall Street investment houses (in particular Goldman Sachs), The Federal Reserve and bullion banks. They say that the bailout of LTCM at the New York Fed's urgent behest was an egregious attempt at what has been a long-time effort to manipulate the price of gold as well as other securities. They believe that Chairman Greenspan has declared himself and the Federal Reserve ready to be part of the efforts to fix the price of gold.

> "Through a well-orchestrated campaign by the bullion banks and certain select financial houses, a virtual 'reign of terror' has brought the gold market to its present demoralized state. Hedging is a legitimate and necessary activity of risk management, but not at the price of destroying an industry. With the Russian default of last summer (1998) and the subsequent collapse of the capital markets, we believe there is strong evidence that gold lending has evolved as the successor of the failed yen-carry trade. While carry trades have provided enormous profits for the bullion banks and the hedge fund community, today the gold carry trade has become more central than ever to the bailout of the financial community. This explains the recent sweetheart gold loans and Wall Street's fierce attempts to control the price of gold. They are desperate to cover-up the true state of our markets and specifically the derivative mess of the gold lending market. Gold lending, once offering some legitimacy, has now become a mechanism for exploiting an industry, violating our laws, and bailing out a bunch of over-leveraged gamblers."[14]

Gold Derivative Banking Crisis

In the summer of 2000, GATA wrote a summary of their extensive research of the gold market covering the preceding 18 months.[15] Members of Congress were informed about the study on May 10, 2000. GATA reached the conclusion that the gold market is recklessly manipulated and now poses a serious risk to the international financial system. GATA requested a full investigation into the matter. GATA believes that the longer the gold price is artificially held down, the bigger the eventual banking crisis will be. Interestingly, there was absolutely no reaction to this shocking report.

Some of GATA's main points were:

"Annual gold demand exceeds mine and scrap gold supply [the latter of which is difficult to measure –auth.] by more than 1,500 tonnes p.a. Commodity prices are rising yet the price of gold has declined steadily. According to the Office of the Controller of Currency, the notional value of the off-balance-sheet gold derivatives on the books of U.S. commercial banks exceed $87 billion, which is greater than the value of the total U.S. official gold reserves of approximately 8,140 tonnes. Gold derivatives surged from $63.4 billion in the third quarter of 1999 to $87.6 billion in the fourth quarter, after the Washington Agreement was announced. The notional amount of off-balance sheet gold derivative contracts on the books of Morgan Guaranty Trust Co. went from $18.36 billion to $38.1 billion in the last six months of 1999. Several prominent New York bullion banks, particularly Goldman Sachs, from which the immediate past Secretary, Robert Rubin, came to the Treasury Department, have moved to suppress the price of gold every time it has rallied over the last year.

Why would anyone want to suppress the price of gold?

Suppressing the price of gold has made it a cheap source of capital for New York bullion banks, which borrow it for as little as one percent per year of its value. Gold is borrowed from central banks [including the Swiss National Bank, – auth.] and sold, and the proceeds are invested in the financial markets that have much greater rates of return. As long as the price of gold remains low, the 'gold carry trade' is a financial bonanza to a privileged few at the expense of many, including the gold producing countries, most of which are poor. If the price of gold was allowed to rise, the effective interest rate on gold loans would become prohibitive.

Suppressing the price of gold gives a false impression of the U.S. dollar's strength as an international reserve asset and a false reading of inflation in the United States.

Too much gold is being consumed [consumption of gold is insignificant, 'transformed' or 'sold' are more to the point. – auth.] at too cheap a price. Massive amounts of derivatives are being used to suppress the gold price. If this situation is not corrected soon, there will be a gold derivative credit and default crisis of epic proportions that will threaten the solvency of the largest international banks and the world standing of the dollar."[16]

The merit of Murphy and Powell is that they want to open the debate and are beginning to shed some light on one of the darkest chapters in financial history. With their report, GATA is trying to draw powerful politicians' and the public's attention to the illegal and harmful game that has been going on for so long. According to GATA, it represents a dangerous threat to the international banking system.

The Washington Agreement on Gold

As mentioned before, after the Bank of England announced it would sell part of its gold reserves, the price of gold dropped to nearly $250 during the summer months of 1999. Then suddenly, on Monday, September 28, 1999, the price in London jumped by $11 to $281.10. A few days later the price in London leapt to $317 and ended the week on Friday, October 1, 1999, at the second fixing at

$307.50. This was an increase of $37.50 in one week! Mining shares showed stronger gains; especially the hard-pressed African gold mines were among the biggest winners. How did this increase come about?

On Sunday September 26, 1999, in a surprise move, fifteen European central banks, including Switzerland, the U.K. and Sweden, made a dramatic announcement. They proclaimed that gold would remain an important element of global monetary reserves, and that they would restrict bullion sales in the next five years to a total of 2,000 tonnes. They also agreed not to expand their gold leasing and their use of gold futures and options over the same five-year period.

The signatories of the so-called Washington Agreement owned a total of 15,941 tonnes of gold at the end of 1999. This is considerably more than the 12,344 tonnes the U.S., the IMF, Japan and the BIS hold in their coffers. Nations outside the agreement, such as Russia, Taiwan, etc., officially own 5,197 tonnes of gold.

What is interesting is that by the end of 1999 central banks still officially owned 33,843 tonnes or only 3,191 tonnes less than in 1975, or 4,300 tonnes less than in 1971, the year in which central bank holdings reached their highest level with 39,102 tonnes. Based on these figures, the notion of a flight out of gold would certainly be a gross exaggeration.

What remains a mystery, however: How could 1,300 tonnes of Swiss gold be included in the Washington Agreement without the SNB having legal authorisation to sell the gold? It has to be noted that at the time until April 30, 2000, there was still a possibility of a referendum. Why the haste? This obviously seems to be the new way of handling things in Switzerland. Sooner or later the Swiss public is going to find out about these sinister manipulations behind closed doors.

What had happened? Some suggest that the European central banks finally realized that the gold they were lending could actually be lost. A dramatic action was needed to get out of the dilemma. Depressing the value of their own holdings by lending them at a ridiculous return of little over 1% had never been done before. By lending they were absurdly putting their most precious asset at risk. Finally, they began to realize what was at stake: Their gold!

The Gold Genie Is Out of the Bottle

The International Harry Schultz Letter, in its October 10, 1999 issue, reports the following:

> "The Central banks did not do this to help gold bulls. But they did not want the bears slain, so they permitted some sales. They had no option. Speculators (e.g., New York bullion banks and the anti-gold mafia) were hammering gold with no regard to the massive supply/demand gap. […] After years of immoral and illegal manipulations by bullion dealers, bullion banks and bullion brokers, aided by certain governments, gold broke loose. The price fixers haven't given up; they still don't want a free market for gold, but they know they are in for a battle royal. But the gold genie is out of bottle.
>
> Gold mines who hedged heavily (sold gold forward or bought puts) found themselves in trouble. Some mines were 'forced' into it by bullion banks who threatened them with lower credit ratings if they didn't. Blackmail! Shows how vicious the greedy price fixers are. "[17]

In some cases, it is known that bankers/lenders requested the mines hedge themselves before loan discussions were even started!

Golden Prosperity Unwanted – Yet!

The increase in the price of gold at the end of September and the beginning of October 1999, did not last long because the major players did not want it.

The bullion firms did not like it, because it threatened their business. The investors in common stocks did not like it, because it hurt the stock market as technology stocks were just taking off like never before. The hedge funds did not like it, because they were short and suddenly had to run for cover. The central banks did not like it, because the gold they had lent out was sold – and some at lower prices. They were beginning to realize that some of the borrowers might never be in a position to repay their gold loans.

Not even some of the major gold mining firms (with the exception of unhedged mines such as Agnico-Eagle) liked it. The fate of Ashanti and Cambior could happen to others. Some said it was just the tip of the iceberg!

Intelligent people who understood the derivative mess and the stock market bubble did not like it either, because they were afraid of the consequences of a banking crisis and hoped everything could be dragged out a bit longer and then somehow resolved.

When it became clear that very few wanted a higher gold price, it was quietly massaged down again to around $275.

The Second Increase

On Monday February 7, 2000, gold opened at $312/315 an ounce in Europe based on preceding Friday's announcement by Canadian mining company Placer Dome that it was suspending its hedging programme. In Asian trading on Monday, gold surged to $318, the highest since October 14, 1999. Later Barrick also announced some tactical changes in its hedging policy.

Although it is important for the gold price that hedging be reduced, it is obvious that very little has changed. The editor of *Mining Journal Ltd.,* in its March 2000 issue, wrote that market commentators who conclude that forward sales are coming to an end are laboring under a misconception. Australian producers even increased their hedging activity. Hedging remains a strategy, even if some producers have become mildly bullish. There is no reason yet to believe that sales will end soon. The *Mining Journal* concludes: Sales – must end soon![18]

Again it was prosperity unwanted and the gold price quietly began to recede again below the $300 level, where it remains so stoically that neither the most bearish nor the most bullish news seems to have any effect.

The Debt Pyramid

Decades ago friend and former central banker John Exter told people to think of all the debtors and creditors in the financial system as being in an upside down pyramid, a vast complex of paper IOU's.

> "It includes not only those in the dollar, but in all currencies, in the whole world monetary system. I shall concentrate today on the dollar debtors, but please remember there are similar debtors in other currencies.

> The pyramid has a flat top, so when turned over it has something to stand on. It stands on a block of gold, the gold in the vaults of the central banks of the world. Before central banks closed their gold windows, all debt in the pyramid was redeemable by central banks freely at $35 an ounce. That is what made fixed exchange rates possible. Since then the gold at the base has increased enormously, close to twenty times, so the pyramid stands on a far bigger base. It is the market's way of taking us back to the gold standard, destroying the value of paper as priced in gold.

> It helps to array the debtors according to their liquidity. Put the most liquid down near the gold base where the pyramid is narrow, and the least liquid at the top where it is wide, all others in-between. The pyramid grows too rapidly and becomes excessively large whenever too many debtors become illiquid by borrowing short and lending long. The number of illiquid debtors of the pyramid grows faster than the number at the bottom, and their solvency is threatened. Today's debt pyramid is by all odds the biggest in history, and has far more illiquid debtors. It dwarfs the one of 1929."[19]

What would John Exter say now, 20 years later, as debt is much higher, a dangerous bubble is prevailing in the stock markets, and we have a world of derivatives that nobody is in a position to measure? This is what Mr. Greenspan means by "systemic risk"!

The Golden Pyramid

U.S. analyst John Hathaway, in a report published in August of 1999, refers to John Exter's pyramid. He says:

> "John Exter was the first to suggest that gold related to paper assets in the form of a pyramid. He described the relationship of gold to paper assets in the form of a pyramid. Currency at one time was a gold derivative. Government issue was backed by physical gold held by central banks. Because currency was a claim on gold, it was in effect a short position against a physical asset that was relatively easy to calculate. Governments had the idea because they could never seem to stop issuing new paper. Even the pretence of a link has long been abandoned. Since currencies no longer have gold backing, and the world still appears to function, nouveau central bankers assert that gold is superfluous. [...] The old currency gold/pyramid has been replaced by a little understood labyrinth of paper claims against gold [...]."[20]

The Advice of Central Banker John Exter

> "So the bottom line for the world economy does not look good. It is more cheerful for you [He means investors in gold. –auth.]. You can do much to protect yourself. Go down the pyramid; get liquid. Federal Reserve currency notes are at the very bottom of the paper part. Hold enough to get through this current liquidity squeeze when banks might close and cash will be king. Treasury bills are good, too. They earn interest, but you cannot spend them in the supermarket. But the best asset of all, whether in inflation or deflation, will be the gold at the base of the pyramid. Accumulate what you can of it, either

above the ground, like coins or bullion, or in the ground, like mining shares."[21]

The Golden Sextant

Reginald H. Howe, wrote in an essay in October 1999:

"To appreciate the potential force of the coming monetary storm, a basic understanding of gold, gold banking, inflation and deflation is essential. Forget the CPI and other such price indices. They are generally lagging indicators. Forget too that most blather about whether gold does better in an inflation or a deflation. Gold is insurance against severe currency or credit destruction, whether its precipitating cause be inflation or deflation. Inflation and deflation are, respectively, expanding and contracting credit relative to some reliable measure of money. Historically, the measure was gold, which does not do well in periods of controlled or hidden inflation precisely because more credit can be built on less gold without arousing widespread public alarm. Measuring inflation is difficult today because what passes for money – unlimited paper currency is itself so intermingled with credit as to make the two virtually indistinguishable. A money market fund is nothing really but short-term credit obligations aggregated to look like what once was a bank account (in a sound bank) by a 40% reserve in gold coin or bullion resting in the vault.

Measuring the amount of real money in the world is no more difficult today than a century ago. It is the total aboveground physical gold stock, now somewhere around 120,000 metric tonnes (excluding double-counting of gold leased by central banks but still on their balance sheets). Going off the classical gold standard and the quasi gold standards that followed has not changed gold's inherent nature as real, permanent, natural money."[22]

At the End of a Century of Hyperinflations

Peter Bernholz, former Professor at the University of Basel, wrote in February of 2000 that the 20th century was the century of hyperinflations. The comparatively low rates of inflation of the 19th century were entirely due to the superior monetary order of a bimetallic and, later, the gold standard. Under the precious metal standard, banknotes were convertible into gold or silver on demand at a fixed exchange rate. This limited the power from governments and central banks and the banks to create money at will. Monetary expansion was limited by the reserve requirements of the gold and silver holdings available.[23] There is no doubt that this system worked and that it worked better than any system that followed:

> "It is an old experience and it has been confirmed again during the 20th century, that low rates of inflation can only be achieved if governments and politicians leave money alone. There were occasions beginning with 1950 where the central banks of the USA, Germany and Switzerland could temporarily pursue an independent monetary policy to keep their respective rates of inflation relatively low. But central banks are never really independent, and inflation rates in these three countries were always higher than they were under the automatic gold standard.
>
> Based on these realities certain doubts arise whether Switzerland's decision to abolish the gold reserve requirement and plans to sell a major part of its gold reserve is really as wise a policy as it is presented to be by its advocates. Dollar holdings [...] can be blocked anytime. This is not the case with gold reserves safely located in Swiss mountains because they are nobody's liability."[24]

Action Is Needed

Those who are de facto in charge of the world's monetary system, the large banks and the large investment banks, will not agree. In this respect, I have no doubt. They are reaping enormous benefits from fiat money—in the U.S. more than $600 billion in 2000 alone—and will not easily relinquish those revenues. But the question remains: Do we want to repeat the catastrophic blunders of the last century or do we want to learn from history and avoid them? That is all. Mainstream thinking is not enough and never will be. All the great people of this world were independent thinkers. Their visions brought progress to civilization. There are plenty of quotations and wise words that could be mentioned here, but let us mention just two of them.

Harry Schultz has given us one of the best definitions of the gold standard.

> "Standards: (Gold and other Kinds):
>
> I have written several times over the last 36 years and I want to restate this principle with force: I am pro-gold *regardless* of the price! I don't fight for gold in order to make a profit on gold shares, bars or coins! Gold is important for far more important reasons and I would be embarrassed to promote gold *only* for monetary gain. Gold is the essential linchpin for our *individual* (not group or nation) freedom. Gold belongs to the monetary system as a *governing* factor. We belong back on the gold standard. I used to compromise and say a *quasi*-gold standard will probably do, a modified Bretton Woods version.
>
> And that may be what will evolve, but in my view we should fight for a pure gold standard, the old-fashioned form, because it worked! And not just for fiscal reasons! It *forced* nations to limit their debt, spending and socialist schemes, which meant sound behavioural *habits* were formed around those limitations, and those *habits* rubbed off on everyone. People were more honest, moral, decent, kind, because the *system* was honest and moral. Cause and effect. Today we have cause and effect of the opposite standard: *no* limits on what governments can do, control, dictate; no limit on government debt,

welfare or socialist schemes. There is no governor on the government.

This habit rubbed off on the public, causing them to go into debt, lose respect for the system and morality. The effect brings us more divorce, fraud, crime, illegitimate births, broken homes. When the money of any country loses its base/backing there is no standard for any behaviour. Money sets a standard that spreads into every area of human activity. No paper money *backing*, no morality. That is why gold coin money worked so well and why the U.S. moved into paper money very slowly, carefully, keeping the paper-$'s backed 100% by gold. But slowly, like slicing a sausage, that backing was removed in stages, 'til now there is none. The effect of this cause is all around us.

Violent films reflect violent society reflect no respect throughout society. Layer by layer, we are corrupted when money loses certainty. Today's stock market bubble is part of the scene as will be tomorrow's mega-crash and mega-recession. Big Brother was made possible through the absence of automatic controls and loss of individual freedom via non-convertible currency. So, pass the word. Fight for gold. Not for profits, though they are helpful and help us fight for individual freedom, but for a future that returns to sanity in various standards. If we have a gold standard we get golden *human standard*! The two are intertwined. They are the ultimate cause and effect. Gold blesses." [25]

Charles de Gaulle, President of France, gave France the greatest gift he could offer: He renewed the country's confidence. On February 4, 1965, he said:

"The time has come to establish the international monetary system on an unquestionable basis that does not bear the stamp of any country in particular. On what basis? Truly, it is hard to imagine that it could be any standard other than gold. Yes, gold whose nature does not alter, which may be formed equally well into ingots, bars or coins; which has no nationality and which has, eternally and universally, been regarded as the unalterable currency par excellence."[26]

Is the Lustre Returning?

The current depression of the gold price is over-extended. It has lasted longer than it would have without the constantly negative media and central bank propaganda, price suppression by central bank sales and lending, arbitrary restriction on IMF member countries linking their currencies to gold, legal tender laws, and speculation by bullion banks. But as long as gold remains the number one store of value, no central bank or bullion bank action, or G-7, G-10 or G-20 conference of the leading economic countries will be powerful enough to have a lasting influence on the long-term trend of gold. In the long run, it is the markets that are the masters. This is even truer today when nobody seems to see the need to move away from a disastrous non-system of irredeemable paper/electronic money and back to the only system that guarantees long-term prosperity – gold as money.

Epilogue

[1] Erich Leverkus, *Evolution und Geist*, (Rahden, Germany: Verlag Marie Leidorf, 1999), 77/78; T. Hofmänner trans.
[2] Ibid.
[3] Blanchard Economic Research in an editorial on www.gold-eagle.com on January 13, 2001.
[4] Ibid.
[5] Ibid.
[6] Ibid.
[7] Ibid.
[8] Ibid.

[9] Otto von Habsburg, "Ethik und Moral des Geldes," *Frankfurter Allgemeine Zeitung*, Supplement "Geld und Geist, 12 April, 1988.
[10] James Dines, *The Invisible Crash*, (New York: Random House, 1975), 88.
[11] Larry Parks, "Economic and Social Perils of our Fraudulent Monetary System," *J. Taylor's Gold & Technology Stocks*, vol. 19, no. 6 (2000), 1-9. (www.miningstocks.com/interviews/larryparks.html)
[12] Bill Murphy, *Gold Derivative Banking Crisis*, (Dallas: Gold Anti-Trust Action Committee, 2000). Available at www.gata.org (GDBC Report).
[13] John D. Meyer, Vice Chairman GATA, personal letter to author, 16 April 1999.
[14] Ibid.
[15] Bill Murphy, *Gold...*
[16] Ibid.
[17] Harry Schultz, *The International Harry Schultz Letter*, 10 October 1999, 7.
[18] "World Gold Sales – must end soon!," Editorial, *Mining Journal*, London, vol.3, no 3 (2000), 3.
[19] "Interview with John Exter," *Blakely's Gold Investment Review*, vol. 1, no. 1 (1989), 9/10.
[20] John Hathaway, "The Golden Pyramid," Tocqueville Asset Management LP, 20 August 1999. Available at www.tocqueville.com/brainstorms/brainstorm0031.shtml .
[21] "Interview... " *Blakely's Gold Investment Review*, 9/10.
[22] Reginald H. Howe, "Real Gold, Paper Gold and Fool's Gold: The Pathology of Inflation," The Golden Sextant, 12 October 1999. Available at www.goldensextant.com/commentary4.html#anchor674427.
[23] Peter Bernholz, "Am Ende eines Jahrhunderts der Hyperinflationen – Golddeckung und Regelbildung als bewährte Stabilisatoren," *Neue Zürcher Zeitung*, 26/27 February 2000, 95.
[24] Ibid.
[25] Harry Schultz, "GOLD vs. the PRICE of Gold", *International Harry Schultz Letter*, 18 June 2000, 3/4.
[26] Jacques Rueff, *The Monetary Sin of the West*, (New York: Mac Millan, 1972), 70 – 74.

Conclusions by a former Private Banker, Security Analyst, Director of Gold Mining Companies, Monetary Historian, Swiss Patriot and worried Citizen of the World:

The Gold War is nothing else than a Third World War. It is not only a most unnecessary but the most destructive of all wars. It should be stopped now.

World War III may have begun with the demise of the classic gold standard of the 19th century. If the countries at war in World War I (WWI) had not hastily and foolishly given up the gold standard, WWI might not have lasted more than six months, because the warring nations would have run out of gold to pay for it, and war taxes would have been resisted. I contend that WWI lasted as long as it did because the gold standard was abandoned. Deficit financing made it possible for it to last over four years, destroying capital wealth, a rich cultural heritage and unnecessarily killing millions of young soldiers and innocent people.

If WWI had lasted only six months, currencies would not have been destroyed. There would have been no Versailles Treaty and no German hyperinflation. The little understood Genoa Convention of 1922 was largely responsible for the boom of the 1920s and the crash of 1929 leading to the crisis of the 1930s. Without the mishandling of gold, there would never have been a Hitler. Neither would there have been a Bolshevik take-over by the likes of a Lenin, nor would Russia have had to endure a Stalin with even more millions of innocents killed. There would never have been a WWII.

Ignoring gold led to the 1944 Bretton Woods system and also to its downfall. Without repeating the mistakes of 1914 or 1922, we never would have had an inflationary crisis in the 1970s. The oil crisis in the 70s and the approaching oil and energy crisis of the twenty-first century are primarily monetary crises. The suppression of gold and the unlimited expansion of fiat money have led to the monetary, economic and political crises and wars of the twentieth century. The end of Bretton Woods gave birth to the ongoing and future derivative crisis, which is at the base of what Alan Greenspan calls "systemic risk". Because the world disregarded gold money, the world's crises were erroneously, but probably intentionally, blamed on gold. That is why we have gold wars.

Financial markets can only function satisfactorily under a gold standard. History has shown that monetary stability was best under the automatism of the classic gold standard. Fiat money can only lead to short-lived financial and economic booms. The end result is inflation and embezzlement of savings at the expense of workers, pensioners and the poor, who are unable to defend themselves against the ongoing fraud.

Well functioning financial markets based on an honest monetary system guarantee the creation of savings. Savings lead to the formation of capital, and are a prerequisite for a steadily rising standard of living. Organic growth in line with the growth of gold mine production is what is needed, not growth of 10% and more per annum financed by the creation of paper/electronic money.

Smoothly functioning financial markets with savings channeled into productive investments bring the world economy to its full potential, increasing employment on a worldwide basis. The catastrophic problem of unemployment could finally be solved, and the growing gap between rich and poor narrowed. It cannot be solved otherwise. If there is full employment in the whole world, there will be fewer wars, less mass immigration, because the world is a beautiful place and its beauty is not limited to just a few rich countries. People would not have to leave their home countries where they have their cultural and religious roots. Mass ethnic and cultural destruction would be a thing of the past.

Politicians should not use coercion, e.g., legal tender laws, to interfere in the gold and silver markets. History has proven that the free market has chosen gold and silver as money. Money cannot and should not be based on faith and promises by government. Only money based on what people freely choose as being trustworthy: gold!

With honest money, people will have confidence in the future efficacy of that money. But it is necessary that they take destiny in their own hands and study monetary archaeology. What has gone wrong, and why has it gone wrong? There is enough historic documentation around, but unfortunately, it is not taught at universities.

Finally, I would like to state that I feel that the world will continue towards an even more precarious situation if nothing is done. As technological advances of all kinds have shown, there are plenty of brilliant minds in the world. There ought to be enough to get us out of the present monetary dark ages.

This approach would lead to full employment and worldwide prosperity and stability, as well as to a renaissance of culture and morals. Law and order would experience a comeback. It would not be the first time for this to happen. It would also lead to a better understanding of human beings amongst themselves and it would end most military confrontations. One historic experience is that human nature never changes. Man will, therefore, always love and respect honest business dealings with a medium of exchange thy can trust: gold. Gold will finally win the war, but why not call an armistice now? Let us hope this will happen before it is too late, before too much time and too many lives are wasted.

The State of Affairs at the Time of Completing this Book

While finishing up this book in Summer 2001, gold bullion is trading below $270 an ounce; the metal is close to or below the cost of production for many mines. Almost no one believes the gold market will ever rally. As cycle analyst Ian Notley puts it: "Gold stocks are moribund, forlorn, forgotten and dismissed from portfolio management consideration." Gold stock indices are oversold more than any time in their 60-year history. The gold industry's market capitalization is a little over $20 billion, which is just somewhat larger than Caterpillar's $15 billion—Caterpillar being the company providing the heavy vehicles for most of the mining companies. By comparison, General Electric's market value is still around $434 billion, Microsoft's $358 billion and Cisco's $141 billion. Meanwhile, a very strong accumulation condition has developed in the precious metals market. According to Ian Notley all is not lost as a once-in-a-lifetime opportunity is quietly and subtly unfolding.[1]

251

Mines are still continuing to hedge. The banks ask them to do it. AngloGold announced that it would continue to hedge half of its production for the next five years. The company expects to mine just over seven million ounces of gold this year. The company takes a dim view on the immediate outlook for gold.

Despite all the depressing news, the situation may not be as negative as it looks. Gold slumps seem to proceed according to a master plan. Supporters are lead to believe that gold will soon become nearly worthless. This drama is only complete when the last believer in gold capitulates by throwing his holdings into the market. Precursors of a recovery are the gently climbing prices of gold mining shares. A different type of buyer is at work here. It's the one who knows very well that a mine has precious assets in the ground, assets that are not going to lose value when stock markets and currencies collapse. This pattern is expected to take place in the next gold bull market.

What will be the basis for this coming bull market? In the great gold bull market of the 1970s, it was investment demand that soared. Because of the breakdown of the fixed-exchange rate system, ailing stock markets, exploding inflation and loss of purchasing power of currencies, investors turned to gold. When real interest rates went below zero because of the Fed's attempts to stimulate the economy, investors began to have second thoughts about their fixed income investments. Therefore, large amounts of capital moved into gold.

A similar situation seems to be developing now. The money supply is exploding due to an unparalleled effort to lower interest rates to avoid further weakness in the stock market and to save the heavily indebted consumers. Consequently, real interest rates are pushing into negative territory again. Negative real interest rates (the U.S. dollar and most stocks still grossly overvalued) will create a situation where an increasing amount of frightened capital will be turning to the metal of kings, thus creating the basis for a new bull market in gold.

Years of study have convinced me that there is a strong and criminal agenda to illegally suppress the price of gold. Unfortunately, it looks as if this agenda is going to be continued under the Bush Administration. But experience has shown that gold is the ultimate custodian of value in times of collapse, especially stock market crashes. Furthermore, gold is a superb hedge against constant loss of capital in times of currency disorder. We are living in an environment of increasing currency and trade wars—a race to the bottom—where every country, even Switzerland, wants to lower the value of its currency in world markets. During such times, the best protection is gold. In recent years, there have been many examples such as the collapsing Asian markets or the economies of Russia, Brazil, Zimbabwe and many other countries where currencies have come under severe pressure.

Central bank and, in particular, Fed actions to master the economy do not inspire a high degree of confidence. The recent, desperate moves to lower interest rates and increase the money supply will probably have dire effects. The bursting of the Nasdaq bubble and its consequences on both consumer spending and investor confidence on a worldwide basis should not be underestimated. As always, the market has the last word, and those who ignore this truth do it at their own risk!

Something to keep an eye on in the future is a lawsuit filed in Boston against the Bank for International Settlements in Basel, Switzerland, Alan Greenspan, William J. McDonough, J. P. Morgan & Co., Inc., Chase Manhattan Corp., Citigroup, Inc., Goldman Sachs Group, Inc., Deutsche Bank AG and Lawrence H. Summers, Secretary of the Treasury. Howe's complaint about manipulative activities in the gold market since 1994 has the potential of putting some government officials and high-ranking bankers in a very embarrassing, if not criminal, spot. Already, alleged improprieties by the Fed, the Treasury and its Exchange Stabilization Fund are published on the Internet or written about in investment newsletters. Who knows, maybe a cleansing storm is building on the shores of Massachusetts? Perhaps, it will put an end to government meddling and interfering in what is supposed to be a free gold market and then return the countries to a solid gold standard. I certainly hope so.

Meanwhile, the world economy continues to sail along precariously with its highly unstable monetary non-system. There can be as many G-7 or G-8 meetings as one can imagine, but nobody has the slightest idea how the monetary system can be restored. Sadly, the knowledge of what an appropriate currency system ought to be has nearly been lost. There are only a precious few left who know that only an honest monetary system with people freely choosing what they prefer as the medium of exchange—for which there are compelling reasons pointing to gold—can remedy the present disastrous currency muddle. The knowledge of those few who have taken the time and effort to study the history of money and man will be needed badly one day. When the time has come, it will serve to end the suffering of mankind and to relaunch the world economy by putting the world financial system back on a safe, golden track.

---

[1] Ian Notley, *Notley's Notes* (January 22, 2001), Yelton Fiscal Inc., Ridgefield, CT 06877 USA.

Selected Bibliography

Books, Monographs and Articles

American Institute for Economic Research (AIER). *Money: A Search for Common Ground*. Lugano: n.p.,1984.

---. *The Pocket Money Book*. N.p. n.p., 1994.

Bernholz, Peter."Am Ende eines Jahrhunderts der Hyperinflation – Golddeckung und Regelbildung als bewährte Stabilisatoren." *Neue Zürcher Zeitung*. 26/28 February 2000, 95.

Bernstein, Peter L. *The Power of Gold*. New York: John Wiley & Sons, Inc., 2000.

Blanchard, James U. *Silver Bonanza*. New York: Simon & Schuster, 1993.

Bresciani-Turroni, Constantino. *The Economics of Inflation*. Northhampton: John Dickens & Co., 1968.

Codevilla, Angelo M. *Between the Alps and a Hard Place*. Washington, DC: Regnery Publishing, Inc., 2000.

Coombs, Charles A. *The Arena of International Finance*. New York, NY: John Wiley & Sons, 1976.

Davidson, James Dale and William Rees-Mogg. *The Great Reckoning*. New York: Summit Books, 1991.

Defoe, Daniel. *Daniel Defoe, His Life and Recently Discovered Writings*. Edited by William Lee. New York: B. Franklin, 1969.

Dines, James. *The Invisible Crash*. New York: Random, n.d.

Ewert, James E. *Money*. Seattle, WA: Principia Publishing Inc., 1998.

Exter, John. "The International Means of Payment." *Inflation and Monetary Crisis*. Edited by G. C. Wiegand. Washington, DC: Public Affairs Press, 1975.

Fabra, Paul A. *Capital for Profit*. Savage, MD: Rowman & Littlefield Publishers, Inc., 1991.

Fekete, Antal E. *Whither Gold*. International Currency Prize Essay. Zurich, Switzerland: Bank Lips AG, 1996.

---. *Gold and Interest*. St. John's, NF: Memorial University of Newfoundland, 1997.

---. *Gold Mining and Hedging*. St. John's, NF: Memorial University of Newfoundland, 1998.

---. *The Subjective Theory of Interest*. St. John's, NF: Memorial University of Newfoundland, 1997.

Galbraith, John K. *The Great Crash* 1929. Boston: Houghton Mifflin Company, 1955.

Gibbon, Edward. *The Decline and the Fall of the Roman Empire*. N.p.: n.p., 1792.

Gleeson, Janet. *The Money Maker*. London: Bantam Books, 1999.

Goethe, Johann Wolfgang von. *Faust, der Komödie erster Teil*.

Goethe, Johann Wolfgang von. *Faust, der Komödie zweiter Teil*.

Goethe, Johann Wolfgang von. *The Tragedy of Faust, Part I*. Translated by Theodore Martin. London: W. Blackwell and Sons, 1865.

Goethe, Johann Wolfgang von. *The Tragedy of Faust, Part II*. Translated by Theodore Martin. London: W. Blackwell and sons, 1865.

Graham, Benjamin and David L. Dodd. *Security Analysis*. New York: McGraw-Hill, 1951.

Grant, James. *The Trouble with Prosperity*. New York: Random House, 1996.

Green, Timothy. *The New World of Gold*. Salford: Walker & Company, 1981.

---. *The Gold Companion*. London: Rosendale Press, 1991.

---. *The Prospect for Gold*. London: Rosendale Press, 1987.

---. *The World of Gold*. London: Rosendale Press, 1993.

Greenspan, Alan. "Gold and Economic Freedom." *Capitalism: The Unknown Ideal*. Ed. Ayn Rand. New York: New American Library, 1967.

Halbrook, Stephen P. *Target Switzerland*. Rockville Center, NY: Sarpedon, 1998.

Hathaway, John. *Gold Investment Review – Annual Review* 1999. Tocqueville Asset Management, L. P., 11 January 2000.

---. "The Golden Pyramid." Paris: Tocqueville Finance SA (20 August 1999). See also www.tocqueville.com/brainstorms/brainstorm0031.shtml .

Holzer, Henry Mark. *Government's Money Monopoly*. New York: Books in Focus, 1981.

---. *How the Americans Lost Their Right to Own Gold and Became Criminals in the Process*. Greenwich, CT: Committee for Monetary Research and Education, Inc., 1981.

Hoppe, Donald J. *How to Invest in Gold Stocks*. New York: Arlington House, 1972.

Howe, Reginald H. *The Golden Sextant*. Zurich, Switzerland: Bank Lips AG, International Currency Prize Essay, 1992.

---. "Gold Unchained by the Swiss; Ready to Rock." Published at www.goldensextant.com on 16 April, 2000.

---. "Real Gold, Paper Gold and Fool's Gold: The Pathology of Inflation." The Golden Sextant (12 October 1999). Available at www.goldensextant.com/commentary4.html#anchor674427

Ingraham, Jane H. "Goodbye Sovereign Switzerland." *The New American* 15, no. 15 (1999).

Jastram, Roy W. *The Golden Constant*. New York: John Wiley & Sons, 1977.

---. *SILVER, The Restless Metal*. New York: John Wiley & Sons, 1981.

Keynes, John Maynard. *The General Theory of Employment, Interest and Money. London*: Macmillan and Co., Ltd., 1936.

---.*The Collected Writings of John Maynard Keynes*. Vol. 2. London: Macmillan and Co., Ltd., 1977.

Kile, Michael. Th*e Case for Gold in the 1990's*. 1991. Perth, Australia: Gold Corporation, 1993.

Klockenbring, Gérard. *Geld – Gold – Gewissen*. Stuttgart: Verlag Urachhaus, 1974.

Lee, William, ed. *Daniel Defoe, His Life and Recently Discovered Writings*. 1869.

Leverkus, Erich. *Evolution und Geist*. Rahden, Germany: Verlag Marie Leidorf, 1999.

---. *Freier Tausch und fauler Zauber*. Frankfurt a/Main: Fritz Knapp Verlag, 1990.

Lips, Ferdinand. *The Book on Investments*. Düsseldorf: ECON Verlag, 1981.

---. *Geld, Gold und die Wahrheit*. Zürich: Fortuna Verlag, 1991.

Mackay, Charles. *Extraordinary Popular Delusions and the Madness of Crowds*. London: Richard Bentley, 1841.

Mencken, H. L., ed. *A New Dictionary of Quotations*. New York: Alfred A. Knopf, 1997.

Menger, Carl. *Grundsätze der Volkswirtschaftslehre*. Wien: Wilhelm Braumüller, 1871.

---. *Principles of Economics*. New York: New York UP., 1981.

---. *The Origin of Money*. Monograph 40. Greenwich, CT: Committee for Monetary Research and Education, Inc., 1984.

Mises, Ludwig von. *Human Action*. New Haven, CT: Yale UP, 1949.

Murphy, Bill. *Gold Derivative Banking Crisis*. Dallas, TX: Gold Anti-Trust Action Committee, 2000.

Palyi, Melchior. *Managed Money on the Crossroads*. Chicago: Henry Regnery Company, 1960.

---. *The Twilight of Gold*. Chicago: Henry Regnery Company, 1972.

---. "A Point of View." *Commercial and Financial Chronicle* (24 July 1969).

Parks, Lawrence. "The Near Death & Resurrection of the Gold Mining Industry." Woodside, NY: *J. Taylor Hard Money Advisor, Inc.*, 2000.

---. "Economic and Social Perils of our Fraudulent Monetary System." *J. Taylor's Gold & Technology Stocks*, vol. 19, no. 6 (2000), 1 – 9. See also www.miningstocks.com/interviews/larryparks.html .

--- *What Does Mr. Greenspan Really Think?*, Foundation for the Advancement of Monetary Education, New York, 2001 See also www.fame.org

Paul, Ron and Lewis Lehrmann. *The Case for Gold – A Minority Report of the U.S. Gold Commission*. Washington, DC: Cato Institute, 1982.

Pick, Franz. *The U.S. Dollar – An Advance Obituary*. New York: Pick Publishing Corporation, 1981.

Rees-Mogg, William. *The Reigning Error*. London: Hamish Hamilton Ltd., 1974.

Reynolds, Alan. *The IMF's Destructive Recipe of Devaluation and Austerity*. Indianapolis, IN: Hudson Institute, 1992.

Ricardo, David. *Complete Works*. Edited by Piero Sraffa. Cambridge: Cambridge UP, 1966.

Roepke, Wilhelm. *Die Lehre von der Wirtschaft.* Erlenbach/Zürich: Eugen Rentsch Verlag, 1958.

---. *Jenseits von Angebot und Nachfrage.* Erlenbach/Zürich: Eugen Rentsch Verlag, 1961.

Rothbard, Murray N. *The Case Against the Fed.* Auburn, AL: Ludwig von Mises Institute, 1994.

Rueff, Jacques. *L'Age de l'Inflation.* Paris: Payot, 1965.

---. *The Monetary Sin of the West.* New York: Mac Millan, 1972.

---. *The Inflationary Impact the Gold Exchange Standard Superimposes on the Bretton Woods System.* Greenwich, CT: Committee for Monetary Research and Education, 1975.

Salsman, Richard M. *Gold and Liberty.* Great Barrington, MA:American Institute for Economic Research, 1995.

Samuelson, Paul E. *Economics.* New York: McGraw-Hill, 1973.

Sarnoff, Paul. The Silver Bulls. Westport, CT: Arlington House, 1980.

Schlüer, U. "Stuart Eizenstats Mässigung." *Schweizerzeit* (13 Juli 2001), 8.

Schultz, Harry. "GOLD vs. the PRICE of Gold." *International Harry Schultz Le*tter (18 June 2000).

Schwartz, Anna J., Christopher Whalen and Walker F. Todd. *Time to Abolish the International Monetary Fund and the Treasury's Exchange Stabilization Fund.* Monograph no. 54. Charlotte, NC: CMRE, December 1998.

Sédillot, René. *Histoire Morale & Immorale de la Monnaie.* Paris: Bordas-Cultures, 1989.

Shirer, William L. *The Rise and the Fall of the Third Reich – A History of Nazi Germany.* London: Secker & Warburg, 1960.

Somary, Felix. *Erinnerungen aus meinem Leben.* Zürich: Manesse Verlag, 1959.

Stamm Luzi, *Der Kniefall der Schweiz,* Zofingen, Switzerland: Verlag Zofinger Tagblatt AG, 1999.

Sutherland, C. H. V. *GOLD, Its Beauty, Power and Allure.* London: Thames & Hudson, 1959.

Veseth, Michael. *Mountains of Debt, Crisis and Change in Renaissance Florence, Victorian Britain and Postwar America.* New York – Oxford: Oxford UP, 1990.

Webster, Pelatiah. *Not Worth a Continental*. 1790. Reprint Irvington on Hudson, NY: Foundation for Economic Education, 1950.

Welker, Ernest P. *"WHY GOLD?" Economic Education Bulletin*. Great Barrington, MA: American Institute for Economic Research, 1981.

White, Andrew Dickson. *Fiat Money Inflation in France, How it Came, What it Brought and How it Ended*. 1914. Reprint Caldwell, ID: Caxton Printers Ltd., 1972.

White, Lawrence H. *Free Banking*. Brookfield, VT: Edward Elgar Publishing, 1993.

Whitting, P. D. *Die Münzen von Byzanz*. München: Ernst Battenberg Verlag, 1973.

Wormser, René. *Conservatively Speaking*. Mendham, NJ: Wayne E. Dorland Company, 1979.

Zweig, Stefan. *The World of Yesterday*. New York: Viking Press Inc., 1943.

Other Sources

American Institute for Economic Research, Great Barrington, MA
     01230

Barron's

Cacciotti, Joseph J. *Investment Letter*. New York: Ingalls & Snyder
     LLC, 61 Broadway, New York, NY 10006-2802.

Chamber of Mines. South Africa, P.O. Box 809, Johannesburg 2001,
     South Africa.

CMRE. Committee for Monetary Research & Education, Inc.

     10004 Greenwood Court, Charlotte, NC 28215-9621.
     cmre@worldnet.att.net

FAME. Foundation for the Advancement of Monetary Education.
     Box 625, FDR Station, New York, NY 10150-0625.
     www.fame.org

Financial Times, London

Finanz & Wirtschaft, Zurich.

GATA Anti-Trust Action Committee Inc., 4718 Cole Ave., Dallas,
     TX 75205.
     www.gata.org

G&M, Gold & Money. Bandulet Verlag GmbH, Kurhausstrasse 12.
     D-97688 Bad Kissingen.

Gold Eagle
     www.gold-eagle.com

Der Goldbrief. J. A. Saiger, Postfach 64, A-5024 Salzburg
     goldbrief@gmx.net

International Harry Schultz Letter, P.O. Box 622, CH-1001
     Lausanne
     hsl.mentor@skynet.be

Les Echos. 46 rue la Boétie, F-75381 Paris Cedex 08

Mining Journal London

Neue Zürcher Zeitung

Paribas International Equity Research, rue d'Antin. F-75078 Paris
Cedex 02.

Swiss Federal Government

Swiss National Bank - www.snb.ch

The Golden Sextant - www.goldsextant.com

The Dines Letter. James Dines & Co., Inc., P.O. Box 22, Belvedere,
CA 94920.

Wall Street Journal

World Gold Council, 45 Pall Mall, London SW1-5JG
www.gold.org

A Monetary Chronology of the United States. Great Barrington, MA:
Economic Education Bulletin AIER, 1994.

Gold and the International Monetary System in a new Era. World
Gold Council Conference, Paris, 19 November 1999.
London: World Gold Council, 1999.

*A Glittering Future? Gold Mining's Importance to Sub-Saharan
Africa and Heavily Indebted Poor Countries.* London:
World Gold Council, June 1999.

Appendix

The Wisdom of …

Henry H. Fowler, U.S. Secretary of Treasury 1965–68 and father of the SDR's:

While in office he repeatedly described the U.S. dollar as "the strongest currency in the world."[1]

Arthur F. Burns, Chairman Federal Reserve 1970–78:

"If long continued, inflation at anything like the present rate would threaten the very foundations of our society."

In an interview given on June 29, 1972:

"The dollar is not in any danger at all."[2]

James Dines, analyst, investment advisor and author. In his book *The Invisible Crash:*

"It is an interesting historical footnote that the private ownership of gold was banned by Lenin, Hitler, Mussolini, Mao Tse Tung and Franklin Delano Roosevelt."[3]

"Presidents Kennedy and Johnson said gold was not necessary for backing the U.S. currency and should be demonetized, because they understood that gold is a brake on the printing press."[4]

Lenin, Soviet revolutionary, collectivist and statesman, is said to have declared:

"When we conquer on a world scale, I think we shall use gold for the purpose of building public lavatories in the streets."[5]

Much more insightful is the following statement

"[…] the best way to destroy the capitalist system was to debauch the currency. By a continuing process of inflation, governments can confiscate, secretly and unobserved, an important part of the wealth of their citizens. By this method they not only confiscate, but they confiscate arbitrarily; and, while the process impoverishes many, it actually enriches some."[6]

John Exter, former U.S. Banker and monetary expert on bonds in a fiat money non-system:

"Bonds are certificates of guaranteed confiscation practiced on innocent citizens living on fixed income."[7]

Lyndon B. Johnson, President of the U.S. in his State of the Union message, January 4, 1965:

"Our balance of payments deficit has declined and the soundness of our dollar is unquestioned. I pledge to keep it that way."[8]

In the following two statements, the wisdom typical for that period and the economic illiteracy of Secretary of the Treasury Connally and that of a president of a major corporation are illustrated:

"When asked in a television interview, what he thought of the consequences of the dollar, Connally replied that a devaluation of the U.S. currency would be 'very, very beneficial to the United States'. He added, 'I don't think the average American will even be conscious of it.'"[9]

At a White House cocktail party, Paul Volcker, then Under Secretary of the Treasury for Monetary Affairs, asked the president of a major U.S. company, "What would be the public reaction to a devaluation of the dollar?" Said the executive, "I don't know anyone who gives a damn."[10]

"Paul A. Volcker, Under Secretary of the Treasury for Monetary Affairs, warned European nations here today not to try to impose their ideas of monetary order on the rest of the world. At the same time, Mr. Volcker reaffirmed in the strongest possible terms the United States determination not to increase the official gold price of $38 an ounce, and eventually, to eliminate gold as a monetary metal."[11]

This superficial nonsense was not limited to U.S. officials, but was uttered in Europe as well.

[1] Henry H. Fowler, in James Dines *The Invisible Crash*, 50.

[2] Arthur F. Burns, "The Superinflation Squeeze" *Money Magazine*, August 1979, as quoted in James Dines *The Invisible Crash*, pp. 74, 115.

[3] James Dines, *The Invisible Crash*, 86.

[4] Ibid., 89.

[5] Vladimir Ilich Lenin, as quoted in John Maynard Keynes, *The Economic Consequences of the Peace*, (1919), reprinted in *The Collected Writings of John Maynard Keynes*, vol. II (London: MacMillan, 1977), 148/149.
In his earlier writings, Keynes showed a strong aversion to inflation. He agreed with Lenin's interpretation of the harmful effects of inflation: "Lenin was certainly right. There is no subtler, no surer means of overturning the existing basis of society than to debauch the currency. The process engages all the hidden forces of economic law on the side of destruction, and does it in a manner which not one man in a million is able to diagnose", p 149.

[6] Vladimir Ilich Lenin, as quoted in John Maynard Keynes, *The Economic Consequences of the Peace*, (1919), reprinted in *The Collected Writings of John Maynard Keynes*, vol. II (London: MacMillan, 1977), 148/149.

[7] John Exter, conversation with the author, Zurich, June 1975; See also, James Dines, *The Invisible Crash*, 97.

[8] Lyndon Baines Johnson, *State of the Union Message*, January 4, 1965 as quoted in James Dines, *The Invisible Crash*, 105.

[9] James Dines *The Invisible Crash*, 113.

[10] Ibid.

[11] Ibid.

Index

221, 241, 244, 245, 246, 249, 250, 253
automatic, 90, 244
classic, 11, 41, 139, 230, 243, 249
dollar, 139
modern, 10, 11
Gold Standard Act, 14, 21
Gold stock indices, 251
Gold Window, 75, 77, 79
Gold/Silver Ratio, **57**, 58
Gold-backed bonds, 173
Gold-backed currency, 180, 190
Goldman, Sachs & Company, 123, 124, 135, 150, 156, 171, 210, 234, 235, 236, 253
Goldsmithery, 156
Gooding, Kenneth, 137, 175
Government debt, 143, 245
Government spending, 36
Graduate Institute of International Studies, 83
Graham, Benjamin, 18, 26
Grant, James, 39, 46
Great Britain, 8, 10, 11, 13, 14, 21, 25, 35, 39, 47, 50, 51, 52, 53, 54, 64, 65, 68, 73, 74, 80, 83, 84, 88, 100, 109, 114, 138, 139, 140, 146, 159, 174, 175, 176, 180, 214, 215, 216, 217, 218, 219, 220, 222, 223, 225, 226, 227, 238, 248, 258, 259, 261, 265
London, 100, 121, 123, 149, 154, 217, 218, 220, 237
Greater Fool Theory, 19
Greco-Roman civilization, 6
Greece, 1, 2, 58
Green, Timothy, 74, 95, 100
Greenback era, 13
Greenspan, Alan, xiv, xvii, xviii, 81, 110, 114, 130, 144, 206, 207, 212, 214, 220, 221, 226, 227, 235, 242, 249, 253, 256, 258
Gross Domestic Product, 155
Gross National Product, 98, 115, 139

Guy, Robert, 223
Guyana, 159
Hague, William, 217
Hancock, Peter, 211
Harmony Gold Mining Ltd., 157, 169
Harrod, Roy, 89
Harvard University, 101
Harwood, E. C., 233
Hathaway, John, 154, 176, 242, 248, 256
Heavily Indebted Poor Countries (HIPCs), 136, 158, 159, 160
Hedge funds, 80, 152, 235, 239
Hedging, xiii, 80, 132, 135, 149, 150, 152, 154, 155, 157, 160, 161, 163, 164, 166, 168, 171, 176, 204, 216, 219, 235, 239, 240, 252, 253
Helvetistan, 182, 223
Henderson, Dale, 131, 175
Hitler, Adolf, 55, 249, 263
HM's Treasury, 32, 216, 218
Hoarding, 29, 31, 58, 62, 88, 89, 90, 91, 93, 107, 184, 223
Hofmänner, H. Thomas, xiv, 247
Holocaust, 192, 195, 202
Holocaust survivors, 193
Holocaust victims, 202
Holocaust victims, special fund for, 195
Holzer, Henry Mark, 28, 29, 45, 256
Homestake Mining, 31
Honest weights and measures, xiv, 19
Hoppe, Donald J., 37, 38, 46, 51, 61, 67, 70, 71, 79, 109, 110, 257
Horace, 70
House Banking Committee, 207, 214
House of Habsburg, 203
House of Saud, 106
Howe, Reginald H., xiii, 174, 175, 208, 212, 213, 219, 225, 243, 248, 253, 257

Printed in the United States
983200003B